HONEYBEES OF SOLOMON

HONEYBEES OF SOLOMON

JUSTICE K.T. THOMAS

Former Judge of the Supreme Court of India

GYAN PUBLISHING HOUSE

NEW DELHI-110002

Honeybees of Solomon

ISBN: 978-81-212-0966-3

Reprint in 2017 in India by
Gyan Publishing House
5, Ansari Road, Darya Ganj,
New Delhi-110002
Phones :011-47034999,9811692060

E-mail: books@gyanbooks.com
Website: www.gyanbooks.com

Printed at: G Print Process, Delhi

Contents

Foreword

[Mr. Justice Y.V. Chandrachud - former CJI]

There is a strong current of social thought which tries to discover and identify a variety of alternatives to litigations in courts. Indeed, justice without law was a living reality for our distinguished patriots and social reformers, centuries ago. My reason for being happy with alternate dispute resolution in the form of arbitration is entirely personal. Were there no arbitrations, I would never have met Mr. Justice K. T. Thomas. And, had I not met Justice Thomas as a co-arbitrator, I would have missed a precious experience. In Justice Thomas as an individual, I met a genial and genuine gentleman. And, in Justice Thomas as a co-arbitrator, I met a painstaking companion who took copious notes of arguments, cited Supreme Court judgments of the cuff and, placed justice on a pedestal higher than what the rigours of the letter of law demand.

2. It has been a pleasure to go through "Honeybees of Solomon". The judgments delivered by Justice Thomas in some of the cases mentioned in the book show that the Almighty did send Honeybees to him whenever he needed guidance to discern the just from the unjust, making his task Divine-oriented. That was what he had said in his reply speech when the Kerala Bar gave him a full Court welcome on his appointment as a Judge of the Kerala High Court. On 16th March 1996 when Justice Thomas was appointed as a Judge of the Supreme Court of India, the President of Kerala Court Advocates Association, Shri S. Gopakumaran Nair said in the farewell function that it is rarely that one comes across a "well balanced combination of a brilliant

judge, a reasonable citizen and a fine person", as one sees in Justice Thomas. My short but sweet association with Justice Thomas tells me how true this compliment is. Incidentally, one common facet of the lives of both of us is that we took to law by chance: in retrospect, a charming chance.

3. Why are Indians, regardless of class or community, one of the most litigious people in the world? Highly placed public men are prone to ascribe the heavy backlogs in our courts to the apathy of the judiciary to the felt necessities of the times in which we live. But then, when one of the big ones has a cause of action, real or assumed, against the other, why does say: "I will show you your proper place by taking you to a Court." The inevitable truth is that, fundamentally, the common men and women seek justice and, aspire to achieve it only through the processes of law, howsoever long and expensive.

4. Finally, I would be failing in my duty if I did not refer to the gracious hospitality of Mrs.Tharuni Thomas. My wife Prabha remembers it nostalgically. I believe, good wives make good husbands, god lawyers make good judges and Honeybees help discern the just from the unjust. I pray that Destiny may continue to bless Justice K.T. Thomas and S. Tharunitai with more and more Honeybees.

MUMBAI
Dated: 8th June 2007

Justice Y. V. CHANDRACHUD
Former Chief Justice of India

Introduction

I never had any intention, nor even the idea, of writing a book until I demitted office as judge of the Supreme Court of India. It was quite usual for judges to aspire assignments after superannuation from judgeship. I felt differently. I longed to go back to my hometown to live the remaining life. But then what would I do there? In that context the idea sprouted in my mind to scribble down the memories of judge-life. Before I embarked on this work a different thought winched to the fore – why not first write about the experiences at the Bar? I was mostly a trial lawyer and hence some of the cases handled by me, civil or criminal, had the trappings of thrill and sensation. So I wrote down, in my mother tongue (Malayalam) a brief account of how I became a lawyer and how the pangs of a junior got eventually transformed into contentment during later years of the profession. Those scrawls crystallized into the shape of a book titled "Before reaching the seat of Justice", It was published by DC Books, a very renowned publisher in Kerala.

Though I started writing the present book soon after retirement from the Supreme Court I could complete it only now, not because of its size but due to other engagements in the meanwhile. On completion I requested Mr. Justice Y.V. Chandrachud, the oldest among the former Chief Justices of India, to write a foreword. He held the office of Chief Justice of India for the longest period in history. I have always enjoyed reading his judgments in simple and decorous diction. I had the good fortune to acquaint myself with him at close quarters in recent years, as we both sat together for long on an arbitration panel. This acquaintance gave me the opportunity to see the noble and graciously humble personality in him. I recall that it was Mr. Justice Chandrachud as Chief Justice of India who approved the recommendation for my elevation as judge of the High Court of Kerala. These are the grounds which persuaded me to request him to write the foreword. I am grateful to him for acceding to my request.

Among the publishers, I chose M/s. Gyan Publishing House, New Delhi as they are among the renowned publishers in this country. I thank them for agreeing to print and publish this.

This book is not an autobiography, because there is no account in it of the major portion of the life I lived thus far. This is only a bunch of recollections of my judicial career. I do not know whether this work will be beneficial or otherwise, interesting or boring, to the readers.

The entire manuscript was taken down and transcribed by Mr. N. Thomaskutty, my secretary. I place on record my appreciation and gratitude to him.

Justice K.T. Thomas

1

The raison d'etre of the nomenclature

I have chosen to title this bunch of memoirs of my years as judge "Honeybees of Solomon" not because Solomon had any inspirational value for my judicial career. Nor because any honeybee had accorded helping guidance to me. This is only with reference to the legend concerning the famous emperor Solomon of Jerusalem, which I had learnt during my childhood days. Some scriptures depicted him as a wise judge, though others have caricatured him as a great monarch, or an imaginative poet flanked by feminine admirers. The queen of one of the neighbouring countries visited his palace hearing about the wisdom of Solomon. Though she was treated as a state guest she ventured to test the wisdom of the host emperor's sagacity to judge. One day she placed two bouquet of identical flowers at a distance from each other, one with real flowers and the other with artificial flowers. She asked Solomon who was standing a little distance away from the bouquet whether he could distinguish between the two and pronounce which among them was real. Solomon's eyes wobbled between the two bunches of flowers and he found it difficult to discern the real from the imitate due to the seemingly striking similarity of the flowers arranged in both bouquets. While looking at to get some clue, his attention reached a honey bee hovering around one of them. Solomon pronounced his judgement by pointing out the bouquet with real flowers. The visiting queen was astounded by the ease with which the judge could distinguish the genuine from the synthetic. Little did the female ruler realise that it was neither the wisdom, nor the intelligence nor any of the cognitive faculties of the judge which helped him to discern the truth from the fake but a guidance sent by the almighty.

When I became a judge of the High Court of Kerala there was a formal welcome function in a full court reference. In my reply speech to the welcome address I quoted the above legend and concluded "if the Almighty would send down such honeybees whenever I need guidance to discern the just from the unjust, my task would be divine oriented". Several years thereafter when the Supreme Court Bar Association offered a farewell to me on the last day of my judicial career, I recounted the above legend in my reply speech and concluded the peroration thus:

"I am beholden to the Almighty for bestowing such honeybees on all occasions when I needed guidance; sometimes such honeybees appeared in the form of an answer to a query. At other times it came in the form of a document or in the form of a flash through my inner mind. I was able to distinguish the just from the unjust not on account of any sagacity of my own or the function of my cognitive faculty but by the guidance of such honeybees".

While contemplating in my mind as to what title I should confer on the recollections of my career as a judge, it occurred to me that "Honeybees of Solomon" would be a more appropriate appellation. Hence the nomenclature.

2

Ascension as a Judge

The career of a person does not by and large, crystallize according to his designs. It is orchestrated often, without his control or even his decisions. He might, perhaps, get an option to repudiate the career destined for him. But such option is rarely exercised.

As in the case of many people I too did not make a choice well in advance, regarding the career to which I eventually got inextricably wedded. Law was not in my mind until I completed my degree course. The desire to go for law was God planted in my mind by some coincidence which happened during the summer vacation of 1959. It happened during the recess between completion of the final examination and publication of the results. After passing the law degree examination I had to choose a senior advocate to undergo a course of apprenticeship and the initial period in the legal profession. It was an irony that I was moved into the chambers of a senior advocate whom I wished to sideline on account of his taciturnity, though he commanded considerable respect from all concerned.

A week before my enrolment as advocate, I received by post a notice requiring me to appear for an interview for a Central Government post. I thought about it seriously. The offer was very tempting to me because I had yet to spend money for the sartorial costumes prescribed for advocates, which at that time was a good amount. The salary scale of that central government post was attractive. In spite of all this I finally decided, after prayerful meditation, not to go for the interview. Even now I am unable to explain why I decided against the job opportunity offered. Had I appeared for the interview, my career most probably, would have been totally different. This according to me, is an experience from which I can write today that the career of the person crystallizes in a manner delineated by an unseen power.

After 17 years of hectic professional activities as an advocate, I availed myself of the opportunity to test whether I could join the judiciary. I opted in favour of appearing for an interview before a panel of three senior judges of the High Court of Kerala. The panel was formed for selecting 2 or 3 persons for direct recruitment from the Bar as District and Sessions Judges. The selection at that time was held only after an interval of about 8 years. Little did I hope then that I would be one of the 3 persons to be finally selected for the post, since the applicants were so large a number. The result of the interview was communicated to me and only then did I know that I topped the list of selectees. My mind wavered; should I abjure the thrill and the lure of the career of a legal practitioner or confine myself to the sequestered columns of a judge or should I sit on the higher dais wearing the vestment and chasuble of a judicial arbiter. I received a divided opinion from those who were concerned for me. One set of people advised me against accepting the assignment, whereas the others were all in favour of my joining the judiciary. Finally I decided to cast the dice in favour of accepting the judicial career.

I took my first oath as judge before Mr. Justice Balakrishna Eradi (who later became judge of the Supreme Court of India) in his chamber in the High Court. Then, I was posted as the District and Sessions Judge, Trichur.

On 15th September 1979, when the clock of the main court hall at Trichur chimed eleven times, I entered the court hall and sat on the seat of the judge of the District Court. A packed court hall witnessed that simple, but solemn ascension. As soon as I sat on the seat I was welcomed by the Public Prosecutor cum Government Pleader (Mr. M.R. Kurup who is no more now). I felt I should reply. Fortunately it went off well, though it was an impromptu reply. Thus commenced my career as a judge which stretched for a long period of nearly a quarter of a century.

During the fairly long period as a judge I had, pleasant as well as unpleasant experiences, though the unpleasant were comparatively few and far between. I had the unique privilege of getting wonderful support from members of the Bar and a galaxy of highly friendly colleagues at all levels of my judicial career. I record this not as a ritualistic acknowledgement, but as an experience of reality.

I could function as the District and Sessions Judge of Trichur only for a short period of eight months, of which the real judicial functions could be performed only for about five months, as the rest of the period was covered by a short and a long vacation. I recollect now the dreams frequently flashing in my sleep during the early months of my judicial career. In such dreams I saw that I had resigned from judgeship and had gone back to being an advocate; and I waited and waited to have at least a stray litigant to engage me but none turned up including my old clients. Such dreams only explained how I would have vacillated to cut short my practice as an advocate.

I wish to put on record two unforgettable experiences I had during the eight moth period mentioned above. One is the opportunity which came to me as a windfall for attending a three weeks training course at the Institute of Criminology, New Delhi. It happened on account of the cancellation of the nomination of another District Judge to the same course for reasons unknown to me. I had to suddenly fly to New Delhi as was required by the High Court.

All the participants in the said training course were judges directly recruited from the Bar but I was the youngest among them.

Most of them later became judges of the High Court in different states. Experiences imparted to us in the training institute were profound and very useful in the discharge of my judicial functions during the years that followed. One of the programmes in the training institute was witnessing a Postmortem Examination. We were taken to the Forensic Medicine Department of a Medical College where the Head of the Department conducted the autopsy on the dead body of a young deceased.

It was an experience of long standing effect. I could see directly how perfectly the postmortem examination could be conducted, and the meticulous manner every detail was observed and noted. It impressed me that autopsy should be held during sun light to get the exact colour of each feature.

During the training period I took care to visit the Supreme Court of India. It was my fortune to attend the proceedings in the court hall of the Chief Justice of India when arguments were addressed by advocate V.B. Ganatra before a Constitution Bench of five judges headed by Chief Justice M.H. Beg. The question related to a nice legal point contained in the Prevention of Food Adulteration Act. When the judgement of the Constitution Bench was later reported in the Law Journal, I could recollect with some thoroughness that I too was a witness when that question was thrashed in the apex court. At that time I never even imagined that one day I would sit on the dais of the highest court in India.

During the same period I was able to find time to attend the proceedings held by "Justice Shah Commission" at the Patiala House, New Delhi. The said commission was appointed by the central government of the post emergency period to enquire into the atrocities committed during the infamous Emergency. It had tremendous political fallout because it involved the actions of various functionaries including Indira Gandhi during the dark days of the emergency. When the Shah Commission was commenced the proceedings were conducted with all din and bustle. It evoked unusual media publicity. But unfortunately it turned out as a war field for Indira Gandhi to fight back. The Commission submitted its report which ran into volumes. But by then Indira Gandhi became victorious in a general election conducted as the Janata Government broke into pieces. When Indira Gandhi came back to power, she put the Shah Commission Report into cold storage. Thus the commission which at the inception was a highly explosive powder keg became a damp squib.

The other experience during my tenure as District Judge, Trichur was purely personal to me and it had no official trapping. Yet I cannot omit it due to its alarming overtures during the infantile months of my judicial life.

3

Moulding up into Judgeship

After I returned from New Delhi, my wife developed a fever. The doctors at Trichur did not diagnose the cause of it at the first instance. As the high temperature persisted for a number of days she had to be hospitalised. Her condition became worse day by day until it reached a critical stage. Then I informed her sister and brother–in-law (Dr. Benjamin Pulimood and Mrs. Dr. Remani Benjamin Pulimood) who were working as doctors at the Christian Medical College Hospital, Vellore. Dr. Benjamin Pulimood rushed down to Trichur. Sensing that her condition was far serious she was taken to the C.M.C. Hospital. She would have developed "peritonitis" within one or two days, had the disease been not diagnosed at Vellore CMC Hospital that she was actually suffering from acute typhoid. Though typhoid is not killer disease now, the delay in diagnosing it in spite of the best efforts made by the doctors at Trichur had brought her in a serious situation and it was a narrow escape from being fatal.

Incidentally I may mention that she had typhoid on an earlier occasion also. It was during the month of our marriage in October 1962. Even on the wedding day my wife was suffering from typhoid. After the wedding function the couple were separated for affording the sick bride time to recuperate from the illness. A few days hence she got recovered but reached normal life only about a couple of months later. We became parents of three sons by the time of my joining judiciary and all of them were then school going children. Little did we reckon that the same disease (typhoid) would once again visit her and that was one of the reasons for not diagnosing it initially. When it visited her on the second occasion, she was saved from the pangs of death by the timely action taken by her elder sister and brother-in-law Dr. Pulimoods, apart from providential help.

About twelve years prior to it we had to pass through a harrowing experience when my wife reached nearest to her end. It happened as the consequence of intra uterine death of a foetus in her second pregnancy. Birth of our eldest son (now Dr. Binu Pratap Thomas) was through a premature confinement. It was a laborious task for the mother to bring up the premature baby to the level of a normal child. So the next pregnancy should have been after an interval of a reasonable period. I cannot recollect whether the interval was sufficient enough for a mother to bear the next child. What ever that be she became pregnant and when it reached six months of growth the intra uterine death happened. But we realised it only one or two months after the death of the foetus. We were all relieved that it happened without much strain. I went to the room in the evening to see her. Since one of the doctors told me that she was alright by then, I had a chat with her and left the room. Hardly an hour passed while I was chatting with her uncle Dr. K.M. Thomas in another wing of the hospital, the information reached me that she started bleeding profusely and that the entire bed became drenched in blood. I rushed to the room which was lit by candescent bulbs. But I heard my wife saying to all around her to switch the lights on as she felt it dark then. The blood in her eyes would have drained off by that time. Almost all the doctors in the hospital, besides a host of staff rushed to the room. From the mood of those people I realised that she was fast falling into a total bloodless condition. Fresh blood transfusion was urgently needed but no precautionary measure had been adopted in advance. Her blood group was B and the only person who had same blood group was my youngest brother (K.T. Jacob who is now the Senior Divisional Manager of the New India Assurance Co.) from among those who are available then. His blood was suddenly collected and within the shortest time group matching test was held and the blood was transfused to her. But the quantity of blood collected from him was insufficient to replenish the lost blood. My wife appeared to have had only a few more minutes to survive. But within a couple of minutes two other youngsters living in the neighborhood of the hospital were traced out by Dr. K.M. Thomas. They had the blood of the same group. When they were brought down to the hospital they demanded a certain sum as price of the blood. They thought that the amount demanded by them was a good price. But in my estimation in the exigency of the situation the demand was only for a paltry sum. The blood so collected was also infused in to her system. The resuscitation of her into life was visibly discernible with massive quantity of blood transfused into her body. The one who was almost dying down was seen winching to the fore of life and within half an hour she opened her eyes. She identified her kith and kin who were all looking at her aghast and in a terrific mood of suspense. After a few days she came back to her normal life. Our second son Bechu Kurian Thomas and third son Bipin Cherian Thomas were born by normal delivery. When I became District Judge all the three sons attained school going age.

My stint as a District Judge at Trichur had a specialty. Most of the District Courts in Kerala had at least one more additional District Court, but for Trichur District there was no such additional court. All the new appointees in the post of District Judge would be additional District and Sessions Judges to start with. But due to a very rare combination of fortuitous circumstances my first posting happened to be at Trichur and hence I was not appointed as Additional District Judge at the first instance. Thus I got exclusive jurisdiction to handle all the cases in the district not only on the civil side but on the criminal side as well. The number of murder cases pending trial in the Sessions

Court Trichur was quite large. Then a Sessions Judge, particularly of a court crammed with sessions cases, was supposed to do fast work. If he could complete the trial of one murder case in a week that was considered to be normal fast work. At Trichur, I realised that if I could maintain only the pace of one sessions case a week it would result in further swelling up on the backlog of murder cases of that court. So I resorted to a speedy course by completing the trial of two murder cases per week. One of those two cases would be comparatively less heavy while the other one would be a normal one or heavier one.

The schedule for examination of witnesses in murder cases was so arranged as to commence it on a Monday and close it on the third day. The trial in the next case commenced on the following Thursday to be closed on the next Saturday. Eventually this became the normal schedule of posting of the case in that court during my tenure though there would have been exceptions whenever cases involving large number of witnesses had to be tried.

I could find time on many days to hear argument in civil appeals also and I could dispose of such cases along with sessions cases besides criminal appeals. The disposal therefore galloped but I took pain to see that the speed was not at the cost of depriving the advocates of the opportunity to argue their cases to their satisfaction.

The High Court of Kerala had the practice of allotting the supervision of judicial work of one District to one senior Judge of the High Court. When I was District Judge of Trichur the supervision of the administration of the district was with Justice G. Balagangadharan Nair. He knew that my initial appointment as the sole District Judge of Trichur would end by the next general transfers but when he noticed that the new District Judge of Trichur had cleared huge backlog of cases, besides attending to all administrative works, (which included giving instructions to the subordinate courts and calendar review of the judgements of the magistrates) he put up a note for the consideration of the other judges of the High Court that if possible I should be retained at Trichur itself even for the period beyond the next general transfers. This fact was disclosed to me later by Mr. Justice Balagangadharan Nair himself. But his effort in that regard did not succeed. However, I had the unique privilege of becoming the administrative head of the entire courts of the Trichur district besides doing the judicial work of the civil as well as criminal wing of the District Court. I doubt whether any other District Judge had enjoyed such a privilege in the first limb of his judicial career.

One of the causes of criminal trials getting delayed in India is on account of the time consumed for recording the depositions of witnesses by writing them down in long hand. This work is being done by the trial judge himself. Unless this practice is substituted by resorting to electronic means for recording depositions the delay in the court procedure would continue to linger on in the trial system.

I have noticed, when I was practicing as an advocate, that most of the trial judges did not read out the deposition after it was recorded and before the deponent affixed his signature on it. Those judges without any qualm of conscience used to write the certificate below that the record of such deposition "was read out in open court and that the deponent agreed that it was truly recorded". It was my resolve not to make any such false certificate on the depositions. Hence it became my unexceptional practice to read out every deposition in open court whether it was long or short. Some of the advocates used to tell me at the first lap of my stint at each station (where I worked as District Judge) that they would take such deposition as read out to the witness so that I could dispense with the task of reading it in open court. They said so with the honest intention of helping me to reduce my work load. But I told them of the statutory necessity and also the injudiciousness involved in signing a certificate which was not true. May I use this context to inform all trial judges that I never felt on any day, that the time consumed for reading out a deposition went waste, or that it involved much time. Even a lengthy deposition could be read out within a few minutes as the scribe of the deposition was myself and I could read it at ease.

During the first week of my tenure as District Judge of Trichur, one Sub Registrar appeared as a witness on the summons issued from the court. He was to give evidence regarding a formal point in a case filed for granting probate with a copy of the will annexed thereto. I was told that the witness was present, though it was on a day scheduled for the trial of a murder case. The advocate, at whose instance the witness was summoned, was not present in court. When the case was taken up another advocate represented that the advocate concerned had applied for adjournment of the case. But I told in emphatic tone that if a witness was present he would not be sent back without examining him, unless such examination was dispensed with by the party concerned. I also made it clear that if the witness was a medical practitioner or a public servant that case would be taken up on a priority basis so that the witness could go back to his work after his evidence was recorded. So saying I called the case in which the Sub Registrar was present. I asked the witness to mount the witness stand and impressed all concerned that if none would turn up to examine the witness in chief, I would pronounce orders closing the evidence of that party. I waited for a couple of minutes and during that time the advocate concerned reached the court hall. I noticed that the said Sub Registrar had appeared in the same case on two prior occasions and the case was adjourned then also without him being examined on the simple ground that a sessions case was also posted for trial on such days. In fact the Sub Registrar submitted that he had no objection to appear in the Court on another day. But I told him that I had objections because his presence in the court would cause his absence in the Sub Registry where many persons would be waiting for him to perform his official duties. The examination of that witness, being only a formal affair, was completed in five minutes time. But the message went all around and thenceforth no occasion was created for any witness to be told to appear again for recording his evidence. I may state here that at all stations I sat as a Judge, no witness was asked to go back without recording his evidence except when his evidence was dispensed with as unnecessary.

It was the regular feature in criminal courts that all the accused have to keep themselves inside dock provided in each court hall for that purpose. I was not able to find any valid reason insisting on it. In my perception, the dock in a court hall was meant only as a token or symbol for the custody of accused. When an accused in a criminal case was not in custody i.e. if he was on bail why should he be required to stand inside the dock of the court ? This question remained in my mind when I was practising as an advocate. After I became a judge I made it clear to inform every accused who was on bail that he was not obliged to stand inside the dock and that he was free to stand outside the dock. Of course some of the accused still continued the old practice and they did not avail themselves of the choice offered by me.

I further thought that accused keeping on standing in court room when the trial in his case was proceeding was a primitive practice, at any rate it was not akin to civilised thinking. Hence I provided seating facilities for the accused in the court hall and informed them that such seats were meant to be occupied by them. Nevertheless some of the accused opted to keep standing.

Whenever an accused in a case had to be questioned by the judge as required by law, I permitted him to consult his advocate even inside the court room regarding the answers to be given by him. It was not fair that the accused should have committed some erroneous answers and the court to use such answers to the detriment of the accused. Therefore, I used to tell the accused in advance about the pattern of questions which would be put to him, and about his right to consult his advocate, whenever he found any question difficult to answer without such consultation.

I was very much concerned about a wrong conviction of accused in any criminal case. But at the same time, I strived very much to avert unmerited acquittals of the accused in criminal cases. With the above subject in mind, I tried to ensure, during trials conducted in my court, that cases which ought to end in conviction should not end in acquittal on account of any lapse on the part of the court or even that of a public prosecutor. I knew that the said attitude created an impression that I was prone to convict the accused in all criminal cases. I feel that formation of such impression was not correct.

During my earlier days as District and Sessions Judge at Trichur, my wife and I felt the pinch of financial strain as I had a good income from a lucrative practice as an advocate. We realised that the salary paid to a District Judge was only a small portion of what I was making at the Bar. Perhaps I was then one of the largest income earning advocates in my district. When the first month's pay packet was received by me as District Judge, my wife looked at me overseeing the difficulties to maintain the household including the difficulty to meet the expenses to educate our three sons who were in the school going age then, and to maintain a car (as the petrol price shot up geometrically during that period). When Babu Paul, I.A.S. (who persuaded me to aspire for judgeship) visited us at Trichur, my wife told him that "when you encouraged my husband to become a judge perhaps you did not know there would be steep fall in the income". He became nonplussed hearing the said comment. Eventually we learned how to live a frugal but dignified life with the limited income. Of course I had a fairly good saving from my Bar practice. That helped me to replenish the deficiency of the salaried income.

4

The first murder case tried in my Court

The first murder trial which I very well remember, having been brought before me as a Sessions judge at Trichur, was a case of patricide (murdering one's own father). To narrate the story I wish to substitute the real names of the parties with fictitious names. The following was the synopsis of the case.

George was the accused. He and his wife with their children were residing in his father's house. His elder brother Jacob and his sisters were residing elsewhere. George was in course of time not well disposed to his aged father for reasons which I am not in a position to remember with exactitude. On the fateful night, when the old man was sleeping, a wicked idea bubbled up in the mind of George, perhaps he was then inebriated. He took up a pestle (rice pounder) from the kitchen and went near the bed of his father. He gave a big blow with it on the head of the sleeping old man. The victim made a feeble sound and died instantaneously. George bathed the dead body and laid it on the coat after clothing him well including typing a turban on the head. He then told all others that his father had a fall on the verandah when he went out to pass urine and died in such fall. As George felt that the pestle remaining outside might create some suspicion, he broke it and dumped it into the commode of his latrine (which was an old model privy).

The old man who died was a respectable person attached to the local parish. The burial of him was conducted in the cemetery of the local church after a ceremonial procession etc. After the burial was over, George heaved a sigh of relief thinking that every body believed that his father's death was due to the accidental fall.

The sisters and the elder brother remained in the house of the departed for a few days more to perform the traditional obsequies in the community. The period of moaning was to end with a feast supplied to all those who shared the sentiments of the bereavement. One of the sisters of George made a search for the rice pounder for pounding rice to prepare some items of food in connection with the feast. As the sisters were very familiar with the rice pounder of the house they preferred that pounder to be used for pounding the rice but it was found missing. Why it was missing, they all made enquiries for it. During the enquiry the responses of the accused to the queries were not spontaneous but suspicious. Next morning when the elder brother went to the latrine, he noticed some thing projecting out of the surface of the commode. He did not leave it like that, and he probed into it and recovered, to his great dismay, a broken pestle from inside the latrine where normally no body used to keep such an object.

The elder brother ruminated over it, he started recounting the peculiar behavior of George at all times after his father's death and he watched his behaviour thenceforth. The answers given by George to any inconvenient question connected with the pestle put to him evoked greater suspicion that it would have had some connection with the death of the old father. On a night, before the brother and sisters finally left the house, George having reached a stage when he could not contain the lump in his chest any more, disclosed to the elder brother and his sisters of what really happened. Though some people in the family tried to keep this great crime a family secret the elder brother could not persuade himself to pardon his younger brother for the murder of his father. So he informed the police. George was arrested and after completing the investigation, the case was charge sheeted against him. The gist of the charge sheet was that George killed his father by beating him with a rice pounder while sleeping.

It was the above case which came up before me for trial, perhaps one of the earliest murder cases which would have been tried in my court.

The case was conducted very seriously by the prosecution and the defence. Mr. Karunakaran conducted the prosecution quite efficiently. Sri. Veerachandra Menon, the most leading criminal lawyer practising at Trichur then, was the defence counsel. He did his part very well. Although many witnesses cited by the prosecution have turned against the prosecution case, the Public Prosecutor did not lose hope. When the elder brother of the accused gave evidence in court, he said that George confessed to him of what happened. That confession contained the admission of the crucial aspect that George dealt a blow on the head of his father with the rice pounder during sleep. That part of the evidence was called, in legal parlance "extra judicial confession" Though such confession was legally admissible in evidence there was a catena of decisions to support the view that extra judicial confession was a weak type of evidence.

The doctor, who conducted postmortem examination on the dead body, said that the extensive comminuted depressed fracture of the skull of the deceased would have happened on sustaining a blow with a heavy object like a rice pounder. The defence lawyer, who was one of the seasoned and experienced criminal lawyers of Trichur Bar, conducted a grilling cross examination of the doctor. He elicited almost successfully that the skull fracture of that type would have happened when that part of the head came into contact with a hard object like the surface of a cemented verandah.

At that stage,. I felt the need to put a question to the doctor, I have learnt while I conducted criminal cases as a defence lawyer that depressed comminuted fracture of the skull would not happen by a mere fall on the ground from a standing position. I put a few questions to the doctor like this;

"Doctor, the skull portion is one of the sturdiest of the human skeleton which is intended to protect the brain as that organ has to carryout the most vital function of the human body. Is it correct ?" The doctor answered in the affirmative.

Next question;

"Doctor, if the skull portion has to be depressively fractured should not that fall on the verandah be from a higher level and not from the standing position ?" Answer of the doctor was again in the affirmative.

Though the defence counsel availed himself of his right to put further questions on the answers given by the doctor to the question put by me, the witness stuck to his position that such a type of fracture of the skull would not be sustained by falling from a standing position.

The most important witness for the prosecution was the elder brother of the accused. The manner in which he gave evidence in court created the impression in me that what he narrated was the true version. When arguments were heard, the advocates felt that my mind was leaning in favour of convincing the accused. The public prosecutor pleaded that death penalty should be awarded to the accused.

I convicted the accused of murder. But I was not inclined to impose death penalty as I was always reluctant to impose that punishment except in very rare cases where the punishment of even life imprisonment would appear to be too inadequate. Personally I consider then and now that death penalty is not a punishment at all. Nevertheless I was bound to award it in rarest of rare cases because I took an oath that I would discharge my functions in accordance with law. So I sentenced him to imprisonment for life.

I must also mention that the accused went up in appeal to the High Court. A division bench of the High Court of Kerala was not inclined to act on the evidence of the brother of the accused. Hence the appeal was allowed and the accused was acquitted.

I could not continue at Trichur beyond the time of the next general transfers which came into effect in the month of May 1977, though I did not complete even one year as District Judge of Trichur. Justice G. Balagangadharan Nair was the judge of the High Court in charge of supervision of the judicial administration of Trichur district. He pleaded with other judges of the High Court to allow me to continue at Trichur as he was very much pleased with my work, despite the fact that I was the junior most District Judge then. But even at the time of my posting at Trichur I was told that it was only for a temporary period till the next general transfers, because quite a number of senior District Judges were looking forward to get posting at Trichur due to its proximity with Guruvayoor, the famous temple town. However, I took enormous satisfaction in that. I could stimulate greater work culture at that station, particularly in the subordinate judiciary.

The punctuality which I maintained with meticulous precision would have conveyed a message of discipline and orderliness in the entire judicial network of the district. I used to peruse almost all the judgements of the magistrates in the district, in order to verify whether revisional powers of the Sessions Judge should be exercised in respect of any such judgement. Invariably I communicated to the authors of such judgements at least one or two remarks about each such judgement. This practice fuelled an impetus to the magistrates and instilled an awareness in them that their judgements were being read by a superior judicial personage. This helped making the quality of their judgements better than earlier.

At the end of the judicial year (before the onset of the summer vacation) I was transferred as the Additional District and Sessions Judge of Calicut. So I left Trichur to take up the post at the new station. Though my tenure at Trichur was far too short a stint, and it was almost my judicial kindergarten tenure I succeeded in forging a good rapport with the members of the Bar. I learned later that many senior advocates of that Bar conveyed their appreciation of my performance as District Judge to some of the judges of the High Court. I have only sweet reminiscences of that short period.

5

Calicut District Court

Calicut city has a heritage of its own. It is a very ancient city on the west coast. It has a unique cosmopolitan atmosphere. It was the Centre of activities of three major religions in India, Hindu, Muslim and Christian. In the past, it was a matter of privilege for a judicial officer to be posted as district judge of Calicut on account of a variety of reasons. One of them was that the district court, Calicut is probably the oldest (except Telicherry District Court) on the west coast. Another is its placement in the judicial set up. Calicut was considered to be one of the important epicenters and was the capital of Malabar province earlier. Before Kerala State was formed in 1956, the District Court of Calicut was within the jurisdiction of Madras High Court, which was one of the four chartered High Courts in India. Calicut District Court was treated, by convention, as the most important judicial Centre, next only to the High Court. A District Judge posted at Calicut was normally the senior most judicial officer and his next step was judge of the Madras High Court.

Another reason is, Calicut Bar had at all times a galaxy of very capable advocates both on the criminal and civil sides of the legal profession. When I was posted at Calicut, the Bar continued to have the same fame which they inherited from the past. I noticed that members of the Bar were very zealous in preserving that name.

My first task at Calicut was to find out a residence, Mr. U.L. Bhat (later Chief Justice U.L. Bhat) was the District judge of Calicut immediately prior to my tenure. He found that the official quarters meant for the District Judge was situated too far away. During those days District Judges did not have official car and they used to maintain vehicles at their own cost. When petrol prices galloped geometrically, Mr. U.L. Bhat shifted to another rented building at Chalappuram which is situated less than two kilometers away from the District Court. When I moved to Calicut, I tried to have the same house rented out to me. The owner of the house was kind enough to oblige me. Sri. A.R. Sreenivasan was the Principal District Judge in Calicut when I was the Additional District Judge, Mr. Sreenivasan had his own house in Calicut where he had his own telephone connection. During those days telephone facility was provided by government only at the residence of the Principal District Judges. I was unable to reconcile with the situation of not having telephone facility in the house occupied by me because I was enjoying telephone connection at my residence for many years before joining judiciary.

Knowing my plight Mr. Srenivasan asked me whether he could seek permission of the High Court to keep the official telephone in my house as he could use his own telephone connection for all official purposes also. In fact, he himself drafted a letter requesting for such permission of the High Court and showed it to me. High Court was kind enough to grant such permission on certain conditions, one of them was that any amount charged by the telephone department in excess of the tariff rate should be borne by me.

It was a great relief to me. It was made possible only because of the noble gesture shown by A.R. Sreenivasan. I do not think that any other Principal District Judge would have sacrificed such official telephone facility for the purpose of accommodating the additional District Judge. Mr. Sreenivasan was a man of few words, a very grave looking personality. In fact, I have appeared before him as an advocate when he was Munsiff at Kottayam during early sixtees and again when he was additional Sessions Judge at Telecherry. The highest degree of judicial rectitude maintained by him was not only visible on his face but permeated inside the court room where he presided over. In the matter of discharge of judicial functions he did not fear any one, not even the High Court. Though he was recluse in social amiability his judicial outfits had out-shone all other special characters. I was very much inspired by his transparent rectitude. The advocates really feared him for his serious out look but respected him for his spotless judicial integrity. In the telephone matter he showed to me that he had one more excellent quality – he was a noble and kind hearted colleague.

A short stint at Manjeri (Malappuram District)

During the middle of the first year as Additional District Judge, Calicut I was compelled to shift to the neighboring district, the headquarters of which was situated at a small town called Manjeri. The reason for such a sudden transfer was that no District Judge was available to be posted at Manjeri in the vacancy caused by the retirement of the former incumbent. Although the High court sent up a panel of names to be promoted to the cadre of District Judges, the Government did not appoint them due to some legal snag. The High Court found it urgently necessary to post somebody as District Judge of Manjeri. Otherwise, the entire district would continue without a District Judge to supervise the administration. It was in that context the High Court decided to close down the additional District Court at Calicut and shift me to Manjeri. As I was told that I would be at Manjeri only for a short duration, I left my family to continue at Calicut itself.

On the first day as District Judge at Manjeri, the Bar Association arranged a tea evening for welcoming me. One young and smart looking advocate then sang a song. He was introduced to me as "Advocate Mr. Mammootty who had acted in films" I told him that I was a regular cinema goer but I had not seen him in any such cinema. However, I wished him well as he appeared to have possessed all promises for a good cinema star. He was then practising as junior of one Sreedhara Menon.

Within a few days thereafter, advocate Mammootty appeared before me in a case only to plead for an adjournment. I was not inclined to adjourn the case and hence, I insisted that he should start arguments. I assured him that if his case turns out to be hard for him to win, the case could be posted to another day so that his senior would address arguments. But Mammootty went on requesting for an adjournment as he was not then prepared to argue the case. I finally yielded and agreed to adjourn the case on a condition that he himself should argue the case on the next posting date. He accepted the condition and the case was adjourned.

On the next posting day Mammootty reported that his senior would very soon reach the court to argue. Then I reminded him of the condition which he accepted on the previous day. Perhaps he would have thought that I had forgotten it, but when I reminded him of it he was in a fix. He started pleading with me to save him from the plight and permit his senior to argue. I do not exactly remember the further details of what happened. Perhaps the senior advocate would have addressed arguments later.

I later found Mammootty playing a hero's role in a cinema. Then onwards his rise on the screen was simply meteoric. He became one of the best actors in the Indian cinema world. He is today a very renowned actor with hectic call sheets. He once visited me at my residence (at Calicut) when we both were invited to a function held at Feroke college, Calicut. I was then described as the chief guest to inaugurate the function. Mammootty was to inaugurate the Arts club. In my speech I told the audience that I was only "the de-jure chief guest" whereas Mammootty was "the de-facto chief guest"

After he became a celebrity actor, Malayala Manorama weekly serially published his autobiography. In one episode so published, he narrated his experiences at the Bar of Manjeri wherein he gave fuller details of how I insisted him to argue the case mentioned above.

Though my period as District and Sessions Judge at Manjeri lasted only for a period of two months. I was able to bring about a substantial turn out of the work there., I disposed of a large number of civil appeals, criminal appeals, rent control revisions and motor accident claims during that period. I succeeded in equipping the members of the Bar at Manjeri to a great extent on certain special legal aspects concerning motor accident claims. This I could do by discussing with the advocates in open court whenever such claims were heard. Since no tribunal was established at Manjeri for dealing with motor accident claims, I could take up such claims having been vested with such powers.

I, well remember the case of a smart boy in his teens who claimed an amount of Rs.40,000/- as compensation on account of amputation of his right leg in its entirety due to an accident when the motor vehicle hit a tree. The accident was admitted by the owner of the vehicle but he pleaded that there was no negligence on the part of the bus driver. So the advocate of the claimant brought a number of witnesses to the court for proving that the driver was negligent. I told the advocates on both sides that a court in such cases would proceed with the presumption that the driver was negligent because of the legal maxim "Res-Ipsa loquitor" (the thing speaks for itself). I told the Bar that no vehicle is expected to hit a standing tree unless one of the three eventualities had occurred. The first is the negligence of the driver, the second is in spite of his exercising extreme care the vehicle went off the road due to failure of any mechanism of the automobile, and the third is that the driver was confronted by a sudden situation where he was forced to adopt the alternative of hitting the vehicle on a stationary object to avert a greater disaster. Among the above three possibilities, the court is expected to presume the first possibility as the most probable one. But if any of the other two events had really happened the man who drove the vehicle is the best person to know it and he has to establish the same to the satisfaction of the court. I persuaded the advocates of the claimant to give up all his witnesses who came to give evidence to prove that the driver of the vehicle was negligent. It appeared to me that the advocates of Manjeri took it as a new approach.

In another case of motor accident claims the defence was one of admitting that the bus capsized but it was not on account of any negligence of the driver, it was due to some latent defect of the vehicle itself which neither the driver nor the owner was aware of. The claimant in that case also brought a number of witnesses to prove that the driver was in fact negligent.

I told the advocates that I would proceed on the assumption that there was latent manufacturing defect in the vehicle. According to me the owner is still liable to pay compensation to the innocent victim because of the principle of "strict liability" propounded in the English law of Torts adumbrated in a very famous decision known as Ryland Vs, Fletcher. It was laid down (using a language for laymen understanding) that the person who brought any artificial object would be liable for all the damages suffered by another on account of it, unless he succeeds in proving one of the five exceptions. I therefore, impressed upon the advocates that once the accident is admitted in such a case, the burden is on the owner of the vehicle to prove the exception and failure to prove the exception would result in a judgement to be passed against him.

Those and many other cases were decided by me at Manjeri within a short period of two months. By then the government approved the new panel for district judges. As I was very eager to get back to Calicut, I exerted some pressure on the Registrar of the High Court to move the file for my re-transfer to Calicut. Mr. K.B. Menon was then the Registrar. He was very considerate to me as he knew me earlier when I was practising as an advocate and he was then either the chief judicial magistrate or district judge. He helped me to have the file moved fast. High Court took the decision to transfer me back

Today the District Judge of Manjeri is Mr. Thomas P. Joseph who was a long time junior of me. He too was directly recruited from the Bar as District Judge. I learned from knowledgeable quarters that he is doing extremely well as District and Sessions Judge, Manjeri, and has cleared a huge backlog of cases.

6

Back in Calicut

After reaching Calicut, I became again Additional District Judge and Mr. A.R. Sreenivasan continued to be the principal District Judge. An incident which happened during that period cannot be forgotten. K. Bhaskaran Nair, a very respected advocate having enormous practice on the criminal as well as labour litigations was also involved in many social activities at Calicut. He was able to train up a number of juniors, some of whom later became renowned judges. (Mr. Justice R. Basant and Ms. Justice Hema, of the Kerala High Court are some of his erstwhile juniors) Mr. Bhaskaran Nair passed away a couple of years ago. The Calicut Bar Association invited me to unveil his portrait in the hall of the Association. It was a very largely attended function. Among others Mr. Justice R. Basant and Mr. Retna Singh (the present Advocate General of Kerala) addressed the gathering. I will now refer to an episode which happened during my first limb as District Judge of Calicut.

Mr. Bhaskaran Nair invited me to address the Rotary Club of Calicut on the subject chosen by him. (Language of the Court) Such a subject was chosen in the background of the Government of Kerala deciding to adopt Malayalam as the language for all trial courts. But the decision was not implemented. I prepared a well reasoned speech to be delivered. I put forward my conviction that

English shall be used as the language of the trial courts. My reasoning in the speech can be summarised thus;

"The policy relating to the language of the court must be resolved with statesmanship and not by any sentimental attachment to a particular language. I too have sentimental attachment to Malayalam because it is my mother tongue. A statesman must weigh the advantages and disadvantages on the balance and then only take the decision seeing which side the scale tilts. So weighed, I found that English language is of far greater advantages if used in the trial courts, than any other language as far as a multi-lingual nation like India is concerned.

The most important reason is that English is the language now used in the Supreme Court. Every advocate in the trial court and every judicial officer must have the ambition to go higher and higher and finally reach the Supreme Court either as senior advocate or judge of the Supreme Court. The only profession, wherein language is indispensable for carrying out its business, is the profession of law. Even medical profession or engineering profession can be carried on without the aid of any language as such but legal profession cannot be conducted without having proficiency in the language used. So the advocates and judicial officers of the lower courts must acquire not only proficiency in English but good command of vocabulary in that language to show excellence in their workmanship. By historical reasons Indian courts are blessed with English typewriters, stenographers who are proficient in English, law books written in English and text books on law written in English. Why should we abandon all those advantages and lean in favour of mere sentimental causes incurring exorbitant expenses to convert the whole system into Malayalam and thereby cause Kerala lawyers to get relegated to back benches".

The above speech was widely reported in the newspapers, particularly English newspapers. On reading the news, the then Chairman of the Official Language institute sent a complaint against me to the Government stating that I violated the Government

Service Conduct Rules by speaking contrary to the government policy. The then chief secretary of Kerala State forwarded the complaint to the High Court recommending disciplinary action to be taken against me. A press cutting containing the report of my speech was also appended therewith.

The High Court decided to start disciplinary proceedings against me. As a first step they called for my remarks in the complaint. In my remarks, I admitted that I had spoken as alleged in the complaint. I pleaded that being a new recruitee to the cadre of District Judge I did not know the particular government rule nor the government decision to have Malayalam as court language. I sought High Court's indulgence in the matter.

The then Chief Justice Mr. Justice Balakrishna Eradi had a soft corner for me. He closed the file without any further orders accepting my explanation. A few days later he told me that his own personal opinion of court language was the same as I expressed, but cautioned me that I would abide by the government rules.

Until I became a judge of the High Court, I did not say anything in public which would have created any controversy. However, once I became a judge of the High Court, I expressed my views on court language in different public meetings. I continued to do so after becoming a judge of the Supreme Court. Even today I maintain the view that English must continue as the language of courts at all levels. I have other reasons also to reach the said conclusion.

The Calicut Bar was studded with very outstanding lawyers and I could get the help of almost all of them in discharging my judicial functions. It is a hard labour to mention the names of all such leading advocates. However, I am mentioning the name of Mr. K. Kunhirama Menon, who was truly one of the very best criminal lawyers I would have experienced in my legal career. I had heard of his name and fame even when I was a student of the Law College, as the best criminal lawyer at Calicut. I learnt that he was usually engaged not by the clients but by the advocates to conduct criminal cases of other clients. Perhaps no other lawyer would have conducted as much criminal trials as Mr. Menon had done. When I reached Calicut that doyen of the criminal Bar was very old but still very active moving from one court to another at ease.

His cross examination of the witnesses was an art to be known only when you were involved in the case. When he cross-examined expert witnesses such as doctors, hand writing specialists, ballistic experts or chemical examiners, I noticed how much extra knowledge Mr. Menon had acquired in the subjects in which those experts gave evidence. He had the habit of not only addressing arguments meticulously but making assertions also. Age did not wither him nor custom stale his infinite variety. He was in his full swing even after he crossed the age of ninety. I liked very much the manner in which he handled the cases and he in turn showed great admiration to my interjections either during examination of witnesses or during arguments. Whenever he conducted criminal trials in my court, the junior section of the Bar used to throng to listen how ably an advocate could withstand the inconvenient questions showered on him by the judge, yet maintaining his composure with absolute dignity and poise. I had several occasions to hear him at Calicut, I could hear his arguments as a judge of the High Court also but I missed the chance to hearing him in the Supreme Court. His demise left an unbridgeable gap in the Bar. To the members of the Bar, he was not merely a senior advocate, he was their mentor, their guardian and even their friend irrespective of the age difference.

He passed away at the very ripe age of 93, but even on the previous week, he was on his legs in one court or the other. I was judge of the Supreme Court when he died, but the Calicut Bar expressed desire to have me at Calicut for unveiling his portrait in their hall. As it was a great privilege conferred on me, I flew down from New Delhi to Calicut to perform the said honoured duty in a packed hall. I gave a speech which was later reported in one or two publications. I flew back to New Delhi to attend my duties in the Supreme Court on the next day itself.

Visiting Lakshadweep Islands:

My wife and I could make an official trip to Lakshadweep Islands in March 1980 as the said group of islands fall within the territorial jurisdiction of the District Court, Calicut. Lakshadweep is an archipelago of small but beautiful islands in the Arabian sea. Those islands are really coconut groves and the population therein consists predominantly of Muslims. The main islands are Kavaratti, Mini Coy, Anthrothu, Aminidweep, Bangaram, Agathi and Kalpeni. Normally every judicial court was to be inspected once in two years, but in the case of courts situated in Lakshadweep Islands such inspection need be conducted only once in three years. Justice K. Bhaskaran was in charge of the supervision of the judicial administration of the courts in Calicut District and when he decided to go Lakshadweep for conducting inspection of the courts I had to accompany him being the District Judge of Calicut. His gracious wife (Ratnam) accompanied him and so I took my wife also with me. (Here I must say a word about Mrs. Bhaskaran. Rarely had I come across a lady as noble as she was. Her behaviour was comprised of a blend of nobility, humility and femineity. She was very talented in drawing, sketching etc. Most of the scenery in Lakshadweep were converted by her into pencil sketches on paper. A couple of years ago she died of degeneration of nervous system. Since then her husband Justice Bhaskaran also became a sick person. I used to visit him as often as I could. He also passed away a few months ago.

We set out on an evening voyage by a vessel called "Aminidivi". Special cabins were provided to all of us in the vessel. That was my first sea voyage. Mr. P.M. Syeed (now he is Union Cabinet Minister) was a Member of Parliament then and he too was on board the ship. While dining with the Captain of the ship as his special invitees I distinctly remember how the Captain reacted to an innocent comment made by Mr. Syeed. Looking at the calm ocean Mr. Syeed said that we were fortunate because the sea was very calm and hence the voyage would be very smooth. Suddenly the Captain remonstrated "Oh God !, such a statement has been made in advance. See the sea would become very rough". I did not believe in any superstition. But as the Captain feared, when the vessel moved forward for three hours the vessel began to swing on either side violently. The Captain was seen very adeptly handling the steering. Justice Bhaskaran and my wife were affected by sea-sickness in a major way and both of them vomited profusely and were not able to lift up their heads. The doctor attached to the ship administered "Avomin tablets" to them for preventing further deterioration of their health condition. It was a mystery that Mrs. Bhaskaran and me were exempted by the sea-sickness. The ocean continued to be turbulent for three hours and thereafter it became calm.

Early next morning when the eastern sky became red heralding the rising of the sun we saw a marvellous site. Hundreds of "Tuna fish" were seen leaping up above the sea surface and swimming down in the depth. The twitching of such huge fish in the air continued for long. We have not seen such a splendid sight elsewhere.

The local people gave us a traditional welcome. One amazing feature of the population was their strict adherence to truth. Only one murder case was charge sheeted in the entire islands until the time of our visit and that too was an accidental attack. Kavaratti island was surrounded by lagoons and a large variety of multi coloured coral fish were growing in the lagoons. To see clusters of such fish gamboling around were visible through the fiber glass fitted on the bottom of the canoes. It was a matter of thrill and joy.

The farthest island was Minicoy. The people of that island had a different civilization and style of living and they spoke a different language though they could speak a little bit of Malayalam. An interesting episode happened at Minicoy. As we arrived there, we were given a welcome by the local people. The tribal chief stood in front of the crowd which thronged to welcome us. Our deffadars (main attenders of the judges) walked in front of us. They were dressed in a special manner with broad red belts and a prominent cross belt which was also red, and a special cap. The local people thought that those Deffadars are the judges. So they garlanded them. When the Deffadars tried to dissuade the locals from doing so through gesticulations we gave indication to go ahead. The local people as a customary welcome took the Deffadars to a big swing. It was funny sight how the unwilling Deffadars yielded to their welcome. It took ten minutes for the people to realise their mistake. Though we enjoyed it fully.

We visited Bengaram by covering a good distance through the sea in a boat. Bengaram was an uninhabited island where no wild life, including reptiles, could be seen. The island was surrounded by a vast stretch of blue lagoons though the water in the lagoons was of considerable depth. We could see white sand at the bottom with a clear vision. That island was an idyllic natural beauty. No wonder it has now become one of the most liked itineraries of tourists the world over.

A period of nearly two decades lapsed between our visit and now. I do not know whether the virginity of the island is still preserved. We left Lekshwadeep and returned to the main land by the same vessel.

During the four year period as District and Sessions Judge of Calicut I was fortunate in dealing with a record number of cases. It is an uphill task to narrate even all the important cases tried in my court. That apart, it would be dull and monotonous for the readers who spent their time reading the details of all such cases. If details are omitted, perhaps the synopsis may skip the core of the cases. Hence I have selected a few among the important cases conducted before me at Calicut to be pinned down here.

7

Betheri Case

The first sessions trial before me at Calicut was a very sensational murder case. The incident had happened in a hilly region of Waynad District which, during those days, formed part of the territorial jurisdiction of the Calicut sessions court. The place where the incident happened was Betheri (it was earlier called Sultan Batteri) which is now a township. It was in this case that I had the first occasion to experience how forcefully the defence in a murder case could be conducted. K. Kunhirama Menon was the main defence lawyer. Another efficient lawyer at Calicut Bar (Kunhirama Poduval) also appeared for some accused along with Mr. Menon. The facts of the case, in brief, are the following:

"A man called Mathai was a small trader at Betheri. He and his wife and his young children were residing in a house situated a couple of miles away from his business place. On a particular night Mathai did not return home and his wife became panicky. On the next morning she informed his elder brother but he comforted her saying that Mathai could be expected by night. But still he did not return. When the police was informed they registered a case as "man missing". After a few days the police arrested certain youngsters and on their disclosure statement the policed came to know that Mathai was forcefully taken to another house by three or four persons and they killed him by tightening a rope around his neck. His dead body was wrapped in a gunny bag. The killers then hired a taxi car, but they told the driver that the cab was needed for transporting some bunches of banana. The driver was asked to take the car to the house where the banana were stored. The three accused carried some banana bunches and also the gunny bag (containing the dead body) to the dickey of the car and asked the driver to proceed to Calicut.

On the way the car had to go down through the mountainous regions of Waynad for which there were eleven "Hairpin bends". When the car reached the 9th Hairpin bend the accused asked the driver to open the dickey. The driver stopped the car and opened the dickey. Then the accused dragged out the gunny bag (containing the dead body) and threw it down into the depth of the ravine. In the course of that process the driver accidentally saw the feet of a human being jutting out of the gunny bag. He became fear stricken and asked the accused why he was deceived by concealing this fact earlier. When the accused realised that the driver knew that the load was a human corpse, they adopted an aggressive posture towards him, and threatened him that he too would be killed if for any reason this information was disclosed to anyone else. The driver then promised to keep it a secret.

It is unnecessary to mention how the police eventually came to know about the accused. After the arrest of the accused, the police knew where the dead body was dumped in. The police reached the 9th Hairpin bend and with the help of some specially skilled persons who climbed down the mountainous ravine the gunny bag was traced out. It was lifted up and the highly decomposed dead body was disinterred therefrom. The body was in a totally unidentifiable condition. The police officer cut out both the thumbs of the corpse and preserved them in a bottle as a precautionary measure. He hoped that the finger impression of the deceased Mathai could be traced out from some official papers. So the police sent the thumbs along with the finger impression of the deceased for expert opinion. The Finger Bureau made a detailed examination and sent up a report holding that the thumb collected from the dead body was that of Mathai when compared with the thumb impression traced out from the official papers. That became the most crucial evidence to prove that Mathai was murdered and his body was dumped into the ravine near the 9th Hairpin bend.

Many witnesses were examined including the widow, the brother and a business partner of Mathai. Two witnesses were very important. One was the driver of the car and the other was a boy (who too was abducted by the accused along with Mathai). In fact, the accused had planned to liquidate the boy also to wipe out all evidence of murder. But later they changed their mind as the boy promised to work under the accused as an employee and keep the entire episode a secret.

The trial of the case prolonged for a long period of 22 days. Each witness was cross-examined threadbare by the advocates, particularly Kunhirama Menon. The arguments were heard at length. Finally I pronounced judgement convicting all the accused and sentenced them to life imprisonment. It was the first criminal case which I conducted at Calicut. But it gave an impression that I was prone to convict the accused in criminal cases. Nonetheless the Bar was happy because they felt that I gave the advocates full opportunity for cross-examining the witnesses and to argue the case.

The criminal cases conducted at Calicut were so many. Most of them had at least one prominent feature to be highlighted. Still I would restrict myself to a very few only, lest the readers might feel it rigmarole and stale.

8

A case of double infanticide

In a village on the eastern terrains of Calicut District a couple lived with their two children. The first was daughter (Liz) aged 5 years and the second was son (Jose) aged 3 years. The parents were Christian settlers emigrated from middle Travancore (central Kerala) to the erstwhile Malabar region (north Kerala). Though I do not remember the names of the parents I wish to call them here as George and Mary. After Jose was born his father George underwent a vasectomy as they wished to limit the members of their children to two. George had a rubber plantation besides his residential compound. His brothers were living in the neighbourhood. The youngest brother Joy was unmarried and was living with one of his brothers.

There was a well in the compound of George which neared completion of its construction, what remained was only its parapet. On the day of occurrence George and Mary had to go to their parish-church in connection with some festival. While they were busy preparing to go to the church, his brother Joy visited him to enquire whether they proposed to go to the church. George's child Jose seeing his young uncle clang to him. Mary (George's wife) supplied him a cup of horlicks and a banana. Joy gave the banana to his nephew and gave him a kiss also. Then he left that house. After a little while George and Mary proceeded to the church leaving the little children at home with a specific instruction not to go near the well.

About a couple of hours later George and Mary returned home. The children were not in the house and the parents assumed that they would have gone to the house of one of their uncles situated close by. When George sat for his breakfast he wished his children also to share it with him and hence he asked his wife to fetch them. Mary, after making some enquiries found to her grief, that the children were not in any of the neighboring houses. Instinctively she ran towards the well and looked into it. She noticed a small picture book (which Liz had with her) floating in it. Mary made a loud scream and many people rushed in. Two of them climbed down into the well and made a search. Finally the dead body of both the children were brought out. The house turned into a cauldron of wailings and lamentations. As the parents were sure that the children had accidentally slipped into the well they were not inclined to have their dead body cut to conduct postmortem examination. So George told one of his brothers to arrange with the police for dispensing with the postmortem examination.

The funeral was scheduled to take place on the next morning. By then all the relatives reached the house from distant places. One of the sisters of George, while hugging the dead body of the children wanted Liz to wear the gold chain presented by her to the child at the time of baptism. Then only Mary (mother of the children) realised that Liz was in fact wearing gold chain when they left home to attend the church function. She also noticed that gold waist chain which Joy wore was also missing. Disappearance of the gold ornaments alerted the people and the funeral was postponed. In the meanwhile a filtering search was made inside the well up to the rock bottom, but in vain. Then all the people smelt suspicion of some serious foul play in the death of the children. The police was moved again and autopsy was conducted by Dr. Guharaj

(Head of the department of Forensic Medicines, Calicut) The doctor found that Liz was strangled to death and Jose was smothered to death.

I do not propose to narrate the further details of investigation except saying that the police after 20 days arrested the young uncle of the children, Joy for the murder of the little ones after robbing them of the gold ornaments.

The trial took place in my court. The local press carried the details of the trial as the case acquired some sensational dimensions. The circumstances presented by the prosecution against the accused were quite sturdy and unassailable. In the end I convicted the accused of murder of the little children.

While considering the sentence to be passed I was not able to persuade myself to award anything less than the maximum sentence prescribed by law. I was personally opposed to death penalty. There are two schools of thought on death penalty. One favours retention of it and the other pleads for its abolition. I have my own reasons to support the latter school of thought. Whatever that be, a Constitution Bench of the Supreme Court of India (five judges) had upheld death penalty as constitutionally valid provided it is awarded only in "rarest of rare cases in which life imprisonment is unquestionably foreclosed". (Bechan Singh Vs. State of Punjab) Once the law was declared by the Supreme Court, I had to treat it as the law. I had to abide by the oath administered to me that I would discharge my functions without any prejudice or predilection. I found this case as the "rarest of rare cases" in which life imprisonment was unquestionably foreclosed. Hence I passed the sentence of death on the accused.

The newspapers next day flashed this news with the photo of the cute children who were killed. This created a big flutter among the readers. None of them would have reconciled with a sentence less than the maximum provided by law to be passed on the accused. Every newspaper described the case with full details.

Though the High Court confirmed the conviction of the accused, the death sentence was altered to life imprisonment only on the ground that the accused was very young in age. Such alteration of sentence relieved me of the heaviness of my heart as I was personally against awarding death penalty as a sentence on any person.

9

How a submerged equity winched to the fore

A typical instance of experiencing the work of the unseen hand can now be narrated. That case was under the Rent Control Law, which remains sticking in my mind among many cases which I would have disposed of. Narration of the facts of the case is necessary to highlight the speciality involved therein.

A Muslim gentleman died in harness leaving behind him his young widow and two little daughters. He had, to his credit one LIC policy the proceeds of which, on his death were collected by his widow. The amount would have been a substantial sum. As she was contemplating how to utilise the amount she was advised by her husband's brother to invest it in the form of a residential building to be built on a small plot of land which belonged to the two minor daughters. The brother supervised the construction of the building which, on completion, became a substantial building. Though many people approached her to have the building on rent, she was not willing to give it to anyone. She asked her brother to look after the building as she thought it would later be a great succor to her when the daughters reached marriageable age. Her husband's brother occupied the building for which he gave a formal rent deed. After many years, when the daughters reached marriageable age, the widow asked the brother to vacate the building. But it was a different brother whom she found then. He refused to vacate the building. Many persons persuaded him, but he did not vacate.

It was in the above background that the widow and her two daughters jointly filed a case under the Rent Control legislation for eviction of the tenant on the ground that the building was needed for their own occupation. The brother was arrayed as the sole respondent in the case. The defence adopted by the brother was something which the widow would never have anticipated. He set up a case that he was a "kudikidappukaran" (meaning hutment dweller) as defined under the Kerala Land Reforms Act. If a person was allowed to occupy a hut (cost of a hut must be below Rs.750) belonging to the landowner he would be a "kudikidappukaran" as per the said Act. Similarly, if the person was permitted by the land owner to erect a "homestead" on the land belonging to another person, that person also would be a "kudikidappukaran". The word "homestead" means a dwelling house whatever be its value.

The stand of the brother in that case was that he was a "kudikidappukaran" as he was permitted to build the homestead on the plot of land. Under the Kerala Land Reforms Act, when a question arises whether a person is a "kudikidappukaran" or not, such question could be decided only by a Land Tribunal. The civil court has no jurisdiction to decide that question at all. So whenever a person claimed that he is a "kudikidappukaran" the civil court lost jurisdiction to decide it and that question has to be referred to the Land Tribunal for decision. The practical consequence in such situation is that once a case is referred to Land Tribunal it would remain there for many years. The Rent Control Court in this case made a reference to the local Land Tribunal to decide that question.

Unfortunately the petitioners or their advocate did not appear in the Land Tribunal at all. The respondent/tenant therefore had a cake walk in the case. He gave evidence on oath before the Land

Tribunal to the effect that he was permitted by the Land owners to erect a homestead thereon. His evidence became unchallenged as nobody represented the widow to cross-examine him. The Land Tribunal decided the question on the strength of that unchallenged evidence by holding that respondent was a "kudikidappukaran". Under the law a "kudikidappukaran" could not be evicted at all. The Rent Control court had no other option and so it dismissed the petition for eviction.

The widow and her children filed an appeal before the Sub Court. The sub judge felt much sympathy towards the widow and her daughters but there was no escape from dismissing the appeal due to the unchallenged evidence given by the tenant in the Land Tribunal. Thereafter the widow and her children filed a revision in the District Court, Calicut. The power of the District Court, in revision, was very much restricted. According to law, no finding on facts made by the trial court (and confirmed by the appellate court) could be interfered with by the District Court in revision, unless the finding was illegal or perverse. When the revision was argued before me, all the parties concerned in that case felt that the tenant's advocate would get an easy win. The advocate for the widow and the children argued for some time. He was not able to point out anything by which the finding of the Land Tribunal and the appeal court could be interfered with. My mind was much vexed because a widow and her daughters had to loose the case in which justice was clearly on their side, but the law was apparently against them. After hearing arguments of their advocate, I felt very sorry that I had to dismiss the revision with a heavy heart by denying justice to the hapless ladies. As there was no chance for them to win, their advocate sat down helplessly.

At that stage I perused the records of the case. The unchallenged evidence of the respondent/tenant was very short and it read like this; "The petitioners (the ladies) permitted me to put up a homestead on the land and hence I erected the house building". The said statement of the respondent had to be accepted in view of the fact that it was not challenged. Permission of the landowner was necessary to construct the building without which no right could be claimed as Kudikidappukaran. The permission must be legally valid. Suddenly I felt a strong doubt in my mind. Whatever be the nature of the permission given by the ladies to the respondent to construct the building it could not be valid at all. The law is clear that if the permission was granted by some one who was not competent to give such permission, the court should treat the permission as null and void. Among the three petitioners who gave the permission, one was a widow and the others were her minor daughters. I put the following questions to the advocate for the respondent:

"Is a widow competent under the Mohammedan Law to act on behalf of her minor children regarding their properties ? Are not the minor daughters incompetent to give permission ? If the permission you rely on was only that which was given by those persons, how could that be a permission at all in the eye of law ?"

The above bunch of questions were a bolt from the blue for the counsel who appeared for the brother. He would never have thought that he would be confronted with such a legal conundrum. He requested for an adjournment to study those aspects of Mohammedan Law. On the next posting day I repeated the same questions to him but he was unable to get over the insurmountable hurdle. He finally sat down. The advocate for the ladies became jubilant though it was the judge who discovered that formidable point which never flashed through his mind.

I wrote a judgement dealing with the factual position and held that there was no valid permission under law for erecting a homestead without which no claim of "kudikidappu" can be laid. I held that the tenant was liable to be evicted under the B.R.C. Act on the ground urged by the widow and her children.

My judgement, though challenged in the High Court, was confirmed. Finally the ladies got the building vacated. My joy was so profound and over flowing in that I could salvage a cause of justice only because of a flash which passed through my mind at the final round, which escaped the notice of the first court as well as the Land Tribunal, nor could the appeal court and also the advocates for the ladies discover it at any stage of the litigation. Could that flash have been a "honeybee" bestowed on me from the ultimate dispenser of Justice.

10

Medical Insanity Vs. Legal Insanity

This is a perplexing subject in the realm of criminal law. Section 84 of the Indian Penal Code says that "nothing is an offence which is done by a person who, at the time of doing it, by reason of unsoundness of mind, is incapable of knowing the nature of the act, or that he is doing what is either wrong or contrary to law". Very often cases arouse wherein the question to be decided was whether the person who caused the death of another could claim the protection of the above Section 84. I do not wish to dwell on the jurisprudential aspect of the subject now, but it would interest the reader to have the narration of two cases, the trial of which were conducted in my court at Calicut. I shall now present the first of those two cases.

The accused in a murder case tried in my court at Calicut was a middle aged man. The case against him was that he beheaded his nephew. The motive for the murder was apparently silly. According to the prosecution version, the accused asked his nephew to buy cigarettes for him, but he did not obey. The accused became angry, he took out a big knife and caught hold of the tuft of nephew's hair and decapitated him. The accused then surrendered to the police.

As the accused did not engage an advocate due to financial incapacity, I appointed a junior advocate to defend him in the court. I forewarned the advocate that the ferocity of the murder might perhaps end in death penalty for the accused, and wanted him to conduct the case as best as possible.

It appeared strange in this case that all members of accused's family including his mother gave evidence against him. They all denied the suggestion of the defence counsel that the accused was suffering from mental illness. On the contrary, all the witnesses said that the accused was sound in mind and his health condition was normal. The manner in which the prosecution evidence progressed gave me an inkling that this case might perhaps turn out to be a "rarest of rare cases", wherein the court might award death penalty to the accused. Nonetheless, I had a lingering feeling that the motive for beheading the nephew was too silly and that something more important had been hidden in the case. During discussion in open court the advocate told me that the accused disclosed to him about a prior incident which took place ten years ago in which the accused inflicted cut injuries on the right arm of his younger brother. That younger brother happened to be present in the court hall as a spectator. I wanted him to be examined as a witness at that moment itself. He was led to the witness stand. When the public prosecutor examined him he said that the accused never had any mental disease. He denied having been attacked by the accused on any former occasion.

At that stage I heard the accused murmuring that the scars of the cut injuries were still visible on his brother's forearm. I asked the witness to remove the sleeves of his shirt. I noticed a few scars of cut injuries on the forearm. I then confronted him with a volley of questions and practically cornered him. He finally admitted that the accused cut him with a big knife about ten years ago and that the accused was taken to the mental hospital at Calicut where he was treated for a long period.

I issued a direction to the Head of the Mental Health Department, Calicut (Dr. Santhakumar) to make an effort to trace out whether a person by this accused's name had been treated there at any time. Next morning Dr. Santhakumar appeared before the court with a bunch of registers and records and reported to me that the accused was treated as an inpatient in the said hospital for a virulent type of schizophrenia and he was sent back home after completing a long course of treatment. The doctor disclosed to me that this accused was brought to the same hospital after the present murder because of the recurrence of his disease. I was convinced that he was suffering from acute mental illness when he beheaded his nephew.

I was taken aback. Why all this backdrop was suppressed by the family members and even by the investigating officer? To my repeated queries, I understood that the members of the family became frustrated by the violent nature of the accused due to recurring schizophrenia and hence they did not mind the court passing a death penalty on him, so that they could get rid of a dangerous member afflicted with homicidal proclivities once and for all.

I felt sad, our society did not give the family members proper counseling to deal with a mentally sick person. When medical science has advanced to appreciable levels prescribing effective treatment for mental diseases, could the court of law afford to liquidate a human being on the mistaken impression that he committed murder knowing the nature of his act. The stark reality was that the accused did not know when he cut the head of his nephew that he was doing it. His cognitive faculties were so paralyzed as to render him incapable of knowing the nature of his acts. If any such person was sentenced to death penalty it would have resulted in a mockery of justice.

In my judgement I held that the accused had done the act but without knowing the nature of what he did due to his mental illness. So I acquitted him but directed him to be kept in the mental hospital until such time as he could be put back to normal life. I passed further directions regarding his treatment as well as the follow up steps to be adopted. I also ordered an enquiry to be conducted to find out the persons responsible for suppressing the mental condition of the accused in the trial court.

I remember the above case with the vivid details and even now I recollect his face as he was standing in the dock of the court. I do not know what happened to him thereafter. Now I shall present the second case.

The trial of one case turned out in its last phase as an acrimonious debate involving the subject of mental health. It was a case of triple murder of a mother and her two children. (I do not exactly remember whether the children slain were three or two) The person accused in the case was the husband of the mother and father of her slain children. As the incident created a big commotion in the district, the state government wanted to appoint an advocate as special public prosecutor to conduct the prosecution in the case. Mr. K. Bhaskaran Nair, a renowned criminal lawyer was appointed as such. But ironically the accused engaged one of his devoted juniors Mr. R. Basant (now Mr. Justice R. Basant). Apart from the fact that Basant was trained by Mr. Bhaskaran Nair as his junior the former was deeply loyal to the senior. By the time the trial took place Basant would have reached take off stage from the fledgling period in his career as a legal practitioner.

When the prosecution witnesses were examined they all stuck to their original version and hence I felt that it would have been a cake-walk for the prosecution particularly because the prosecution could adduce overwhelming evidence to prove that the accused inflicted cut injuries on all the deceased persons with a chopper. The questions put by the defence counsel were easily answered by the witnesses during cross-examination. I noticed that Mr. Basant put questions without disputing the core of the case that the accused inflicted cut injuries. However, I could discern that the defence counsel was trying to make out a plea of insanity of the accused. But all prosecution witnesses gave answers to the effect that the accused did not have any mental disease.

The prosecution was conducted in a very efficient manner by a very experienced criminal lawyer. The defence lawyer was almost a raw junior. Hence it appeared to me at first that it was a combat between a seasoned gladiator and a rookie.

When the accused was questioned by me regarding all circumstances which appeared against him in the case he answered mainly pleading that he had no knowledge about anything which happened on the night in question. He offered to give defence evidence. Mr. Basant filed a list of four witnesses and all of them were doctors attached to the mental health wing of the Medical College, Calicut. Finally he chose only three of them to be examined.

The first witness examined on the defence side was Dr. Vasudevan Namboothiri. Mr. Basant produced a chart containing a large number of human conduct features and requested me to mark it as an exhibit for the sake of convenience. I did so. He gave that chart to Dr. Namboothiri and asked him thus:

"I am putting a hypothetical question to you, if you examined a person who was brought to you and then you came across from him that he had shown all the symptoms contained in the chart, what would be the diagnosis you make from such features ?"

The doctor answered; "My diagnosis would be that the person who had all those features was suffering from paranoid schizophrenia". On a perusal of the chart I noticed that all the symptoms enumerated therein were brought out by Basant during his cross-examination of prosecution witnesses as the demeanor noticed in the conduct of the accused. The special public prosecutor Bhaskaran Nair then sensed that the case of the prosecution had taken a reverse turn in favour of the defence. Though he cross-examined Dr. Namboothiri, the witness stuck to his original stand. The next witness Dr. Vijayan who had even higher academic qualifications than Dr. Namboothiri concurred with the opinion expressed by Dr. Namboothiri. But when R. Basant examined Dr. Santhakumar who was then the senior most doctor of the mental health department in the Medical College, Calicut, he answered in such a manner as to considerably diluting the opinions expressed by the other two doctors. According to Dr. Santhakumar the symptoms enumerated in the chart were not enough for him to reach the diagnosis that the patient was suffering from paranoid schizophrenia.

I felt that R. Basant though a raw junior was adopting new techniques in criminal trials while defending the accused. Never did I come across such forensic techniques having been adopted by other defence counsel.

Though the case initially was very strong for the prosecution it turned out to be a closely fought battle. Of course ultimately I accepted the prosecution case and rejected the defence theory and convicted the accused and sentenced him to imprisonment for life.

At the end of my tenure as Sessions Judge at Calicut I called R. Basant to my chambers and encouraged him to strive forward and think of becoming a District and Sessions Judge directly recruited from the Bar. A few years thereafter, when I was judge of the High Court, Mr. Basant was one of the successful candidates selected to the cadre of District Judges. He later became a judge of the High Court of Kerala.

The other junior of Mr. K. Bhaskaran Nair, Ms. Hema (mentioned above), also became District and Sessions Judge directly recruited from the Bar. It was my good fortune to have been one of the five Judges who formed the panel for selecting such direct recruitees and in the selection the above two persons were found to be quite suitable for appointment as District and Sessions Judges. Ms. Hema had a very tumultuous career as a District Judge. As she was appointed first in a district, which was under my administrative supervision, I had occasions to give her guidance and directions without least interfering with her judicial independence. She used to recollect them with gratitude. I noticed her as the very studious and hardworking judicial officer committed to her work. She got a rare opportunity to undergo a training in England for Family Law. I understood from Mr. Justice B.N. Kirpal, a former Chief Justice of India (who attended the training course and delivered the valedictory address) that Ms. Hema from Kerala was adjudged to be the best participant in that training course. On returning to India she was assigned to discharge duties as Judge of the Family Court, Ernakulam. She was elevated as Judge of the High Court of Kerala. Mr. Justice R. Basant and Ms. Justice Hema are two proud products of Calicut Bar.

11

Winding up life in Calicut

There were many episodes which took place during my four year tenure in Calicut which had influenced my thoughts and perceptions. It is difficult to narrate all of them. I changed three houses during the said four years as there was no official quarters even for the District Judge, Calicut. But I could accomplish an achievement of commencing the work of providing residential quarters for all the judicial officers at Calicut. The project was completed within the scheduled time. Now all the judicial officers posted at Calicut are lucky as they deed not wander about in search of residential houses. For the accomplishment of the above project I owe much to the free hand given to me by Mr. Justice K. Bhaskaran of the Kerala High Court who was then in charge of the aqdministrative supervision of the District. Mr. P.P. Thomas was the Superintending Engineer, PWD (who later retired as Chief Engineer, Kerala) and Mr. K.M. Balakrishnan, the District Collector. Both of them were of tremendous help for completing the project.

I enjoyed morning strolls along the beach road of Calicut. During half of my tenure my walking-mate was Mr. C.J. Robin who was my class-mate as well as hostel-mate while we were studying law at Madras Law College. After leaving the Law College Mr. Robbin set up practice at Calicut mostly as a tax practitioner, while

I set up practice at Kottayam. Though we both were deeply immersed in politics during our early days, I gradually drifted out from that field, but Mr. Robin continued in active politics and he later became Mayor of the City Corporation of Calicut. We both used to go up to the water of the sea when fishermen returned with their catch and quite often we made purchases of fish directly from them. We both enjoyed such fish purchase.

During the second half of my tenure, I had the fortune to have Mr. K.K. Nayar as my walking-mate. He had his education in England and joined the Forest Department in Kerala and retired as Chief Conservator in Forest. Whenever the name of Mr. K.K. Nayar was mentioned, he was described as the most honest and upright forest official of the state. His juniors trembled when K.K. Nayar set out for supervision of forests. It was said about him that he could identify every tree in the forest. He was perhaps the rarest commodity in a department which was notorious for being studded with corrupt officials. I recollect the rejuvenating morning walks and our conversation provided enough pabulum for moulding up a proper perceptive towards forest laws in the later years of my official career.

I wish to cut short my experience as District Judge of Calicut by mentioning an episode which would have been a disaster for members of two families but for the providential escape.

The eastern parts of the then district of Calicut consist of the hilly regions of the present Wayanad district. A large area of forest was also included in that region. By the middle of twentieth century there was a large migration of people from the plains to the above hilly regions before people migrated to this area the forests were the natural habitat of wild life. Those people made extensive plantations such as rubber, tea, coffee etc. Eventually those area became very rich and the people also prospered in wealth. There was then demand for carving out those regions to form a new district called Wayanad. The court was established at Kalpetta which is now a big township as the center of Wayanad district. When it was part of Calicut district, it was the duty of the District Judge of Calicut to conduct annual inspection of the administrative work of the courts at Wayanad.

Sri. A.V. Haridas was then Munsiff of Kalpetta (he is today the Vice Chairman of the Central Administrative Tribunal) He requested me to have a visit of the forest areas of Bandipur. I thought of availing myself of the special opportunity of seeing the interiors of the forest areas of Wayanad district. My wife and children accompanied me to Kalpetta. Mr. Haridas persuaded his wife and children also to join our trip to the forest.

After the inspection work was over at Kalpetta, we set out in two vehicles to Bandipur. Two forest guards came with us for showing the exact direction to proceed.

The children and one guard were in one vehicle driven by a professional driver. We the elders and other guard were in the next vehicle which was driven by another driver. As we entered into the thick forest area we saw a herd of elephants gracing themselves. For two reasons we thought of standing out to have a better view of the wild elephants. First is that the forest guards assured us that the wild elephants, when they were in a herd, would never harm to human beings. Second is that the elephants were then quiet far away from the road and we could see them better through binoculars. We therefore stopped the car and all of us got out. It was a good sight particularly when we saw some baby elephants in the herd clinging on to their mother elephants. After a couple of minutes one of the mother elephants sighted us from a distance. Unexpectedly that wild animal was seen galloping towards us. Impulsively we all jumped into the vehicle and the drivers started the engine and moved forward as fast as they could. The elephant instead of stopping, chased the cars for a good distance, but our drivers applied their feet on the accelerator for gaining greater speed. Chasing elephants was a "dreadful" sight to those who flee to escape. It was not possible for the elephants to reach near the cars and thereafter it gave up the chase after galloping for some distance.

We proceeded towards the interior of the forest. Though it was a kacha road, we could reach the den of the forest area and thought that we escaped from the possible vision of the angry elephants. All the elders were under terrible tension, our children were fearstriken and even the two drivers were then seen shivering. As the place where we reached was a cul-de-sac we remained there for nearly two hours hoping that the elephants would have gone far away. We then undertook our return journey through the same road.

As we neared the place where we first saw the herd of elephants, we were relieved in noticing that there was not a single elephant anywhere near visibility. With that sense of relief we proceeded to some more distance. Suddenly we spotted one elephant climbing up from a stream or a pond about two or three furlongs away from our cars which was followed by another elephant and then another one. I was certain that the same herd of elephants were moving on. I then asked the driver not to slow down the vehicle but to speed up. Within two minutes the same mother elephant spotting out our convoy, started to gallop with a big trumpet. The vehicles took greater momentum and the wild elephants took speedier pace. The elephants chased our vehicles for a distance of nearly half a mile and found that they were unable to catch up with speeding automobiles. Hence they gave up the chase after making another outcry. Our vehicles continued to ply at the same speed until we felt assured that we crossed the Rubicon and thus out of the zone of danger.

After heaving a great sigh of relief, I asked the forest guard why he assured of no danger from elephants while they were in a herd. His answer was that it was because of the mother elephants, as it concerned for its calves. I told him that my position was also the same that my concern was for my children. Thus, ended a jaunt which would have been a terrible disaster.

On completion of four years of stint at Calicut, I was transferred as District Judge at Quilon. Members of Bar at Calicut arranged a farewell meeting in their court hall which was crammed with advocates. Another farewell function was arranged on the night at Alagapuri Hotel followed by a dinner which too was attended by a number of advocates. At both functions selected representatives of advocates spoke very touchingly. In my reply I said, among other things, that I became so attached to Calicut Bar that I felt to have become a non subscribing member of that Bar. The affection and regard which the members of the Calicut Bar showered on me continued even for many years thereafter. Even today they express their sentiments very lavishly whenever they get an occasion to do so.

12

District Judge, Quilon

The official residence of the District Judge, Quilon (renamed as Kollam) is situated on the shore of a huge lake. The site of District Judge's bungalow at Quilon is perhaps the best among all the official residences of District Judges in Kerala. Even the High Court Judge's official bungalows do not have such a beautiful location. Sitting on the balcony of the bungalow at Quilon, looking at the lake (Ashtamudi Kayal) during night one can have an ecstatic sight, the canoes lit with hurricane lamps moving steadily through the waters of the lake. For two years, I enjoyed the sight staying in the said bungalow as District and Sessions Judge, Quilon. The territorial extent of that district then was perhaps the vastest as it comprised almost the entire territories which now formed another revenue district (Pathanamthitta).

Sri. A. R. Vijayan and Sri. L. Manoharan (who later became Justice L. Manoharan) were the first and second Additional District Judges of Quilon during my tenure. We three used to have regular morning walk which gave us enough time to understand each other's court and its problems. We were able to work in unison.

My first task was to find admission for my three sons in the educational institutions at Quilon. Then my youngest son was offered a seat in a primary class in one of the aided private schools. The Mother Superior who was the head of the institution told me that I had to pay a certain amount by way of "donation" besides the prescribed fees. I was not willing to pay such an amount except the fees as I considered collection of such amount in the name of donation was unethical and un-Christian. She tried to convince me by pointing out some big buildings put up in the school compound with the money collected through such "donation". I told her that even dacoits of Champal valley utilised the money extracted through extortion for feeding many poor tribal people. I also told her that I would take my child to other schools for admission where no amount would be extracted in the name of "donation". But I made a rider saying that if all such schools collected donations I might go back to the same school on the realization that the above idealism is an unworkable proposition in practical terms and that I could not afford to spoil the future of my son by pursuing such kind of idealism.

I then went to one of the renowned schools at Quilon (Infant Jesus School). Rev. Fr. Ferdinand Kayavil, the Principal agreed to admit my son in that school. He mentioned about the fees to be paid. I then asked him whether they collect any amount by way of donation. His answer was clear and dignified. He told me that not even a pie would be collected as donation either from me or from anybody else. I was very much impressed by the behaviour of the Principal and also by his firm stand not to accept any amount other than the prescribed fees.

My son joined the school. We arranged a rickshaw to carry him and his friends who were residing in the same locality to go to the school. Within a few weeks the Principal sent a letter to all students mentioning that the school would conduct a bus service and any one desiring to avail himself of the facilities of a school bus might advance a loan of Rs. 3000/-. I readily gave the amount of Rs. 3000/- though I did not expect that the loan amount would ever be returned. But I wish to record here that on completion of my tenure at Quilon the school authorities not only sent the Transfer

Certificate for my son but a cheque as well for the amount of Rs. 3000/- together with the interest at the same rate as a nationalized bank charged for the savings bank account deposit.

The dignified manner in which the authorities of "Infant Jesus School, Quilon" conducted themselves should be a model to others. As years rolled on many private aided schools have gone astray by collecting huge money calling it "donation" at the time of admitting students. Such collections were made even by schools run by religious minorities which enjoyed the protection of Article 30 of the Constitution. Aided educational institutions also collect beneath the table, huge amount of money from persons appointed as teachers. It is very unfortunate that the said nefarious practice is on the increase now. In educational institutions, which were beacon lights fifty years ago have become profit making commercialised institutions, wherein the marketable commodity is learning. Fifty years ago such schools were opened to the people belonging to middle class families of all communities. Training graduates from middle class families could reasonably aspire to become teachers or lecturers of such institutions. But now those institutions have become approachable only to those who can afford to pay huge money to the management of such institutions calling it 'donations'. I believe that a day would come when people may organise to stop those commercialization of education.

I remember the vivid details of the first murder case tried in my court at Quilon. The story of the prosecution was this:- A man called Budhan was a hawker in cloth materials. Besides that work he was doing illicit arrack business in partnership with the main accused in this case. While the business flourished, the accused developed illicit sexual relationship with Budhan's wife Laila. After some time Budhan came to know about it and he thrashed the accused left and right and sent him out of the business. The accused was a cunning person. After a few months, he succeeded in winning Budhan over again. So Budhan restored him to the partnership. As the joint business continued for some time the accused again developed illicit liaison with Laila very secretly. When Laila cautioned him he disclosed to her of his plan to finish Budhan and then to marry Laila to which Laila gave a nod of approval.

One day the accused told Budhan that a rival arrack manufacturer was doing illicit work at a particular place and sought the help of Budhan to trace it out. Budhan was persuaded to go with him to a place called "Karikkathilkadavu". Another employ of the accused was also with them. When they reached the place the accused dug the bank of the river and spotted the utensils etc. employed by the said rival for manufacturing arrack. They collected all those materials in a basket for removing them to a distant place and to destroy them. While the basket load was carried by Budhan on his head the other two accused tied a long towel around his neck abruptly and tightened it until Budhan was dead. They dumped the dead body in the same pit and buried it and planted collocasia thereon. On the same night the accused visited Laila and reported to her about it and had liaison with her. Subsequently she told her neighbours that her husband had gone to Telegu states for hawking cloth materials.

As Budhan was missing from the locality for a long period his brothers made some enquiries. They became suspicious of the role of his business partner in eliminating Budhan and so they complained to the police. To cut short the story, the police officials arrested the accused and elicited all the details from him regarding the occurrence. They took him to the place where Budhan was buried. As law required that in such a case the inquest must be held only by an Executive Magistrate, the police requisitioned the services of the local R.D.O. who was the Executive Magistrate also. The skeleton of Budhan was disinterred from the pit, and the inquest was held accordingly.

Dr. Umadethan, Professor of Forensic Medicine conducted "photographic superimposition tests" with the photo of the skull along with a passport size photo of Budhan (which was collected from the files of the Excise Department as they used to keep the photos of the suspected persons indulging in illicit arrack). Finally the police charge sheeted the accused and his employee as second accused, besides Laila as third accused alleging that they all entered into a criminal conspiracy to finish Budhan. The skull of Budhan was produced in the court. I thought of keeping the skull on the table of the dias of the court hall in such a manner as it faced the accused. It would have been a dreadful sight for all the accused, particularly Laila to see the skull of Budhan grinning at all of them and at all times during the trial.

It was a case of circumstantial evidence, but almost all witnesses for the prosecution, except the official witnesses, were won over by the accused. Yet I did not feel that it was a hopeless case for the prosecution because one timber trader testified to a conversation between him and the accused after consuming liquor a few days prior to the murder. The evidence of that person was that in their chat the accused told him that he and Laila had decided to marry each other and that anyone standing in the way would be eliminated.

When the Executive Magistrate was examined in court I noticed that he was in a "don't care" mood. I knew that his evidence would have been crucial for the prosecution as the place where the dead body was buried was spotted out by the accused to the Executive Magistrate. But when the Magistrate started his evidence he answered in a very casual manner and said that he did not remember all the details. Then I thought it was time for me to interject. I remonstrated at him for the casualness with which he was giving evidence in a murder case. I asked him whether he had brought his file and he answered in the negative. I warned him that adverse comments might be passed in the judgment exposing his irresponsibility. He then appealed to me to give him one more day. I thought I should not miss that opportunity. I asked him to execute a bond undertaking to reach the court on the next day with the file concerned. He would have refreshed himself reading the files. Next day the R.D.O. appeared in court as a totally different person. He gave evidence seriously that the place of burial was spotted out by the accused. When the public prosecutor closed the evidence I pointed out that he had not proved that the photocopy collected from the file of the Excise Department was that of Budhan. I also told him that if he failed to establish the important link he had no chance to bring the case to conviction. Sensing the said lacuna the Public Prosecutor filed a petition seeking permission to examine the brother of Budhan. Without any wavering I granted permission and the brother of Budhan was recalled and re-examined. The only point elicited from the witness this time was, that the photo was that of his brother Budhan.

The first accused was defended by Sri. Puthur Gopalakrishna Pillai who was one of the best criminal lawyers of Kollam Bar. He sensed that in spite of winning almost all witnesses he was facing a very stiff court. When I pronounced judgement I held the accused guilty of murdering Budhan and sentenced him to imprisonment for life. Due to want of evidence I acquitted Laila. But her real punishment was that she had to remain in court looking at her husband's skull grinning at her throughout the trial period. It was indeed unbearable to her.

Appeal was filed by the accused before the High Court of Kerala. It was heard by a division bench of the High Court (Justice T.K. Thomman and Justice M.M. Pareed Pillai) They refused to believe the evidence of the timber merchant. When that was excluded the remaining evidence was not sufficient to convict the accused, according to those two Judges. Hence the accused succeeded in finally escaping from conviction.

Whenever the High Court had confirmed my judgment, I did not rejoice at it and whenever the High Court reversed my judgement it did not make me unhappy. All that I was concerned about, whenever I passed judgments, was that I should reach the conclusion conscientiously on the facts and that it should be in accordance with law. When a case goes before a higher court in appeal the matter gets a still fuller consideration and the judges would reach either the same conclusion or a different conclusion. If they reached the same conclusion, it is no tribute to the first judgement and if they reached a different conclusion it is no censure to the first judgement. This is one of the principles in judicial dispensation. For attaining near perfection for a judicial exercise every cause must have at least one more fresh consideration at a higher level. It is advisable that such fresh consideration should be made by a different personage. A second hearing which is called appeal is thus intended and provided for a fresh look of the facts. Some judges showed euphoria whenever their judgements were confirmed by the High Court or Supreme Court as though it was their victory and some judges showed frustration when the superior courts reached a different conclusion as though it was their defeat. A mature judge is one who is least concerned about the outcome regarding his own judgement when the same is reconsidered judicially by a higher judicial forum.

13

The Dead body giving birth to a child

In a murder case tried in the Sessions Court, Quilon, the facts contained a very strange episode wherein a dead body gave birth to a child. Its synopsis is thus: On the morning hours of a particular day the watchman of a rubber estate came across the dead body of a woman lying in one of the uncultivated areas inside the estate. The watchman, instead of reporting the matter to the manager of the estate or to the police, applied for leave for a week and disappeared from the scene. But he went to the spot stealthily on the next morning to know what happened to the dead body. He was startled seeing a newborn baby huddled to the corpse. He was quite sure that on the previous day there was no child near the dead body. Hence seeing the dead body with a child he ran away from the scene. However he disclosed this to someone else from whom eventually the superintendent of the estate knew about it. The police was informed about this matter without delay.

The postmortem examination revealed that it was the dead body of a young teenaged pregnant girl who was strangulated to death and thereafter the child was born dead or alive and died immediately after birth.

For a long time the investigation officer did not get any clue as to the identity of the murdered girl. One Mr. M. Wahab, Circle Inspector of Police, took up the investigation. At the first instance the police arrested the watchmen of the estate. But on being interrogated the police found him innocent. The reason for his ducking down immediately on seeing the dead body was investigated and found to be true. About eight years ago this watchman came across another decomposed dead body somewhere else in the same estate and he was deputed by the management to inform the police about it. After the police reached the spot the watchman had to undergo a lot of tribulations besides loss of huge money for arranging the postmortem examination and cremation of the dead body etc. Though he applied to the management for refund of all the expenses borne by him, not a single paise was paid to him. He was thus aware of all the consequences befalling him for giving the first information to the police regarding the dead body involved in an offence. Hence he decided not to commit such a folly once again and that is the reason for his disappearing from the scene when he saw the dead body of the pregnant woman in this case.

Mr. Wahab conducted the investigation in a very admirable manner. He traced out the identity of the dead body as that of a Nair girl who was the daughter of a workman attached to a tea estate at Vandiperiyar (situated about 150 KM away from the place where the dead body was found). Mr. Wahab came to know of the following facts:- The Nair girl fell in love with a Christian youngster. They had frequent meetings together and had sexual life also until she became pregnant. When her parents came to know that their young daughter was pregnant they questioned her about the paternity of the child and she revealed to them that it was the accused. They brought him to their house and confronted him with the situation. He then agreed to marry her with the consent of his parents. Though his parents did not at first agree they had to yield to the pressure of the people of the locality and the marriage was conducted in an informal manner.

When the girl reached the final months of her pregnancy the boy thought of eliminating her for which he evolved a plan secretly. He coaxed the girl to go with him to his sister's house (situated a few miles away from the place where the dead body was found) under the pretext of a customary visit during post wedding days. The accused, after reaching the locality by bus, led her through the thick wooded areas of the rubber plantation by making her believe that such route was a short cut to reach his sister's house. It was night and no body was in the vicinity when they reached the particular spot inside the estate. He suddenly transformed himself into a cruel murderer and strangulated her with a ligature until she died. He left the dead body at that spot and ran away. He visited his sister and had dinner with her without disclosing that he left the house with his bride. Yet his sister noticed him gasping and asked him the reason for it to which he gave an evasive reply.

Mr. N. Vasudevan was the Public Prosecutor who conducted the prosecution in the above case. He did his work very ably and sincerely. I was quite sure that he got all assistance from Wahab, the Circle Inspector for conducting the prosecution. The advocate who appeared for the defence was unable to make any dent in the prosecution structure, though he seemed to have entertained high hopes on account of a wrong description of the place of occurrence mentioned in the charge framed by the court.

At the final stage the defence advocate took out his trump card. He argued that the accused was called upon to defend an accusation that he committed murder of that girl at the place called 'X', but the entire evidence was to the effect that the murder took place at a far distant place called 'Y'. He pleaded for an acquittal solely on that ground. But I found no difficulty whatsoever to tide over the imbroglio. I knew that it was due to some mistake somewhere that a wrong description was given as for the place of occurrence. I decided to correct it. I exercised the power of the court for amending the charge, and incorporated the place of occurrence as 'X' in the place of 'Y' and asked the accused whether he pleaded guilty to the amended charge. The advocate then advised the accused to declare that he lost faith in the court. But that strategy had no effect on me. I then replied to him and his advocate that it was open to them to move the High Court to transfer the trial of the case to some other court. The advocate knew well that he would not get a favourable order from High Court even if he had moved for the same. When they declined to accept my offer I proceeded to the next stage. But then the advocate insisted on recalling all the prosecution witnesses already examined for further cross-examination. I informed him that as per the recent amendment of the law, the court had a discretion in the matter and I would recall only such witnesses as would be necessary for the defence in the light of the amendment of the charge and wanted him to convince me about the necessity of bringing back any witness again. As he failed to convince me I did not allow any witness to be recalled.

That case had two hurdles for the prosecution to surmount. First was the suspicious conduct of the watchman of the estate for entering on a long leave immediately after the dead body was found in the estate. That watchman was examined as a prosecution witness. He narrated all the vivid details of the previous occasion when another dead body was found by him in the same estate about eight or ten years ago. To satisfy the judicial conscience the Circle Inspector produced the records of that earlier case to enable me to peruse the same. I had no doubt that the watchman only wanted to escape from all the hardships and expenses which he might have to incur had he informed the police about the dead body. The second hurdle was the unusual phenomenon of a dead body virtually giving birth to a child as mentioned above. To satisfy the court that it was not a different dead body the prosecution examined an expert who said that such a development could take place in the case of a woman dying in advanced stage of pregnancy. He said that due to postmortem prolapsing of the uterus a fetus could be expelled by the mother corpse.

As the deck was cleared, I had no reason to doubt about the truth of the prosecution version. There was no serious flaw affecting the structure of the case, in spite of the seeming odds which came up. I pronounced my judgement and convicted the accused of the offence of murder. However, I did not agree with the arguments of the Public Prosecutor that death penalty should be awarded to the accused. He pleaded for death penalty to be awarded to the accused on the ground that the accused made all the preparations well in advance for liquidating a very innocent girl who reposed utmost trust in the accused at every stage from the beginning of his love affair. However, I could not count this case as "rarest of rare cases" for imposing death penalty on the accused. In spite of all what the Public Prosecutor argued, I imposed a punishment of imprisonment for life.

In my judgement I paid encomiums to Mr. Wahab, the Circle Inspector of Police for the efficient manner in which he conducted the investigation of such a complex murder case, the ramifications of which spread over to distant localities. I was told later that the encomiums paid by me became the basis for the state government to grant some service benefits to him in his official career.

The accused filed an appeal before the High Court of Kerala. The same advocate, who argued for the accused before me went to the High Court and argued the appeal also. However, a Division Bench of the High Court confirmed the conviction and sentence.

14

Half burnt dead body of a pregnant woman

The people of a small village, where population was relatively sparse, were taken aback on the morning of a particular day seeing a semi-charred dead body of a woman lying in the middle of a sugarcane field. Though the police took up investigation in right earnest they could not trace out the identity of that woman. But the postmortem examination conducted on the dead body revealed two special features. One was that the woman was in the early stage of pregnancy. The other was, her neck was cut with a heavy cutting weapon like a chopper. The police naturally concluded that this was a cold-blooded murder and that there would have been an attempt to destroy the evidence of such murder.

The first task of the investigation officer was to find out the identity of the murdered woman. As no woman was found missing in the locality, the police officer widened the radius of the territorial limits of his enquiry day after day, but even after stretching it as wide as 50 KM there was no report of a missing woman.

Incidentally the police came to know of a jeep bearing a particular registration number reaching the sugarcane field on the night in question. The police came to know that the said jeep belonged to the manager of Ratnagiri estate which was situated about 60 KM away from the sugarcane field. When the police made enquiries how the jeep reached the place of occurrence they came to know that one Harijan woman who was the wife of the watchman of Ratnagiri estate was missing from the locality for some days. After conducting hectic investigation for a number of days the police realised that the dead body found in the sugarcane field was that of the same Harijan woman. On completion of the investigation the police charge sheeted the case against three accused. First accused was described as a mercenary killer (a hired assassin) and the second accused was employed by him for assisting him in murdering the victim. The manager of the Ratnagiri estate was arrayed as the 3rd accused.

The story of the prosecution can be summarised as follows: The watchman of the Ratnagiri estate was above middle age, but his wife Ammini was a young woman, almost half of his age. She had a voluptuous charm, but her husband was old looking. They were living in the Harijan colony which was situated two furlongs away from the Retnagiri estate. They had a daughter aged five. The third accused was living alone in the bungalow earmarked for the superintendent of the estate and his wife and children were left at his hometown for the children's education. Ammini was engaged to sweep the bungalow every day for which the third accused used to pay her some remuneration. As there was none else in the bungalow the third accused felt infatuated towards Ammini. He enticed her to have sexual relationship with him almost on all days. Once she disclosed to him that she became pregnant and wanted him to adopt some measures to abort it as her husband had undergone vasectomy. The third accused with the help of some quacks applied measures to get the pregnancy aborted, but all such efforts failed. As days passed Ammini became panicky and once threatened the third accused that she would disclose the truth to everybody unless he resorted to better and effective measures to abort the pregnancy.

In the above background the third accused decided to liquidate Ammini. He contacted the first accused and entered into a conspiracy for liquidating her. Handsome amount was offered to the first accused in return. A plan was chalked out for murdering her. The third accused procured a big chopper and gave it to the first accused and told Ammini to fully co-operate with the first accused for aborting the pregnancy.

On the evening of the already fixed day Ammini left her house without her child. A1 and A2 joined her at the bus stop and they proceeded to a different village. After alighting from the bus they covered a long distance on foot through a coco plantation. When it was night time they asked Ammini to stop as the place was quite suitable for carrying out the abortion. Ammini was compelled to yield to the lust of first and second accused before carrying out the promised abortion. First accused thereafter took out the chopper from his gunny bag and suddenly cut the neck of Ammini. She fell down and died. Her body was then wrapped in the gunny bag. First accused walked up to the Ratnagiri estate and gave a pre-arranged signal to the third accused. The time was around 1'Oclock in the night. Third accused took out his jeep and reached the coco plantation. All the three accused together carried the dead body into the jeep and they drove far away to the place where the dead body was found in the charred condition as mentioned first. They would have tried to set fire to the body but due to some odds it burnt only half.

It was a case of circumstantial evidence. The circumstances were very well presented by the Public Prosecutor (N. Vasudevan), though most of the unofficial witnesses were won over by the third accused who was very rich.

During the trial one unusual development took place. A witness by name Shajahan was examined to say that he visited the estate bungalow one afternoon and then he happened to see the third accused and Ammini lying together on the same cot. But Shajahan was won over by the accused and hence he said in court that he did not even know any one of the accused. But by a slip of his tongue he referred to the third accused in that rank i.e. "3rd accused in the case". I then asked him; "Who is the third accused in this case?" The witness then pointed out the third accused correctly. I asked him "How do you know that he is the third accused in this case?" The witness was really caught trapped. I found him perspiring, finally he said in the court that the third accused told him to say so. I reminded him that he had taken an oath before starting his evidence. (He had taken oath in the name of 'Allah' before starting this evidence that he would speak only the truth). I found him trembling but within a couple of minutes he fell down from the witness box. Though I became nervous I did not show it out. Instead I gathered composure and asked the court staff to carry him outside the court hall and to give him water or anything he needed to reach normal condition. Then I proceeded with the examination of other witnesses in this case. About an hour later Shajahan expressed a desire to speak out and I allowed him to do so. He said that he wished to give evidence. Then I allowed him to be examined again. He then said that he was supplying milk to the bungalow and that one after noon when he went with the milk to the bungalow he noticed that every door remained closed from inside and there was no indication of anyone remaining inside, then he moved to the kitchen side and noticed that one door was not bolted from inside. He stepped into the kitchen and placed the milk bottle inside. Then he heard the hissing sound of somebody from inside. He then cautiously moved forward to the inner rooms. He told the court that he saw the third accused and Ammini lying together on a cot in liaison.

The defence advocate cross-examined him during which he was asked about his first statement in court. He said that when he fell unconscious he felt Allah telling him not to speak untruth in court particularly after taking oath by keeping hand on the Quran. His narration thereafter was impressive. There were other items of evidence also as against the accused.

Finally I concluded that the first accused inflicted a cut injury on the neck of the deceased Ammini and killed her. It was a difficult process for me to fix up the penal liability of the second accused. Could he have thought that the first accused had sought his assistance only for causing mis-carriage of the pregnancy of Ammini and first accused escorted her only for that purpose and not to kill her? I did not find any material on the evidence to reach a conclusion that he also shared an intention to kill Ammini. The fact that he assisted the first accused for removing the dead body of Ammini was not enough for me to conclude that he also shared the intention to kill her. Perhaps the first accused would have prevailed upon him, after the murder to believe that unless he also helped him in removing the dead body he too might have to bear the whole liability. Thinking all the different aspects I thought it safe to convict the second accused only of the offence of destroying the evidence of murder.

Though I had no doubt in my mind subjectively that the on a cot accused was the 'villain' of the lot, there was total dearth of evidence to show that he had instigated the first accused to kill her. The fact that he helped the other accused to remove the dead body was not enough to conclude that the third accused was privy to the murder. So I convicted the third accused only of the offence of destroying the evidence of murder. However I imposed the maximum sentence prescribed by law for that offence i.e. rigorous imprisonment for seven years.

The accused went in appeal before the High Court. A Division Bench of the High Court confirmed the conviction and sentence. I do not know whether any one of them moved the Supreme Court in appeal. Thus, ended the case of the half burnt dead body.

15

Two cases of restoration of gender justice

Though I had to deal with matrimonial causes in many matters, I well remember the facts of two cases which came before my judicial decision when I was District Judge of Quilon (now Kollam). I have to maintain the anonymity of the personalities involved in both cases and therefore I will make an endeavour not to give even a hint of the parties in those cases.

The Indian Divorce Act was meant to apply to Christians but the Act as it then stood was in a very conservative level. The grounds available to a husband or wife who wanted a decree of divorce from the court were very scarce. The plight of a wife under the said enactment was worse than that of the husband. One of the rare grounds for seeking a decree of divorce under the said Act was that the wife concerned was guilty of adultery. But now the situation has changed as Parliament has amended the Divorce Act in 2000 by adding more grounds for getting a decree of divorce. The case which I narrate below was tried at a time when the law remained before such amendment.

A husband filed the suit for divorce on the ground that his wife was living in adultery. Strangely I noticed that the wife admitted the said allegation in her counter statement. When the husband was examined as a witness in the court the wife was also present with her child. The husband was an officer of a nationalized bank and was stationed at a town in the northern side of Kerala. He said in his evidence that when he heard about the extra-marital affairs of his wife he thought of catching her red-handed. So one day he visited his wife's house without prior notice. He said in court that as soon as he reached his wife's house he saw a stranger just going out of her bedroom and she bade him good night. His wife, according to him, was then wearing only a nighty. This was one of the episodes narrated by the husband in the court for supporting his allegation that his wife was living in adultery.

But the strange thing was that the advocate who appeared for the wife, when asked to cross-examine the above version of the petitioner, reported "no cross". I noticed tears rolling down over her cheeks. So I asked her counsel why he did not want to cross examine the husband. As his answer was not satisfactory I asked the wife to mount the witness stand then itself. I put certain questions to her, in the weight of such questions the lid on the cauldron of her lamentations was blown off and she started narrating a woeful story, how she was prevailed upon by her husband not to contest the case. From her narration I realised that the reality was different from what the husband said. This is what I understood:

One day she and her child went to the place where her husband was working. On an enquiry made by her, she learnt that her husband was keeping a mistress. She returned to her native place heart-broken. Her near relations thereupon persuaded her to resort to some legal action. Hence she filed a petition in the Magistrate's court claiming maintenance allowance for herself and the child. The Magistrate allowed the claim and ordered the husband to pay Rs. 400/- per month. When the husband evaded all court processes for a very long time the arrears of maintenance swelled up to Rs. 16,000/- (which during then was a substantial amount) She moved the Magistrate's Court for taking distress proceedings against the husband for realisation of the amount. At that stage he went down to her place and prevailed upon her to capitulate to his terms for accepting Rs. 16,000/- on condition that she would not contest the suit which the husband proposed to file for securing divorce from her. The poor lady out of her dire necessity to get some financial succour yielded to his pressure.

That is how the matter reached the aforesaid stage in my court. I was greatly moved in favour of the deserted wife. I felt it my duty to avert a gross miscarriage of justice. I told all concerned that I would put questions to the husband. Then I started putting searching questions to her husband and he had to admit that his wife was compelled to submit to the present state of affairs.

The advocate of the husband became angry by the manner in which I grilled his client in open court. I heard him muttering; "if the plaintiff and defendant agree together why should the court worry about it". I told the advocate that under the provisions of the Indian Divorce Act the court has a duty to satisfy itself of absence of collusion between the parties. He was not satisfied with my explanation, but he did not choose to take up the cue with me.

The petitioner examined two more witnesses. But they too were not cross-examined by the advocate for the lady, but I put grilling questions to them also. When arguments started the advocate for the petitioner had to face a volley of questions put by me. He was in an angry mood sensing that he was addressing a hostile court. In fact, I was hostile to the cause espoused by his client, yet I was willing to be persuaded otherwise. Though the advocate tried his best, in a very strident voice he failed to change my conviction even by a bit. In my judgement I held that it was false that his wife was living in adultery but on the contrary the petitioner was living in adultery. I also held that the petitioner exerted undue coercion and influence on his wife to compel her to desist from contesting his false allegations and the poor lady, out of her dire need for money, had succumbed to his muscle power.

I found the above conduct amounting to collusion in law. Finally I dismissed the petition for divorce. I also directed him to pay her the entire costs incurred, besides payment of alimony to her and the child.

I felt very much gratified, in that I could save a poor lady from the tentacles of a wily and insidious husband. The husband approached the High Court in appeal but I learnt that my judgment was confirmed by a division bench.

The above case was soon followed by another matrimonial case, wherein a young bride claimed decree of divorce (or nullity of marriage), on the ground that her husband was impotent. She produced a certificate issued by one lady doctor stating that the bride remained virgin even two years after her marriage. The husband contested the matter very aggressively. He engaged the same advocate who appeared for the husband in the previous case narrated above. The advocate mainly raised two contentions, one was that the marriage was consummated and the couple continued to have sexual cohabitation, and the other was that the lady doctor who issued the certificate of virginity was not sufficiently qualified to give such an opinion. He thereupon insisted that the couple should undergo a medical check up by another doctor of his choice. I offered that they could be subjected to a medical examination of a doctor chosen by me. Some how, the advocate for the husband was not willing to accede to this offer. He produced a certificate issued by another doctor to show that the husband was capable of sexual cohabitation with the opposite gender. But when that doctor was cross-examined, it was elicited from him that he was a close relative of the husband and that his reasons for concluding about the sexual capacity of the husband were not sound.

The interesting development of this case was that the advocate for the husband produced a portion of one of the letters written by the wife to the mother of the husband. If one were to read only that portion, he might feel that she did not have any grievance regarding her husband's sexual incapacity. But the young wife, when confronted with the portion of the letter, suddenly said that she had retained a copy of the full letter with her and that she was prepared to produce the same in court. I asked that young bride whether it was quite improbable to keep a copy of the letter written to her mother-in-law. She then explained that after writing the letter she showed it to her brother and he advised her to keep its copy with her for any future use. In order to test the veracity of her version, I permitted her to go home and return on the same day with the copy of the letter. To the great surprise of all concerned, she returned within an hour with the copy of a very lengthy letter which she had written to her mother in law. On reading the whole letter it was very clear to me that she had expressed her grievance for not enjoying the connubial life with her husband. The truncated portion of the original letter produced by the husband's advocate was torn out from the original letter in such a way that the remaining portion should not be seen by the court. So production of the copy of the full letter became a turning point in the case. The bomb which the husband's advocate whipped out, (that truncated letter) for exploding the case of the wife turned out to be a damp squib. In the aforesaid circumstances, I had no difficulty to grant a decree of nullity of marriage on the ground that the husband was impotent as far as that particular lady was concerned. Instances of relative impotency were reported in law journals and this could have been a case of such relative importance.

The decree passed by me was challenged by the husband before the High Court of Kerala. A Division Bench headed by the then Chief Justice upheld the decree passed by me. I learned later that the young lady was married to another person subsequently and she eventually became mother of two children in the second marriage. Had it not flashed in my mind to permit the lady to produce the copy of the full letter which she offered to produce on that day itself, perhaps the result of the case would have been different on account of the truncated portion of the letter produced by the husband's advocate.

The Indian Divorce Act, which was solely applicable to Christians in India during the period of the above cases, was very unhelpful to those married people who reeled under the scourge of matrimonial breakdowns, as the Act permitted divorce only on very limited grounds. Though the women organisations raised their voice to bring out a new law in substitution of that Act, the church leaders were insensitive to the demand for reforming the law. Church leadership at all times was prone to huddle to orthodoxy and they preferred conservatism to human realities. When I was Judge of the High Court of Kerala, I used one occasion to direct the Union of India to take a decision regarding updating the Indian Divorce Act. But the response of the Union Government then was very disappointing. They said that unless there was demand from the community they were not disposed to interfere with the personal law of Christians. However, the situation was changed when Arun Jaitely became Law Minister. He piloted for very significant amendments to the Indian Divorce Act and now the law has improved considerably in favour of gender justice.

16

Assignments declined, but became a litigant

The Registrar of the High Court is then and now the chief executive officer of the judiciary of the State. There was a time when Kerala High Court had only one post of Registrar. Later it became two and now there are four Registrars, ranking according to their seniority. In some other states such post has been multiplied into five and even six, depending on the strength and size of the High Court. The said posts were usually held by senior District Judges. During yester years the post of a Registrar of the High Court was considered to be a very honoured one next only to the judges of the High Court. Chief Justice P.T. Raman Nair (ICS) who was always considered to be one of the most eminent judges of the Kerala High Court was once Registrar of High Court of Madras. There was a tradition in that High Court, during British period, that the post of Registrar of the High Court was the stepping stone for elevation to judgeship of the High Court. But in due course of time the respectability of the post of Registrar has been devalued. Some of the judges of the High Court were responsible for the degradation of that post by allocating certain types of work to the Registrar which were unconnected with his executive duties.

When Justice Subramonian Potti became the Chief Justice of the Kerala High Court he wished to restore the pristine honour of the post of Registrar of the High Court. When I was District Judge at Quilon he called me and offered the post of Registrar to me. But I entreated with him to spare me from accepting the post. He then offered the post to K. Sreedharan who was the next senior most District Judge after me. (He later became Chief Justice of Punjab and Haryana High Court and also of Gujarat High Court). But he also declined the offer to become Registrar of the High Court. We both suggested the names of some other senior District Judges who were not only willing but eager to become the Registrar of the High Court. Then Justice Subramonian Potti told us that he would appoint only such person as he considered fit for the post and not any person who desired it. He wanted Justice U.L. Bhatt to persuade me to accept the post of Registrar of the High Court. When Justice Bhatt spoke to me about it I reminded him that he too was in a similar situation and he declined the offer of Registrarship. I also told him that the reasons which prevailed upon him then to decline the identical offer were valid to me also.

Among the Government Secretaries in different department the post of Law Secretary was always held by a senior District Judge on deputation from judicial service. Law Secretary is a post of considerable weight and it could influence the decision making in all matters of Governmental activities. The practice followed for selecting the District Judge to be sent as Law Secretary was the same then and now. The Government would request the High Court to send a panel of names of District Judges whom the High Court considered competent enough to be appointed as Law Secretary out of which the government would choose one. Usually there would be many aspirants among the District Judges for the post of Law Secretary.

When I was District Judge of Quilon, I was one of the senior most Judges in the state subordinate judiciary. The then Chief Minister (K. Karunakaran) desired the High Court to send my name for the post of Law Secretary. When it was sounded to me I expressed my disinclination. The Chief Minister directed the then Advocate General (P.V. Ayyappan) to intercede with me to accept the post. The Advocate General had a talk with me on the subject. I told him that even if the post of Chief Secretary was offered to me I would only decline it because of the very urge behind my leaving a lucrative legal practice at the Bar was to do judicial work and not to have bureaucratic assignments. The Advocate General therefore did not make any further attempt to persuade me but a couple of days later Justice P. Sivaraman Nair (He and Mrs. K. Karunakaran were relatives) called me over the phone and told me that Chief Minister wanted him to persuade me to accept the post of Law Secretary on deputation and assured me that it would not in any manner affect the prospects of my becoming a judge of the High Court. I requested him to spare me from it. The Chief Minister would have been apprised of my firm disinclination in the matter. The Chief Minister then chose K. Sreedharan as Law Secretary. When he gave consent for being appointed, Justice Subramonian Potti expressed his resentment as Mr. Sreedharan had earlier declined the post of Registrar of the High Court on the premise that he wished to do judicial work. As Justice Potti was transferred to Gujarat High Court as Chief Justice, Mr. Sreedharan escaped from the wrath of Justice Potti. However, we both were later elevated as Judges of the High Court and K. Sreedharan held the post of Law Secretary until his elevation.

It was during my tenure at Quilon that I became a party to one litigation which was filed in the High Court of Kerala. Before Mr. Sreedharan and I were appointed as District Judges one Anandasubramonia Iyer was appointed by promoting him to the cadre from the post of Sub Judge. A few Sub Judges were earlier promoted as District Judges with a rider attached to the order of promotion that such promotion was subject to "the claims of the direct recruitees". When we were appointed as District Judges, it became necessary to find vacant posts for us and hence two of the junior-most promotee District Judges had to be reverted to the post of Sub Judge. That misfortune fell on Anandasubramonia Iyer and another person. But Mr. Iyer was fortunate in having been promoted within two weeks of our appointment. Nonetheless he remained our junior for the rest of his career. We were again promoted to a higher grade called "Selection grade District Judges". At that time it occurred to Anandasubramonia Iyer that he should challenge our promotion on a ground which he thought to be sound. As per the rules of promotion a District Judge should have held judicial office for a period of three years before he was promoted to the selection grade. According to Mr. Anandasubramonia Iyer the said three year period could be counted only from the date of expiry of the probation period as judicial officers. If it was so counted, myself and Sreedharan should have waited for promotion to the selection grade for two more years. Mr. Anandasubramonia Iyer had already completed his probation period as a judicial officer (even as a Munsiff) and hence he was eligible to be promoted to the selection grade. According to Mr. Iyer if things had happened like that he would have obtained seniority over us.

Mr. Anandasubramonia Iyer therefore filed a writ petition in the Kerala High Court making me and Mr. Sreedharan as respondents and he prayed for quashing our promotion to the selection grade and also for a direction to promote him to the selection grade.

When we received notice from the High Court I needed the services of an advocate. I have no one in mind other than Advocate Sri. C.K. Sivasankara Panicker ("Sri. Panicker", for short). He was formerly the Advocate General of Kerala. He was one of the best advocates of Kerala Bar from all standards of profession, either from the point of view of equipment, or erudition or perfect court manners. I have yet another reason to select him. I had occasion to observe him and his splendid advocacy even during the earlier days of my practice as he had appeared in selected cases before the courts at Kottayam. When I progressed in legal profession I suggested to many of my clients who needed the services of a High Court advocate, to engage Mr. Panicker. It was in that background I approached him with a request to appear for me in the High Court.

Sri. Panicker drafted the counter affidavit in answer to the averments of the writ petition with meticulous care. He called me to put my signature thereon. Then I asked him about the prospects of winning the case. He told me to go home and sleep well forgetting the case. Such was the optimism which he evinced then. In the meanwhile, Anandasubramonia Iyer became the Registrar of the High Court. Despite we being the opposite parties in a litigation we maintained very cordial relationship with each other. We used to chat together through telephone on many occasions. One day he called me from the High Court and told me that arguments were going on in the High Court on the writ petition filed by him. He expressed great confidence of victory in that litigation. I told him not to be so confident as Sri. Panicker assured me that victory would be mine only. He told me that his advocate was absolutely certain about his victory. About a couple of hours thereafter he called me again over phone and told me that I won the case and he lost it. He congratulated me but I consoled him saying "you can expect a victory in some other litigation if you choose to file it later".

My next task was to pay the fees to Sri. Panicker. Knowing well that he would not mention any amount, but would leave to me to pay him, I sent a cheque for a certain sum with a letter requesting him to send the bill so that I could pay the balance amount very soon. I got a reply from him stating that the amount covered by the cheque was quite sufficient and that no further amount need be paid by me. I was satisfied that my advocate was paid to his satisfaction.

At the end of that financial year when my bank passbook was updated I noticed that the cheque sent to Sri. Panicker remained unencashed. I called his son who was practicing as his junior (now Mr. Justice K.S. Radhakarishnan) and reminded him of the cheque remaining unencashed. He then disclosed to me that his father had instructed the office not to encash the said cheque and said, "Let Thomas feel that he paid the fees to me". I felt beholden to the height of his nobility !

I cannot part with this topic without mentioning one more aspect concerning Sri. Panicker. By the beginning of 1995 his son (K.S. Radhakrishnan) was recommended to be a judge of the High Court. Sri. Panicker had a very lucrative practice even during that period but when the President of India proclaimed the notification appointing K.S. Radhakrishnan as judge of the Kerala High Court, Sri. Panicker announced that he stopped practising as an advocate. Many persons tried to persuade him to reconsider the decision, but he stood firm. Within a few days he and his wife shifted their residence to a hill resort situated about 40 K.M. away from Cochin where he had a farm house and a small estate having a large number of fruit bearing trees. He believed that if he continued practice as an advocate it might cause embarrassment to his son and also to the other judges of the High Court as well as to many members of Bar, besides embarrassment to himself.

I used to visit him at least once a year in the said farm house and we used to chat for hours together. I also enjoyed the hospitality showered by Mrs. Panicker. Both of them are not alive now.

I wish to mention about a small but significant episode which happened when I was District Judge at Quilon. I have pointed out earlier that A.R. Vijayan, was the Additional District Judge of Quilon during my period until he was shifted as District Judge of Kottayam. A.R. Vijayan, like his brother A.R. Sreenivasan was very strong and sensitive about his judicial rectitude and aloofness. They never allowed anyone to speak to them on any matter pending judicial decision except in open court when opportunity for it arose. In this respect, these brothers did not allow even the High Court Judges to mention to them on any matter pending before them whether directly or indirectly.

When A.R. Vijayan was Additional District Judge he once passed an order granting bail or anticipatory bail to a particular accused. The order happened to be very short. When the order was challenged by the state in a revision filed before the High Court, it came up for consideration before Justice M.P. Menon (one of the very best Judges of the Kerala High Court, who scored first rank in his academic pursuits and a gold medal in the Bar

Council examination). Justice Menon found that the order passed by A.R. Vijayan was too short and that the reasons for granting bail were not stated in the order. He then directed the Registrar of the High Court to obtain the remarks of A.R.Vijayan for "the cryptic order passed". A.R. Vijayan, in his remarks, said only one sentence which was this: "That order was passed by me on the judicial side, hence I will not offer any remarks about it". When the above reply was placed before Justice M.P. Menon the great judge ordered that the proceedings against A.R. Vijayan would stand closed with the observations, "The Additional Sessions Judge is right and I was wrong".

In the above episode two characters loomed much large. One is the bold subordinate judicial officer who showed the mettle by informing the High Court Judge that he would refuse to offer any remark as the order was passed on the judicial side. This was a model to those subordinate judicial officers who genuflect before some High Court Judges just for appeasing them. The second character is the High Court Judge Justice M. P. Menon who had shown the greatness and nobility by admiring the fortitude exhibited by the subordinate judicial officer. Both are worthy of emulation.

Though a District Judge could remain at one station for a period of three years, I had to leave Quilon on completion of two years. This happened because the post of District Judge, Trivandrum fell vacant and the High Court wanted a senior district judge to hold that office. High Court considered me for that post on account of different aspects. The Committee of the judges of the High Court dealing with transfer of subordinate judiciary ascertained whether I was willing to go to Trivandrum (though such willingness is seldom ascertained now). I conveyed my consent as I thought I would not otherwise get the chance to be in the capital city of Kerala. Thus I was transferred and posted as District Judge at Trivandrum.

17

District and Sessions Judge, Trivandrum

The city of Trivandrum remained in my mind as one of the most beautiful cities in India. I still recollect my first visit to that city when it was capital of the state of Travancore. The Maharaja of Travancore was the reigning King of the state. The city was then known as the "Rajadhani". During my childhood it was the dream of every child to visit Trivandrum to see the important landmarks such as the Kawadiar palace, Shanmukham beach, the Zoo, the Museum, the magnificent Sreepadmanabha temple, the Observatory, the Aquarium, the University Stadium, the Boulevards etc. which made the city strikingly beautiful. During the period of the reign of Maharajah of Travancore the city of Trivandrum was a dream place for the people of that state. Kanyakumari the cape and Padmanabhapuram palace, as well as Sucheendram Temple are situated at short distance drive from Trivandrum. They were all the parts of the state of Travancore, but now they have become parts of the state of Tamilnadu. The above picture was regarding the Trivandrum of the glorious period. But now the city has lost that ancient charm. It has become a very crowded and polluted city.

The District Court and other courts attached thereto are housed at Trivandrum in a sprawling building which was built in the true Kerala architectural style. It had a compound of nearly six acres surrounding the main building. That building once housed the High Court of Travancore. The District Court has a spacious court hall, situated on the first floor of the building wherein all the offices attached to the court are also accommodated. The District Judge has to enter into his chambers by walking through the passage through the court hall. A long screen made of teak wood separated the said passage.

On the first day of joining the office as District Judge of Trivandrum I observed that the above wooden screen had never been polished after it was brought there many years ago. It was fully dust stricken and untidy. The various items of furniture inside the court hall were also of the same condition, the canes of many chairs had caved in and the chairs became unusable. I asked the chief ministerial officer of the court (Sheristadar) why the screen and furniture were like that. He put forward the usual excuse that the P.W.D. was addressed to do the work and reminders were sent, but they did not carry out the work. I also noticed hundreds of used plastic bags strewn on the compound which was even otherwise replete with wild growth of bushes. Nobody had paid any attention to such things for several years. The garbage of plastic bags would have snowballed into huge piles when members of the staff were dumping down such bags because almost all of them used to bring their meals by wrapping in plastic bags.

I called the peons of the court and asked them whether they would polish the wooden screen and clean the compound if they were paid for it. I offered to supply polish and sand papers. I also offered my services for the work. But they dissuaded me from joining them and agreed to carry out the work for a certain amount which was not much.

They all did the work as a team on a weekend utilising one Friday evening and whole of a Saturday and Sunday. The wooden screen and furniture thereafter became sparkling. The compound became very clean and some flower plants were also planted therein. The cost incurred by the court for this much of cleaning work was a paltry pelf.

To prevent the staff members throwing the plastic bags into the compound I brought a dozen plastic buckets and placed them at different locations on the first floor. I issued a memo to all staff urging them to dump the plastic and other wrappers into those buckets. Despite all these directions, I noticed that those were again strewn in the compound even on the very next working day. So I decided to catch the wrong doers red-handed. I remained incognito during lunch interval and found out many members of the staff, including women, instinctively throwing down the wrappers of the lunch packets. After tracing out the identity of the persons, I called them and politely told them of the need to maintain cleanliness inside and outside the court and appealed to them to desist from such a habit. They apologised for it and promised to refrain from doing so. I took no action on any member of the staff for such a trivial delinquency. I was glad that thereafter none of them used to dump such things as they did earlier, at least until I continued as District Judge of Trivandrum.

On the second day of my tenure as District Judge of Trivandrum I noticed some of the lady advocates appearing in the court without wearing the prescribed sartorial insignia and in a casual outfit. I told them that I would not give audience to such persons in my court unless they came in proper sartorial attire. I also told them of my experience with Calicut Bar where lady advocates appeared elegantly dressed and in the prescribed costume and insignia. I am glad to point out that on the next day all lawyers started appearing in the court in the manner desired by me.

I do not wish to narrate the cases which were tried in my court in Trivandrum except one case as it had certain unexpected turns and developments.

It was a murder case in which the accused were, one uncle and his two nephews. The case of the prosecution was that all the three accused chased a young man who ran for his life through the public road to escape from the revengeful fury of the assailants who were armed with iron rods and chopper. They chased him and succeeded in capturing him. He fell down after receiving some blows from behind, thereafter all the accused inflicted blows with iron rods, chopper etc. He died at the spot.

The above case might appear to be a simple and common type murder case in Kerala. But its special features were at the trial stage. The widow of the deceased engaged an advocate to assist the Public Prosecutor. The trial was to start on a Monday in my court. A couple of days prior to it the advocate of the widow called on me with a strange request that I must assign the case to the additional Sessions Judge as the kith and kin of the deceased had no faith in the Public Prosecutor attached to my court. I told him that he could approach the District Collector for necessary direction to assign the prosecution work to another Public Prosecutor. However, I refused to accede to the request for transferring the case to another court. When the trial was about to start another Public Prosecutor reported to me that he would conduct the prosecution and that he would be assisted by the advocate engaged by the widow of the deceased.

The first eye witness for the prosecution gave evidence which was entirely in favour of the prosecution version. He appeared to me, prima-facie, an independent witness having no bias to either side. He said that he belonged to a distant place, settled down in Trivandrum about 5 years ago as he was employed by a building contractor. He happened to see the incident while working on the top floor of a building under construction. As he heard a hubbub he looked down and saw a person running crying and within a few seconds he saw three other persons running after him carrying iron rods and chopper. He saw the first person being caught from behind by the armed assailants who dealt incessant blows on him with iron rods and chopper. The witness identified the three accused in the court as the assailants who attacked the deceased.

All the three accused together engaged one advocate. He was a soft spoken, but experienced and efficient criminal lawyer. In his cross-examination he asked the witness whether he was an accused in a murder case earlier. The witness answered in the negative. The witness then turned to me with folded hands and said " I am in a court for the first time in my life". The advocate continued his cross-examination but the evidence of the witness remained unshaken. When he was asked whether he paid property tax to the corporation for the house which he claimed to have purchased at Trivandrum, he answered in the affirmative. Then again he turned to me and said that he was prepared to produce all its receipts if the court required them. His evidence was apparently impressive to me. The cross-examination continued till 4.30 p.m. When I asked the defence advocate how long he proposed to continue, he said that he might take a couple of hours more. I stopped the case for the day and read out the deposition already recorded, and directed the witness to be present on the next day with the property tax receipts.

When the court proceedings commenced on the next day, one advocate represented to me that the witness fell sick on his way to court and he was admitted in the government hospital. He sought for two days time. At that stage the defence advocate entered the court hall and in a gasping voice said thus: "Yesterday I could collect proof to show that the witness was in fact an accused in a murder case and was convicted and sentenced to imprisonment for life and that he served the jail sentence and was released from the jail only a few years ago. He knew that I got all the proof and to escape from further examination he got himself admitted in a hospital. Unless he was brought to court today itself he might even abscond".

I ordered the Police to guard the said witness in the hospital. After lunch recess the advocate of the witness made a plea to withdraw the police guard at the hospital as the witness had high B.P. and the sight of the police could aggravate the B.P. condition of the witness. The advocate also said that he would personally undertake to produce the witness on the next day and requested to act on his word. As a judge I had always acted on the statements made by any advocate at the Bar on a matter concerning his personal knowledge and I had always respected the undertakings given by advocates in open court. So I acceded to the request made by the advocate and ordered withdrawal of the police from the place where the witness was admitted in the hospital.

But on the next day neither the witness nor his advocate was present in the court. I was told that his advocate was simply sitting in another court. I sent a peon to him, but he told the peon to mention to me that he was arguing in that court. I sent a message to the judge of that court to inform the advocate to present himself before my court. However, within five minutes he appeared in my court. I politely asked him where is the witness whom you undertook to produce ?" He was unruffled and he put a question back to me. "How can I produce the witness who was absconding ?" I maintained my composure in spite of such provocative submissions.

I ordered non-bailable warrant of arrest against the witness. Then I proceeded to examine the other witnesses for the prosecution. This episode relating to the witness gave me a strong impression that the prosecution story was not true. While the other eye witnesses were examined, I ventured to put grilling and piercing questions to every one of them over and above the questions put by the defence counsel.

Propounders of the adversarial system might frown at me on reading this because the judge questioning the witnesses might be a feature of the inquisitorial system. Yet I dared to do so as I was anxious to avert a miscarriage of justice. In the meanwhile, I ordered sterner steps to catch the absconding witness.

The advocate who appeared for the widow of the deceased showed his resentment when I put cross questions to all witnesses. His party filed a petition before the High Court praying that the case be transferred from my court. I did not know what was the allegation made by him in support of the prayer for such transfer. When the transfer petition came up before Justice V. Bhaskaran Nambiar he dismissed it. The plea made by the advocate to call for my remarks was turned down by the judge. Here I must point out that I had no personal acquaintance with Justice Bhaskaran Nambiar during those days. All that I knew about him was that he had an impressive academic career securing highest marks in Law from Madras University during the first year of his course in Law. He became the Advocate General of Kerala State which office he held quite admirably. As judge he wrote well reasoned judgments in idiomatic style. After I became a judge of the High Court I asked him why he did not call for my remarks in that transfer petition. He replied that since he learnt that the judicial officer against whom those allegations were made was an upright judge. Even the calling for of his remarks might demoralise him.

In fact I did not know that such a transfer petition was filed until I pronounced the judgement in the case. I could therefore hear the arguments with the same tempo as I grilled the witnesses. In my judgement I disbelieved all the occurrence witnesses and acquitted the accused.

Within a fortnight I got an official communication from the High Court directing me to offer my remarks on a petition filed against me by one named person. His complaint in the petition ran like this:

"I happened to visit the sessions court of Trivandrum when a murder case was tried there. Then I viewed a very strange scene that the judge was putting questions to the witnesses when the accused's advocate was not able to put any such questions. I felt that this is not the way a judge should function".

The above complaint was forwarded to me for my remarks. I was a little distressed that being the senior most judge of the subordinate judiciary, I was called upon to offer remarks on a complaint filed by a veritable wayfarer, that too about my judicial performance in open court. I wrote in my remarks that the name of the complainant was pseudonymous and it was filed at the instance of someone deeply interested in convicting the accused in the case; that I firmly believed that the trial judge should not sit silent when he was convinced that the concocted case was presented in his court and the witnesses were perjuring. I believed in the legal perception that the role of a judge was to administer criminal justice and not to pronounce finally who among the two rival sides played their role better in the combat. In my remarks I quoted certain observations made by Mr. Justice O. Chennappa Reddy a judge of the Supreme Court of India that a judge should play a dynamic role during trial to reach the final object of criminal justice. I concluded my remarks expressing my sorrow in having been called upon to offer such remarks on a seemingly fictitious petition. Any way nothing further happened in respect of that complaint.

It would have been closed by the High Court. Barring this episode I had a very comfortable period at Trivandrum. Members of the Bar at Trivandrum by and large were very cordial and cooperative. They helped me in solving some of the sensitive problems.

18

Judge of the High Court

When Justice K. Bhaskaran became the Chief Justice of Kerala High Court, the Central Law Ministry sent a communication to the Chief Justice to recommend persons for filling up the vacancies of Judges of the High Court. The communication mentioned that the quota for District Judges had not been sufficiently taken care of in the then existing appointments. Hence Justice Bhaskaran recommended the names of three District Judges including me. Since only two vacancies existed then he recommended my name as an alternative because he apprehended that one of the two recommendees, perhaps, might not be appointed by the government due to certain reasons. However there was no exigency to resort to the alternative as the first two names were cleared and they were appointed.

Subsequently, when another vacancy arose in the High Court, Chief Justice Bhaskaran again recommended my name. By then I became the senior most District Judge in the state judiciary, though I had by then put in only eight years of judicial service. Within a month Chief Justice recommended, for another vacancy, the name of K. Sreedharan, who was next in rank in the cadre of District Judges. We both expected that the Governor of Kerala would approve our names very soon under the advice of

Chief Minister. But we got a secrete information that the Governor would not send his approval as the Chief Minister did not give his advice in our favour. We conveyed the said information to the Chief Justice when he visited Trivandrum. Chief Justice Bhaskaran then had a discussion with the Chief Minister who pointed out the existence of one more vacancy which arose in the meantime. The Chief Justice recommended the name of Mr. K.G. Balakrishnan for that vacancy. (He became judge of the High Court and later the Chief Justice of Gujarat High Court and still later the Chief Justice of Madras High Court. Now he adorns the bench of the Supreme Court of India. I have every reason to hope and wish that he would become the Chief Justice of India in January 2007). Very soon the Chief Minister forwarded his advice to the Governor regarding all the three of us. The Governor in turn concurred with the recommendations made by the Chief Justice.

Mr. Justice Y. V. Chandrachud was the Chief Justice of India at that time. He upheld the three recommendations made by the Chief Justice of Kerala. Finally the Government of India approved the recommendations and we three were on the verge of being appointed by the President of India as Judges of the High Court. At that time, two events happened which could have created problems for our appointment. One was a writ petition filed in challenge of an order passed by the Government of Kerala. How that writ petition could have created hurdles in the way of our elevation to the High Court can be briefly narrated below:

The cadre of District Judges had two tiers. One is called "District and Sessions Judges" and the other is called "Selection grade District and Sessions Judges". The latter is a promotion post from the former. I was promoted to the higher tier in 1981 and during that period the strength of "Selection grade District Judges" was only five. The Judicial Officers Association petitioned before the authorities that the strength of the "Selection grade District Judges" should be increased to ten, but the Government did not accede to that demand for a long time. However, in the meanwhile, the Kerala State Pay Commission of 1983 made recommendations for pay revision of all government employees as well as judicial officers. There were many anomalies in the pay commission report as far as the judicial officers were concerned. So the Association presented a charter of demands for rectification of such anomalies, including the strength of "Selection grade District Judges". The bureaucracy, particularly the I.A.S. officers, did not favour granting such demands in the charter and therefore the department never placed those demands for consideration of the cabinet. In fact, most of the Ministers were in favour of granting such demands, but they could not help the judiciary as the file was not placed before the cabinet.

The Association filed a writ petition in the High Court for a direction to the Government that a decision be taken on the charter of demands. A Division Bench of the High Court issued a direction to the government to take a decision on the charter of demands. Immediately the matter was processed at the secretarial level and finally they were presented for consideration of the Cabinet. The moment such charter of demands reached the cabinet for consideration, the Ministers approved them as per a one sentence order, sometime in 1985.

One of the results of the Government decision was that the number of "Selection Grade District Judges" was increased to ten. It did not matter to me as I was already in the selection grade and I was already recommended to be a judge of the High Court being the senior most in the cadre. So far so good.

But the government decision granting the charter of demands was made with retrospective effect from 1978 as requested by the Association. Apparently the government order gave substantial financial benefits to the District Judges particularly to the Selection Grade District Judges. But a sugar coated danger was involved in it as far as me and K. Sreedharan were concerned, which we did not notice at the first blush. Soon after the government pronounced that order, five of the District Judges, who were in rank below us, filed a petition before the High Court praying that the seniority rank should be recast because the "Selection Grade District Judges" should have been ten in number from 1978 onwards. It may be noted that myself and K. Sreedharan were just appointed as District Judges in 1978 and hence we were not eligible for promotion to the cadre of Selection Grade at that time. On seeing the said petition the then Registrar of the High Court (M.C. Madhavan) realised the danger befalling us. Though Mr. Madhavan was not a District Judge, he was thorough with all High Court rules, circulars and procedures. He counted the entire ramifications of the decision of the government with reference to the points raised in the memorandum of those five judges. Mr. M.C. Madhavan had a special concern for me and in fact he was longing to see me elevated to the High Court. On receipt of the memorandum for recasting the seniority list he conveyed to the Chief Justice (Justice Bhaskaran) that five juniors of us were to be placed above us in the seniority list. If it happened It would amount to those five persons becoming entitled to claim elevation to the High Court ahead of us. Mr. Madhavan conveyed the above developments to me and said that even the government would not have anticipated this much of consequences when they simply approved the charter of demands with retrospective effect.

Immediately, myself and Sreedharan moved the government for rectification of the defect. As Mr. Sreedharan was then the Law Secretary, he had a special advantage to apprise the Chief Secretary and the Finance Secretary as well as the Chief Minister regarding the implications of the order. Within two days an "erratum notification" was issued by the government clarifying that the increase of the strength of the "Selection Grade District Judges" would only be prospective. Thus we both heaved a sigh of relief as we thought that a potential danger was averted.

The District Judges who moved for recasting the seniority list filed a writ petition on the judicial side of the High Court for quashing the erratum notification issued by the Government. We learnt that the single judge of the High Court, while hearing argument in the writ petition remarked that the erratum notification was illegal as the main decision was adopted by the Cabinet and the decision to issue an erratum was decided by the Chief Minister alone. The single judge who heard the writ petition adjourned it sine die reserving his judgement.

Within a month the President of India issued the proclamation appointing me and Sreedharan as Judges of the High Court of Kerala. The judgement in the writ petition was pronounced only a few months later and the erratum notification was quashed. However, that judgement did not affect our appointment at all and we escaped it narrowly.

The second event was another writ petition filed by a person called Nawab Rajendran in the Delhi High Court. (Nawab Rajendran was a fighter against persons in authority; He had launched many litigations, some of which really caused far reaching ripples in the political scenario of the State of Kerala. He attained fame when he fought cases in the High Court against the Chief Minister and another Minister on certain sensitive issues. He is not alive now, but he had acquired many fans who admired him for his relentless fight for public causes). In the writ petition filed by him against me and Justice Sreedharan he prayed for a declaration that we both did not acquire the qualification for being appointed judges of the High Court. The premise of the writ petition was that, under Article 217(2) of the Constitution of India "a person shall not be qualified for appointment as a judge of a High Court unless he has, for at least ten years, held a judicial office in the territory of India". As we both held judicial office only for eight years, we were not qualified to be appointed, according to the petitioner Nawab Rajendran. The writ petition was filed before the Delhi High Court, instead of the Kerala High Court, as those who helped Nawab Rajendran in filing the writ petition would have feared that no useful orders would come out of the Kerala High Court. The writ petitioner prayed for an interim order prohibiting the President of India from appointing both of us. The writ petition came up before Mr. Justice Ranganathan of the Delhi High Court. He pointed out to the counsel for Nawab Rajendran that the alternative clause under Article 217(2) provided that if the person recommended "has for at least 10 years being an advocate of a High Court" he too was qualified to be appointed as judge of the High Court. The learned judge of the Delhi High Court enquired whether the respondents were directly recruited to the cadre of District Judges. When it was answered he pointed out that even at that time the respondents had acquired the qualification for appointment as Judges of the High Court. The single Judge himself started his judicial career as directly recruited District Judge and he was elevated to the High Court before completing ten years in Judicial service. This was pointed out by him to the writ petitioner. He therefore dismissed the writ petition in limine.

But Nawab Rajendran, being a good fighter did not stop there. He went to the Supreme Court of India and filed a Special Leave Petition. He pleaded that the petition be taken up out of turn. The Chief Justice of India was almost ready to take it up. I was told that the Chief Justice of India would have granted some interim orders but for a flash in his mind and he asked the petitioner whether the respondents were direct recruitees. When he was told of the real fact he did not grant any interim relief nor even a posting out of turn. Our appointment was confirmed by the President of India within a week thereof. Thus we passed through stages of suspense and drama before we reached the High Court as judges. The Presidential order appointing me as judge of the Kerala High Court was issued from the Rashtrapathi Bhavan, New Delhi on 6.8.1985. Though the President signed the appointing order of three persons including me the warrant of appointment was released only in my case at the first instance, as there was only one vacancy available then in the High Court of Kerala. The appointment of Justice Sreedharan was issued a month thereafter and Justice K.G.Balakrishnan was appointed within another fortnight.

On 12.9.1985 at 11 a.m., I was sworn in by the Chief Justice K. Bhaskaran in the main court hall, being the most spacious hall, of the High Court of Kerala. The function was attended by a large crowd including advocates of the High Court and also from Kottayam Bar. My mother was then aged 72 and she could attend the function, but my father was quite sick and hence could only get reports of the function from my mother, as he could not attend. My father's brother who was an octogenarian and also my sole surviving maternal uncle and my in-laws (father-in-law Dr. Rev. T.C. Thomas was Principal of four colleges at four different times) and my family members were also present besides a large number of friends. As a customary practice in the High Court of Kerala all the judges of the High Court proceeded from the Chief Justice's chamber in a procession through the corridors of the sprawling building, preceded by mace holding daffadars who added colour and lustre to the procession. After the swearing in ceremony, the President of the Bar Association (N. Dharmadan) delivered a welcome address. He was followed by the Advocate General (P.V. Ayyappan) who made touching references to his experiences while conducting cases in my courts as Sessions Judge. In my reply I expressed gratitude to Chief Justice Bhaskaran for recommending me and then to my parents and gurus and all persons who mattered in my career. I narrated the story of Solomon's honeybees and closed the speech invoking guidance from the Almighty. I vividly remember, when the procession reached near the portico of the High Court, Chief Justice Bhaskaran disclosed to me in a sentimental tone "you know, how long have I been looking forward to seeing you as my colleague". It was very touching to me. Many years later when I was officiating as Chief Justice of the Kerala High Court, I came across the letter which he sent to the Chief Justice of India recommending me as judge of the High Court. In that letter he wrote very high about my performance as a District Judge. I am beholden to him.

19

Nascency on the Bench of the High Court

I was 48 years old when I became judge of the High Court. My well wishers thought that I would continue to be judge of the High Court for a long period of nearly 14 years and that I would be the Chief Justice of Kerala High Court from September 1995 till 29th January 1999. This thinking was based on a calculation reckoning the date of retirement of my immediate senior judge as Chief Justice vis-à-vis the date predicted for my retirement as shown in the calendar. But this calculation went awry due to vast changes which took place within a couple of months of my appointment. The Union Government adopted a new policy that every High Court in India shall have Chief Justice from outside the state. This policy was adopted on account of two reasons; one was, perhaps, the office of Chief Justice of a High Court became more powerful over the years as he could singularly recommend persons to be judges of the High Court. Some of the Chief Justices used the said power to promote persons not on merits but on personal, communal and political considerations. Second was, some of the Chief Justices had established clout with the Chief Ministers of the state concerned and when such states were ruled by political parties other than the party in power at the Centre, a local Chief Justice could be used by a strong Chief Minister to fill up vacancies with persons liked by such Chief Minister due to extraneous reasons. Whatever that be, the new policy of outside Chief Justices was implemented and justice K. Bhaskaran was transferred as Chief Justice of Andhra Pradesh High Court within two months of my elevation as High Court Judge. In his place Justice V.S. Malimath (Chief Justice of Karnataka High Court) was appointed by transfer.

My appointment along with Justice Sreedharan and Justice K.G. Balakrishnan would have been well augured for the higher judiciary due to another development which took place within a couple of months of my appointment as Judge of the High Court. The salary of a High Court Judge, at the time of our appointment was just Rs. 3500/- per month. This became so on account of a provision made in the Indian Constitution as back in 1949 when the rupee value remained unchanged. At the time it was fixed as Rs. 3500/- it had a value on a par with at least Rs. 1 lac in the year 1985. But from 1950 to 1985, during which time the money value of the rupee plummeted lamentably, the figure Rs. 3500/- remained unchanged, while its value became far lower. Thus the amount of Rs. 3500/- became grossly inadequate for any judge of the High Court to lead a reasonable standard of living. Of course in 1982 the Government of India sanctioned dearness allowance to the High Court Judges which made the total wages at Rs.7500/- per month. But even that amount was far too low for a High Court Judge to have a decent living by maintaining a car and other necessities of life. In spite of repeated requests made by the judges as well as the Bar, the Union Government did not bother to update the wages of judges. It came to a stage when no advocate with an average income practising in Bombay, Delhi or Calicut gave consent to be elevated from the Bar to the bench of the High Court. Thus Judgeship of even the High Court became so unattractive a post to the advocates despite the vast Constitutional powers conferred on him. In some of the chartered High Courts the vacancies were filled up mostly from lower judiciary. It is no exaggeration to say that in the early 1980's the High Court Judges were living a life of near penury. I admire many of them who scarified their very lucrative practice and joined judgeship of the Kerala High Court during those period.

In August 1985 the Prime Minister of India (Rajiv Gandhi) convened a conference of all Chief Justices of the High Courts and all the Chief Ministers of various states. They took decisions to substantially increase the salary of the High Court Judges and to afford vast perquisites to them. A legislation was made for that purpose. Thereafter a High Court Judge became entitled, apart from a substantial increase in the salaries, to free electricity, a rent free bungalow, a chauffer driven car with free fuel up to a good limit, a sumptuary allowance, reimbursement of all medical expenses and lastly LTC (leave travel concession) to go to any place in India with his spouse as well as dependent children twice a year. No judge could thereafter justifiably grudge about the remuneration now being paid to him.

But it is very unfortunate that some of the judges have only enjoyed the benefits in fullest measure without performing their obligations. When vast majority of judges were very alert in quickly disposing of the cases heard by them, a handful of judges earned bad name for the judiciary by not pronouncing judgments even months (at times years) after conclusion of arguments. Still they chose to enjoy all the benefits and perquisites without any qualm of conscience.

I learnt that when Chief Justice Malimath was proposed to be transferred to Kerala High Court he was at first unwilling to accept the transfer. He was the Advocate General of Karnataka High Court when he was aged 38 or 39. When he became a judge of the High Court at a young age, many counted him to be the future Chief Justice of India. When he became Chief Justice of the Karnataka High Court he and others thought that he would continue in that post for a very long period at least until his elevation to the Supreme Court. But the transfer policy came into being during his period as Chief Justice of Karnataka High Court. He pleaded with the Law Ministry of India that if his transfer to another High Court was indispensable he might be transferred to a larger High Court. But when Justice Bhaskaran was transferred and posted as Chief Justice of Andhra Pradesh High Court, there was no vacancy in any other larger High Courts to which Justice Malimath could go as Chief Justice. Finally he reconciled himself, though much against his wishes, to becoming the Chief Justice of the Kerala High Court.

Without fear of contradiction I can state that Justice Malimath was signally successful as Chief Justice of Kerala High Court. Perhaps it was partly because of two advantages he wielded. One was the long tenure ahead of him as Chief Justice and the other was that at the outset of his tenure every body in the Kerala High Court and even the members of the Bar were strangers to him. Apart from these advantages he had a sense of commitment and he did his work with the motivation that he should have a niche in the wall of fame and he acquired it. Due to his efforts the judge strength of the Kerala High Court was increased from 18 to 29 and he made recommendations to fill up all such posts without delay. Most of his recommendations were applauded by the Bar. But when he partitioned the court halls with asbestos sheets for accommodating the increased number of courts there was criticism against him. The strongest criticism was mounted by the next senior-most judge Dr. Justice T.K. Kochuthommen, who later became judge of the Supreme Court of India. He wrote a sharply worded letter to the Chief Justice with copies marked to all other colleagues. But Justice Malimath went ahead with his scheme undaunted by any such criticism. Looking back, I feel that Justice Malimath was justified in partitioning the large court hall for creating more court rooms. In the particular setup he had no other alternative.

The practice followed in most of the states, as also in the Kerala State, regarding appointments to judicial offices at lower judiciary level, was to depend upon the Public Service Commission (PSC in short) which prepared list of candidates for such appointments. But the functioning of the PSC was grossly unsatisfactory and this caused a large number of judicial posts to remain unfilled for a long period. Consequently, such vacancies were manned by temporary hands who had no experience as practicing Advocate. Eventually, a large number of judicial posts came to be occupied by such less qualified temporary appointees who held the office for a long time. It led to a very disquieting situation. In spite of repeated reminders dispatched to the PSC, the response was very lethargic and hence the situation remained unchanged. When Justice Malimath became the Chief Justice of Kerala, he successfully persuaded the Chief Minister to hand over the power of selecting the judicial officers, from the PSC to the High Court.

All the vacancies were soon filled up with candidates selected from the Bar through a rigorous written examination and a thoroughly orchestrated viva voce conducted by the judges of the High Court which brought about a sea change in the functioning of the subordinate judiciary in Kerala state. In fact, Kerala acquired a name as the pioneer in that field.

Justice Malimath codified the rules for selecting District Judges through direct recruitment from the Bar which till then was not governed by any such rules. He conducted the selection process for recruiting advocates as District Judges. He formed a panel of five judges of the High Court with himself as Chairman, for processing the selection through a very tedious oral interview. Though I was one of the junior most Judges of the High Court then, he included me also in the panel. (Many years later when I became a judge of the Supreme Court I had occasion to ask him why he thought of me as a member of the panel by excluding several senior judges of the High Court. His answer was typical of him; "At least now you know why I did so"). Our selection exercise was a fantastic endeavour and we selected six advocates on merits to fill up open as well as reservation vacancies. Some of the selected persons turned out to be very efficient judges.

Justice Malimath created a Directorate of Training in the High Court to train judicial officers. He succeeded in eliciting full support from Justice U.L. Bhat who was one of the most efficient judges with proven administrative as well as organisational abilities.

I have seldom seen judges who could make such amount of homework dealing with administrative matters as Justice U.L. Bhat did. He later became the Chief Justice of Gauhati High Court and was subsequently transferred as Chief Justice of Madhya Pradesh High Court. I heard from the judicial personages as well as from the members of the Bar of those two High Courts speaking in adulatory terms of the contributions rendered by Justice U.L. Bhat in those High Courts. Everybody including me expected that he would be elevated to the Supreme Court of India but he was sidelined for reasons which I did not know precisely.

Justice K.S. Paripoornan was the first Chairman of the three Member Training Committee in which I too was included as a member. Justice Paripoornan has many qualities including a strong voice and look. It had earned much utility for the training programme during its infantile period. He was regarded as a wizard in Income Tax Law and his knowledge in Hindu Philosophy is amazingly prodigious. I took much advantage of it in my work. He was later elevated to Supreme Court. I had the rare privilege of being his colleague both as High Court Judge and as Supreme Court Judge. The Directorate of Training formed in the High Court of Kerala, eventually became the pioneer for the concept of Judicial Academy in various states in India where judges of the subordinate judiciary are being trained up.

I had the opportunity to sit with many outstanding Judges of the Kerala High Court either in Division Bench or in Full Bench of three judges. But none of the Chief Justices of the Kerala High Court (except Justice K. Bhaskaran) had associated me as his bench mate. I sat as a junior partner on the bench headed by Justices U.L. Bhat, K.S. Paripoornan, K. Sukumaran and P.C. Balakrishna Menon. Thereafter, I was the senior partner of Division Benches sitting with other judges.

The control and supervision of subordinate judiciary are vested in the High Court as per the Constitution. The Kerala High Court evolved a scheme for exercising such control and supervision. It was Justice P.T. Raman Nair who orchestrated the scheme. He was an ICS personnel and one of the most efficient administrators on the judicial side. As per the said scheme, each judicial district was placed under special supervision of one of the judges of the High Court. When I took charge of the supervision of Ernakulam judicial district, I found that the arrears of cases pending in all the courts in that district were alarmingly high. I could identify three main causes which contributed to this huge arrears. One, the judicial officers had no time to deal with individual cases since "calling work" (Roll call of cases) itself had consumed the entire forenoon of the day. Second, much time was wasted for dictating long to very long orders/judgements. The third cause for the huge arrears was due to spending fresh hours for hearing the arguments on interlocutory applications.

I convened a conference of all the Judicial officers of Ernakulam District. After discussing with them, I chalked out some measures to bring down the arrears. One was the decision that no interlocutory application would be taken up until 3 p.m., of the day. Another was that all orders on interlocutory applications would be written by the judge in his own hand so that each interlocutory order could be finished with a few sentences. The third was, the time for calling work was limited to 20 or maximum 30 minutes. (Some of the judicial officers hinted that thirty minutes time was too short for completing the calling work. It was decided that in future the posting book for each day should contain only that much of cases as could be finished its roll-call work within a maximum period of thirty minutes) Certain other practical measures were also evolved to save the time for doing judicial work.

Within one month of the said conference I noticed that the above exercise yielded very good results. The backlog of cases started plummeting rapidly. The Arrears Committee set up by the Law Ministry of India made a special reference to Ernakulam District for achieving, during that period, the largest clearance of backlog.

20

A few among the memorable cases

During the long period of eleven years of my judgeship of the Kerala High Court I could deal with important and less important, as well as very important subjects in different cases. Some of the sensational and very sensational cases were also dealt with by me either singly or with other companion judges. No writer would normally dwell on cases of petty nature. But I venture to make a reference to one case which might look, at the first blush, a small case, but it had very wide range of ramifications. Even today its ripple is live.

(1) Survodaya leader – M.P. Manmadhan

That case was filed against M.P. Manmadhan, a very renowned Survodaya leader of Kerala. He was one of the most famous orators in Malayalam and he could keep his audience spell bound for hours together. He was one of those who were detained without trial during the infamous emergency. After his release he addressed well attended public meetings and the people became conscious of the perils of suspension of the fundamental rights during the Emergency. However, he did not contest any election. He spearheaded a campaign for eschewing alcoholic drinking as one of his social programmes. As part of the said propaganda he and his followers picketed liquor shops for preventing the customers from entering into such shops. The liquor barons of

Kerala organized themselves to meet the situation. On a fixed day, M.P. Manmadhan, in the company of a large number of Survodaya volunteers stood in front of a liquor shop keeping hand in hand with others calling out slogans. The police force moved fast and arrested him and his followers. An F.I.R. was registered against him for the offence of "wrongful restraint". The arrested persons were released on bail while the investigation was pending. At that stage Manmadhan and others filed a petition in the High Court praying that the criminal case against them be quashed on the ground that picketing of liquor shops would not amount to an offence at all.

On behalf of Police the Public Prosecutor contended that if one prevented any other person from proceeding to any place where the latter had a right to go such action would be an offence of wrongful restraint as per section 341 of I.P.C. The offence is defined as "voluntarily obstructing any person so as to prevent that person from proceeding in any direction in which that person has a right to proceed". Apparently, the action of Manmadhan fell under the purview of the said definition. But my judicial mind woke up to protect the accused. I passed my judgement quashing the criminal case against Manmadhan and his companions for which I advanced mainly two reasons. One was, even if the volunteers picketed the liquor shop the consequence was too insignificant and trivial for a criminal court to spend its valuable time. I quoted an English dictum "if you dip your pen in the inkpot of another the action may technically amount to theft, but it is too trivial for a criminal court to take cognizance". Second was, after all what was the intention of the picketers? They were only trying to spearhead a campaign which was most dear to Mahatma Gandhi who led the freedom struggle. Under Article 51 A of the Constitution of India, it is the fundamental duty of a citizen "to cherish and follow the noble ideals which inspired the national struggle for freedom". The acts of the accused were done only with the intention to dissuade those who were prone to alcoholic drinks from consuming liquor, though they could not enter into the liquor house. I declared that the acts of M.P. Manmadhan and his followers did not amount to the offence of wrongful restraint. Hence I quashed all the criminal proceedings against him and his companions.

The said judgement was hailed all over India particularly by the people involved in Survodaya movement. A journal published in the state of Gujarat where prohibition was in force highlighted the judgement by quoting excerpts therefrom copiously.

(2) Sandwiched Potassium Cyanide

One murder case became very sensational, it was in respect of an incident which happened at Alwaye (a small town near Cochin) on 23.6.1980. In that incident a mother and her three children of a middle class family died of eating sandwiched potassium cyanide. When the father of the children (Tomy) returned home at night after closing his textile shop, he found his wife and children lying dead. When the police reached the spot they found that death was due to consumption of sandwiches smeared with potassium cyanide. The police initially took it as a case of suicide committed by all of them, but the surviving father was not prepared to reconcile with the theory of suicide. He persisted in pressurising the police to conduct a detailed investigation. Finally the police detected that it was a well planned criminal conspiracy to exterminate the entire family including the father. The conspiracy was hatched by Tomy's sister-in-law Ammini (his elder brother's wife) in collaboration with her paramour as she felt that all the business started by her late husband had eventually been captured by Tomy. She became vengeful towards Tomy and family when the monthly allowance given to her from the textile business was only a pittance. She felt that a major share of the profit from the business should have been given to her. Charge sheet was filed by the police after investigation in which Ammini was figured as first accused, her paramour as second accused and some other persons as co-accused.

The trial of the case in the sessions court was a very prolonged one as the witnesses examined were quite a large number. Major portion of the evidence was recorded by one sessions judge and thereafter another sessions judge who succeeded him recorded the remaining evidence. It was the third sessions judge who heard arguments and pronounced judgement of the trial court. But all the accused were acquitted by him.

The state preferred an appeal against the order of acquittal. That appeal was heard first by a bench of two Judges of the High Court. During arguments one of the judges expressed certain observations clearly indicating that the acquittal was wrong, but the other judge made dissenting observations. The judges as between themselves realised that they might finally write two different verdicts. Hence they cut short the arguments and referred the case to be heard by a bench of three Judges (Full Bench). Justices S. Padmanabhan, K.G. Balakrishnan and myself were nominated on the full bench. The arguments were started before us by the then Advocate General (M.B. Kurup) who himself was a good criminal lawyer. For the accused a leading criminal lawyer from North Paravur Bar (Isac Thomas), who defended the accused in the trial court appeared before us and addressed arguments for two or three days. At this stage I should say that Isac Thomas must be regarded as one of the best criminal lawyers of the state. It was a pleasure to hear him arguing the case. But on account of a development during the course of arguments, Isac Thomas withdrew himself from the case. It was the following:

M.B. Kurup produced a photo of the accused Ammini before us. He collected it from a file kept with him. He produced it for convincing us that Ammini used to wear specs. Suddenly Isac Thomas sprang on his feet and protested in a strident tone that Advocate General was trying to mislead and contaminate the mind of the Judges by showing a document which was not part of the evidence in the trial court. The soft spoken M.B. Kurup became dump-founded. I noticed that he was terribly nonplussed at this tirade made against him. We three Judges felt initially that the point of objection raised by Isac Thomas was very valid.

But in a split second a flash passed through my mind as I felt that the Advocate General was in order by showing the photo to us. I pointed out to Isac Thomas that If the Advocate General felt that the said document was of such importance as to establish the identity of Ammini with reference to the specs, it was open to him to convince us that its non-production in the trial court was either wrong or by a mistake. It is open to the court to allow that document to be produced in the appeal court. Under section 391 of the Cr.P.C. the appeal court has power to take additional evidence. I pointed out that according to one witness, a spectacle worn woman was walking in the vicinity of the house of occurrence. I told Isac Thomas that the interjection made by him was too premature and it resulted in foreclosing the Advocate General from proceeding further with his arguments on that point.

Isac Thomas had no answer to what I pointed out then. Hence I told the Advocate General to proceed with the arguments. When arguments were resumed next day Isac Thomas was not present. Another advocate on his behalf submitted that "Mr. Isac Thomas would not like to continue to appear in this court for health reasons". (I was told that Isac Thomas had some cardiac problems even earlier). We felt that we are deprived of the formidable arguments of an efficient criminal lawyer at that stage. We three judges permitted the new advocate to take over the arguments. Both sides consumed about 10 days to complete the arguments and we reserved the judgement. The senior judge (Justice S. Padmanabhan) wished me to write the judgement.

For the Full Bench, I authored the judgement reversing the verdict of the trial court and we convicted the four accused for criminal conspiracy and murder etc. In regard to the penalty to be imposed Justice Padmanabhan suggested to me that death penalty might be imposed on all the four accused. Myself and Justice K.G. Balakrishnan persuaded him to agree for the lesser penalty of life imprisonment. Finally he yielded to our persuasion. In the judgement authored by me I dealt with the punishment part as follows:

"Now we come to the last duty in this case – passing sentence on the accused. The fiendish manner in which the murders were perpetrated does persuade us to give a sentence less than the maximum allowed by law, particularly to Ammini who acted as the linchpin of the machinations which culminated in the horrendous drama played on 23.6.1980 in Tomy's house. The other accused joined the criminal conspiracy only at the behest of Ammini. The murders were so planned as to make them appear to the outer world as a case of suicide committed by all the members of Tomy's family. But for the unforeseen snag, which developed, perhaps the deaths would have been written off like that. Ammini looked on like a virago to see how her henchman implemented the murderous scheme on Merly, and then she turned to the innocent children to whom she was but the senior aunt. The aunt suddenly turned into wicked demon and spouted the lethal venom into the little ones and finished them off in seconds. She had the wiliness to join the mourners next day feigning bereavement without even a semblance of any qualm. In the normal course the punishment she deserves, in the circumstances, is the maximum provided by law. But one factor dissuades us from imposing that sentence. She has two sons and a daughter who lost their father twelve years ago. Capital punishment to A1 will make those children destitutes. That seems to us to be the solitary consideration dissuading us from imposing the capital punishment on her"

Next day the print media carried news of the judgement on the front page with a big coverage perhaps due to the high degree of sensation which that case had generated at all stages. The judgement was reported in most of the Law Reports in India as it overruled a few legal dictum which held the field till then and made certain innovative propositions in criminal law. About a decade thereafter, I was invited to address the members of the judicial academy of the Bombay High Court (Nagapur Bench) when I was Judge of the Supreme Court. I then noticed how the trainees were well equipped with the legal propositions adumbrated in the above mentioned judgement. It is reported in All India Reports 1988 Kerala, page 1 (it is also reported in 1988 Criminal Law Journal 107 as State Vs. Ammini).

Before passing I may mentioned a few words about Justice Padmanabhan. He was one of the best judges with very shrewd insight and a treasure of practical knowledge. He was very strong in his judicial orientations. His judicial disposition transcended any other personal consideration. His equity-oriented conclusions were well known to the Bar. His judgement in Vypin liquor tragedy case (wherein the trial court acquitted all the accused including some of the liquor tycoons, but the High Court reversed it and convicted all the big guns to long term imprisonment) attracted very vide coverage in all the newspapers in India. It was a pleasure to sit with him. He never hesitated to correct himself whenever he was convinced of a view point. We both continued to be very close friends.

(3) Majeendran Case

One film producer by name Majeendran was shot dead in his own house at Cochin on the dawn of 9.10.1981 by a hired assassin. The incident created a lot of sensation in and around the city. On 26.10.1981 police arrested a prominent liquor merchant (who was made the second accused) as the person who hired one Vijayan (who was arrayed as the first accused) for liquidating Majeendran. The first accused ducked down and the police began to prowl for him. He succeeded in evading the police for a long period of three years. But finally he surrendered before the court.

The case acquired a lot of publicity presumably because the deceased and the main accused were rich men and also because the incident happened in a thickly habitated residential locality of the city. The short story of the case was this:

The second accused and the deceased Majeendran were friends at first and both together enjoyed financial support from one Ramakrishnan, but eventually the second accused felt that he was not favoured by the financier as much as he favoured Majeendran. The germ of hostility so burgeoned in the mind of second accused grew up day by day and it reached the stage where he took the decision to finish his rival off. He elicited the help of Vijayan for it and taught him how to operate a revolver. On the early morning of the scheduled day the first accused entered the house of Majeendran. He pressed the calling bell and the servant-made appeared at the door. When she asked for what the bell was rung the visitor told her that he wanted to see Majeendran. When this was conveyed to the wife of Majeendran who in turn woke him up from sleep and informed him of the visitor. As soon as Majeendran went up to the door the visitor opened the revolver and shot him down. The assassin ran away and Majeendran fell down and died within minutes. Just before he breathed his last he disclosed to his wife that he had suspicion about second accused as having a hand in this incident.

After trial, the Sessions Judge acquitted both accused. Hence the state filed an appeal in the High Court. A Division Bench of the High Court consisting of me and Justice Shamsudeen heard arguments in a very detailed manner. The entire case rested on the evidence of the maid-servant who identified the assassin at the door step. She saw him for the first time in her life only when he arrived at the house of occurrence and she had only a glimpse of him. When she said in her evidence that it was accused Vijayan whom she saw, the only question to be decided was whether her evidence could be believed. After the shooting she saw him once more when a test identification parade was conducted by the police with the first accused and ten other persons. The Sessions Judge did not accept her evidence. But we, in the High Court, felt that the Sessions Judge was too credulous in upholding the argument that she could not have remembered the face of the assailants. In the judgment of the Bench which I authored the following reasons were given for reversing the findings of the sessions judge regarding her evidence. "She conversed with the assailant, though it was only one or two sentences exchanged between them. Her mind was such that a witness like her could, in all probabilities retain the image of the intruder who killed her master, if she had seen him. We had no doubt that she had seen the assailant. That face would have left an indelible image in her mind. The court need not expect the witness to enumerate the facial features of the assailant with meticulous precision. There may not be any traceable distinct features for an assailant, yet the witness who had a glimpse of his face would be able to remember and identify him since that person was associated with an event of unusual importance for the witness".

We were inclined to believe her version as some other evidence lent assurance to us that the first accused Vijayan visited the house on the morning. Accepting her evidence as believable, the prosecution version made a big leap forward and rendered the whole case believable. We dissented from the session judge's approach and concluded that it was Vijayan the first accused who shot down Majeendran. That conclusion led us to the next inevitable conclusion that Vijayan was employed by the liquor baron (second accused) to kill Majeendran. We therefore, set aside the acquittal and convicted both the accused and sentenced them to imprisonment for life. Our judgement was reported in many law journals including the first volume of 1992 Kerala Law Times at page 878 besides Indian Law Reports 1992 first volume (Kerala) at page 705.

The convicted accused had a right of appeal to the Supreme Court as they were first acquitted by the trial court. The Supreme Court, however, dissented from our finding regarding the evidence of the maid-servant and restored the acquittal. The decision of the Supreme Court is reported in All India Reports 1999 Supreme Court 1086.

(4) Panur Soman Case

This is a memorable case in my judicial career. It is lingering in my mind mostly on account of its impact on me even years after the case was disposed of. It acquired great sensation right from the date of death of Soman who was a Sub Inspector of Police then attached to Panur Police Station situated on the northern range of Kerala State. He died of bullet injuries inside the police station. The sensation it generated had snowballed into a wide dimension.

On the morning of the day of occurrence, Sub Inspector Soman arrived at Panur Police Station as usual for his duties. There were six police constables who were present at the station then. After Soman sat on his seat, sound of gun shots was heard outside. When people rushed in they found Soman lying on his seat. All the six constables then took him in a jeep and drove him to the nearest hospital, but he was declared dead. There were three bullet injuries on his chest. As he was wearing a kaki uniform, the bullets had pierced through that outfit.

The above case was investigated by the local police at the first instance, but due to the agitation launched by the local people the investigation was transferred to the state Crime Branch police. Even that was not satisfactory to the agitationists and they mounted pressure for entrusting the investigation to the Central Bureau of Investigation (CBI). At last the Government yielded to the pressure and ordered the CBI to conduct the investigation.

Once the CBI started the investigation the route of the case took a new turn with the help of expert opinion regarding the range of the shots and also with the help of some other materials. The CBI concluded that Soman was shot dead by the constables who conspired together to kill him, as Soman became a stumbling block to the constables getting money from the people. All the six constables were arrested for criminal conspiracy and murder. The case was charge-sheeted against all of them on completion of investigation. The trial of the case was held at Sessions Court, Tellicherry. Ratna Singh (who is the present Advocate General of Kerala) was appointed as Special Public Prosecutor for the case. Some of the accused engaged the most renowned criminal lawyer of the state, K. Kunhirama Menon. The other accused engaged M.K. Damodaran (who later became the Advocate General of Kerala) to defend the accused. The trial was a prolonged one. After completing the trial the Sessions Judge postponed the date for pronouncement of the judgement on three different occasions as he could not complete writing the judgement. The Sessions Judge wrote a bulky judgment and he convicted four out of six constables for the offences of criminal conspiracy and murder and they were sentenced to life imprisonment. However, he acquitted the other two constables.

There were two appeals against the judgement of the sessions court. One was filed by the four convicted constables and the other was filed by the C.B.I. against the acquittal of the two constables. Both appeals were heard together by a Bench of the High Court consisting of Justice K. Sukumaran and Justice G. Rajasekharan. Arguments were heard by them for a number of days. When they finally pronounced the judgement it was a split verdict. Justice Sukumaran confirmed the conviction of four constables. He enhanced the punishment of the first accused to death penalty. He also reversed the acquittal of the other two constables and convicted them also and sentenced them to life imprisonment. But Justice Rajasekharan totally dissented from that judgement and wrote a separate one by which he acquitted all the accused. Since the two opinions were sharply divided verdicts, the appeals were referred to a three judge bench. The convicted accused remained in jail ever since they were convicted by the trial court.

The three judge bench constituted for that purpose was headed by me with Justices P.K. Shamsudeen and B.M. Thulasi Das as the other judges. Very detailed arguments were addressed by K. Kunhirama Menon who appeared for some of the accused and then by M.K. Damodaran who appeared for the remaining accused. T.R. Raman Pillai, a senior advocate argued for the C.B.I.. He succeeded in creating an impression in our mind that Soman was shot dead in the police station.

We then told the advocates for the accused that if the prosecution succeeded in satisfying the judges that Soman was shot dead instead of the defence version that he committed suicide, none of the constables could possibly escape conviction because all of them were present in the station when the incident happened and it would not have been possible to kill Soman without the express consent of all of them and without all of them conspiring together.

There were certain formidable hurdles for the defence advocate to get over in order to make the judges believe that death of Soman would have been by suicide. The report of the ballistic expert was very damaging to the defence version. There were three bullet holes on the kaki uniform of the dead body, tattooing (marks by carbon deposit) was present around two of such holes while the third hole did not contain any carbon deposit at all. This was the finding of the chemical analyst who tested the kaki uniform. On the basis of that finding the ballistic expert gave his report that the bullet which created the said third hole would have been fired only from a distance of beyond 35 cm. This opinion of the expert ruled out the possibility of the bullet being fired by a suicidee himself on account of three premises. One, the range of at least one shot was so much that the victim could not have used his own hands. Second, no suicidee could have fired three shots from a firearm on his own chest. Third, the route of the bullets travelling inside the chest was downwards and that was not at all possible if the victim had pulled the trigger when the mouth of the revolver was focused on his own chest.

However, the sole basis of the conclusion that the revolver was fired from a distance beyond 35 c.m was the report of the chemical analyst which showed that there was no carbon deposit on one of the holes on the uniform. But two doctors who conducted the joint autopsy had noticed that all the three holes on the kaki uniform were surrounded by carbon deposit. We were told that the uniform would have been folded and unfolded many tiles before it reached the hands of the chemical analyst. It was possible that the carbon particles of at least one of the holes would have been dropped off during these stages. Hence we thought that it was an unsafe basis to reach a conclusion regarding the range of the shot. As for the contention that three bullets could not have been fired by a suicide, the advocate read out passages from some books of ballistic experts wherein illustration of suicidees firing multiplicity of shots have been cited when the revolver is of a caliber used in this case. Regarding the downward track of the bullets inside the chest which really baffled all of us, Kunhirama Menon demonstrated before us by sitting on a chair of the same height and resting his elbows on a table of the same height, using the same revolver by employing both hands, that such downward track is quite possible.

There were many other items of evidence. All of them could be used in support of either the theory of suicide or homicide. But there was one circumstance which appeared to us to be very incompatible with the theory of homicide. It was why all the police men rushed the injured S.I. to the hospital, if he was shot by them. Would they take such a risk if the S.I. was not dead by the time he reached the hospital he would have disclosed to all that he was shot by the constables.

Soman's wife was examined by the prosecution and she said that Soman had no reason to commit suicide and also that he left the house on the morning saying that he would be back for lunch. One Damu Vakil was cited by the prosecution as a witness since he was engaged by Soman to defend him in the departmental proceedings initiated against Soman. Damu Vakil was expected to say in court that Soman had no cause for committing suicide. But he was not examined by the prosecution for reasons not known to us. It is interesting to note that Damu Vakil was cited by the accused as a defence witness, but in spite of summons being served on him and five or six postings being given for his examination, he did not turn up. Finally he was given up. I cannot say now as to why the trial court did not take other steps to compel his presence in court.

Our mind wobbled between two alternatives – whether to confirm conviction or to acquit the accused. At the end of the detailed arguments we thought that the safer course is to give the benefit of doubt to the accused and hence we acquitted the accused, though we had doubts about the theory of suicide.

But certain information, which reached me a few weeks after the judgement was pronounced, made me aghast. In a garden party, M.K. Damodaran (who argued for some of the accused) asked me why I wobbled for a long time to reach a conclusion and that the defence advocates were terribly disturbed when they noticed that the judges were contemplating to convict the accused. Damodaran said that he was absolutely certain that Soman committed suicide. As an experienced criminal lawyer he had his own good reasons to believe the version given to him by his clients. When this conversation went on Ratna Singh (who argued for the CBI in the trial court) was standing a little away. Hence, I confronted him with what Damodaran told me. He discretely told me that what Damodaran said was true. This information haunted me for some days as we felt that we narrowly escaped because we were contemplating the idea of convicting the accused, though we changed it at the last minute. Had we not changed like that, we would have been privy to the commission of a terrible calamity in the sense that six innocent constables would have ended up in jail for the rest of their life for no fault on their part, particularly when there was not even a homicide intention to end his life, and that Damu Vakil took great pains to persuade him not to do any such harsh steps. The above information had further added to what I have gathered from M.K. Damodaran which I mentioned above. I became deeply grateful to my God for saving me from a great catastrophe. Had we not changed our mind at the last moment we would have committed the greatest injustice in my judicial career. I called Kunhirama Menon and told him of all the informations I gathered in the matter. He then disclosed to me that he never had the habit of eliciting the truth of any case from his clients because he believed that his only role as a defense lawyer was to impress upon the court that the prosecution did not succeed in proving the case. Nonetheless, he in this case had occasion to be thoroughly satisfied that it was a case of suicide. He quoted to me what one of the accused told him. It was this; "When we saw the Sub Inspector pointing the revolver on his chest, we instinctively leaned forward yelling out "don't do it, don't do it", but within seconds he fired all the shots on himself".

Whatever be the approaches of anybody else on subsequent events, I became absolutely certain from what I narrated above that death of Soman was a case of suicide. On any other occasion I would not have bothered myself as to what the superior court had pronounced the verdict regarding my judgments. But when CBI filed a Special Leave Petition in the Supreme Court against our judgment in Soman case I was very much anxious to know what would happened. I prayed earnestly that the judges of the Supreme Court should be guided to find out the truth. The SLP was heard by Justice M.M. Punchi and Justice Jayachandra Reddy. Both were very well experienced in criminal cases. When I learned later that the Supreme Court dismissed the SLP filed by the CBI, I heaved a sigh of relief.

Should I have bothered myself so much ? I told Kunhirama Menon that if my judgement ended in conviction of the accused and had I come to know of all the subsequent informations (narrated supra), most probably I would not have continued as a judge. It would have been greatly difficult for me to continue to sit on the seat of justice if six innocent persons had to languish in prison on account of my inability to discern such a vital truth concerning them, with the consequences of six families entering into perennial misery. In a meeting held at the Badakara Bar Association in connection with its jubilee celebrations, Kunhirama Menon mentioned this fact to the audience in my presence.

The mysterious transformation of Sukumarakurup's corpse as Chacko's body

I think no other murder case would have instilled more suspense and thrill in the minds of the people of this state than the case in which one Sukumarakurup became the focus point. He was believed to be the victim of a murder and the body was found in flame in a motor car inferno. But later it was revealed that the body was not of Sukumarakurup, but of one Chacko and that Sukumarakurup played the role as kingpin in a diabolic plot to make a façade that he was killed. It was done with the rapacious motive of inveigling a whopping sum covered by an insurance policy subscribed to by himself at Abudabi. This is the nub of the prosecution story.

Though the police nabbed all others believed to have been involved in the conspiracy, the one who eluded from the dragnet of the police is Sukumarakurup himself. So the case was charge sheeted without him as the accused. One of the culprits was transposed as an approver and was examined as an eye witness. Sukumarakurup's brother-in-law (wife's sister's husband) and his driver were arrayed as the first and second accused respectively. Sukumarakurup's wife and her sister were arraigned as third and fourth accused respectively. The Sessions Judge convicted the first and second accused of murder, criminal conspiracy and destruction of evidence, but the remaining accused were acquitted.

Synopsis of the prosecution story, having the silhouette of a crime thriller screen play, is the following: Sukumarakurup belonged to Cheriyandadu (near Chengannur in Kerala) and was employed in Abudabi where he was living with his wife. A greedy thought burgeoned in his mind for becoming fabulously rich overnight. Pursuant thereto he took a policy of insurance at Abudabi in a total sum of 301616 Dirhams (roughly thirty lakhs rupees) He decided to make it appear to all concerned that he got involved in a motor accident and died so that the entire insurance amount could be collected by his wife. This nebulous idea became crystallised into an orchestrated scheme in which his brother-in-law (first accused), his loyal driver (second accused) and an attender in his company at Abudabi were enlisted as participants. For the successful execution of their scheme a small quantity of 'ether' was procured from the laboratory of Alleppey Medical College.

Sukumarakurup and the first accused along with the attender landed at Trivandrum during the first week of January 1984. The four conspirators (Sukumarakurup and the above mentioned first and second accused as well as the attender) met together at "Smitha Bhavan", Cheriyanadu (which is the house of

Sukumarakurup's wife) and carefully worked out details regarding implementation of the plot. They fixed 21.1.1984 as the D-day for the final operation.

On 21.1.1984 all the four met together at Kalpakavadi (a tourist hotel on the National Highway located about 20 Kms. south of Alleppey town). Sukumarakurup reached there in his Ambassador car (KLY 5959). Others reached there in the car of the first accused (KLY 7831). They proceeded from there (Sukumarakurup in one car and others in the other car) southwards on the National Highway hoping to come across somebody having resemblance with Sukumarakurup. But even after covering a distance of about 23 Kms (upto a place called Oachira) they could not find out any such person. They drove back through the same route. When they reached Karuvatta (about 13 Kms. from Oachira) deceased Chacko who was waiting for a vehicle to go home, raised his hand as a signal soliciting for a lift. The conspirators noticed that this stranger had resemblance with Sukumarakurup, hence they offered him a lift in the car KLY 5959.

While the vehicles were on the move, first accused offered a drink to the deceased but he declined. First accused persisted in persuading him and after mixing brandy with ether in one glass he succeeded as the victim drank it. Within a few moments first accused put a towel around his neck and began to strangulate him and then he slouched his head.

The vehicle then proceeded to Smitha Bhavan. The victim's body was carried to one of the rooms and his clothes were substituted with the shirt and lunki of Sukumarakurup. After dumping the body in the dickey of KLY 5959 they proceeded towards north in the two cars. When they reached a place called Kollakadavu they placed the body on the driver's seat of KLQ 7831. They pushed that car down to the adjoining paddy field. Petrol was sprinkled inside and outside the car and the vehicle was set ablaze. But in that operation first and second accused sustained some burns. However, they all scampered away from the scene in the other car (KLY 5959). In that hurry the gloves fell on the ground and in a second they all ran out of site. The time was then 3 a.m.

During the early hours some people saw an automobile inferno and they rushed to the scene. They came across a pair of gloves lying near the car and hence they suspected this to be graver than mere accidental fire. So one among them gave First Information Statement to the nearby police station.

Two of the accused were arrested which helped the police to shape the final case. The attender of Sukumarakurup was made an approver and he gave evidence as the first witness for the prosecution. He narrated all the facts as they happened. We believed his evidence as it was supported by many other circumstances.

Two arguments which became very important were – if the dead body was that of Sukumarakurup then the accused cannot be convicted. To meet that contention it was enough to make out that Sukumarakurup was found alive in flesh and blood on the next day of the murder. By referring to a number of circumstances it was possible for us to show that two witnesses saw Sukumarakurup hale and strong on the succeeding day. To meet the next argument (that it was not proved, the murdered person was Chacko), we held that law does not require that the murdered person should be an identifiable human being, it is enough that the victim of the murder was a human being. The following is the dictum laid down by us for the above purpose.

It is not an invariable rule that in all murder cases prosecution must establish the identity of the deceased. The rule that identity of the corpus delicti must be established, has just exceptions. In the Penal Code the expression used for murder is "whoever causes death by doing an act". S. 46 of the Penal Code says that the word "death denotes the death of a human being". For the offences relating to culpable homicide whether amounting to murder or not, death of a human being is necessary but the Penal Code does not require that such death must have been in respect of an identified human being. If there is unimpeachable evidence in a given case that 'A' has murdered a human being, but identity of that human being could not be established, 'A' would still be liable to conviction of the offence.

We confirmed the conviction and sentence passed on the accused. But Sukumara kurup has not yet been caught. The police department made repeated efforts and schemed different operations to catch him, still he succeeded in escaping at all times. Some people believe that he is already dead and some others believe that he is living in disguise and is moving from place to place. So far none is reported to have seen him ever since, he was made an accused in this case. However, he remains an enigma. The print media occasionally flashes some news about him. Thus the public is kept alive of the great crime thriller story ever played in the history of Kerala police investigation.

A number of murder cases dealt with by me along with one or the other judge in the High Court was quite large among which included such sensational cases as reproduced above. It is an uphill task to deal with all such cases

Two public servants involved in a charge of corruption

One of the criminal appeals filed in the Kerala High Court and heard by me was a case in which one professor of government engineering college and the Controller of Examinations were convicted of the offence of corruption under the Prevention of Corruption Act. Both of them filed separate appeals and they were separately heard. The allegations made against them were the following:-

In one of the examinations conducted by the university for the Engineering course, a large number of students wrote the written tests. After valuation of the answer papers final mark list had to be prepared by the Controller of Examinations. During that stage one of the professors of the Engineering College (he can be referred to as "the professor") alerted some of the students saying that "the Controller is a corrupt person and none of you will win unless you meet him and pay him money". On that advice the some students met the Controller secretly and gave him the amount which they considered sufficient to satisfy him. But one student was very unhappy as he thought that he worked hard and fared well in the examination and hence why should he pay bribe to any one to win much less to the Controller of Examinations ? It may be mentioned incidentally that the Controller was formerly a Principal or (at least) the Head of department of one Engineering College. The student who was hesitant to bribe the Controller entertained a fear that the Controller might not award pass marks to him and that all others who paid bribe would be given pass mark. Finally he informed the Anti Corruption Bureau about the corrupt activities of the Controller and offered to help the Bureau to catch the corrupt official.

Anti Corruption Bureau arranged a trap for catching the Controller red-handed. The trap was orchestrated as per their usual scheme. The complainant, pursuant to that scheme, went to the house of the Controller and paid him Rs. 5,000/-. Once the money was accepted by the Controller the complainant gave the pre-designed signal to the police people who were hovering around the house during the operation. The trap worked successfully and the Controller was caught with the bribe money. But when the case was charge-sheeted the professor was also indicted along with the Controller. The charge against the Professor was that he "abetted" the commission of the offence.

All the students who were examined as witnesses said that the Professor told them like what is quoted above. At the end of the trial the judge of the Special Court convicted the Controller for the main offence, and the Professor for abetment of the offence. Both were sentenced to rigorous imprisonment for two years. Hence the appeals were filed by both of them in the High Court.

The advocate who argued was assisted by his client, the Controller in open court. I well remember that the Controller was superbly thorough with the evidence in the case. On all occasions when I put questions to the advocate regarding any aspect of the evidence the advocate was found turning to his client (the Controller) for help and in a split second the Controller was found reaching the exact page of the relevant portion from out of the voluminous records. I do not remember to have seen any other litigant who marshalled the evidence of the case with as much thoroughness as the Controller did in this case.

But the advocate for the Controller failed to impress me regarding any of the contentions advanced in his defence. I told him that the evidence against the Controller was so clinging that it was an uphill task for the Controller to escape from conviction. So the Controller and his advocate were certain that I was inclined to confirm the conviction and sentence.

All the student witnesses narrated how the Professor impressed on them that the Controller was a greedy person and that unless his greed was satisfied the concerned student would fail to get the required marks. The witnesses further said that they met the Controller and paid him the amount and then the Controller gave enough marks to them. When the advocate who appeared for the Professor began to address arguments, I cautioned him of the futility of contending that the testimony of the student witnesses is not reliable because none of the students had any particular animosity towards the Professor. The advocate then felt that there was no usefulness in arguing further.

However, I had a feeling that the role played by the Professor was not substantially different from what other people would tell their friends or relatives. e.g. if we know that a particular doctor is very greedy, we may caution our friends or relatives who go to the doctor for treatment that he is a greedy man and you have to pay him what he requires. If that is a normal conduct for people at large, could the professor be singled out for holding him guilty of the offence just because of cautioning the students regarding the greedy inclinations of the Controller. When that line of thinking was flashed in my mind I asked the advocate about the possible interpretations of the definition of the offence of "abetment". I granted two days' time for making reflections on this line of thinking. Thereafter I heard the council and the Public Prosecutor again.

In the judgment which I pronounced the conviction and sentence passed on the Controller of Examinations were confirmed and dismissed his appeal. But I was not satisfied of the conviction passed on the Professor. Abetment as defined in Section 107 of the IPC included "intentionally aiding the doing of an act, by any act or illegal omission". In the second Explanation given to the definition it was said that "whoever, prior to the commission of an act, does anything in order to facilitate the commission of that act, is said to aid the doing of that act".

Prima-facie it appeared to be sufficient to make the act done by the Professor as amounting to abetment of the offence. But I interpreted the definition in such a way as to save persons who made similar remarks as the Professor did. I was not satisfied that the Professor told the students that the Controller is a greedy person with the main intention to facilitate the commission of the offence. All that the Professor did was to save the students from the injustice which the controller would have inflicted on them if they did not give bribery to him. I gave my detailed reasoning to distinguish the acts done by the Professor from the act of "intentionally aiding" the commission of the offence. Ultimately I acquitted the Professor. The Controller of the Examinations was thus sent to jail to suffer the jail sentence imposed on him. I do not know what happened to both the accused subsequently.

A few weeks thereafter, one sessions judge who belonged to the same district where the incident happened paid a visit to me in connection with some other matter. During the conversation he confided to me that Damu Vakil had disclosed to him even on the very day of Soman's death that on the previous night Soman was very much disturbed on account of a departmental proceeding against him. (he was charge-sheeted by the department for cheating) and that Soman told Damu Vakil of his

21

Divorces granted by Church Tribunals

Divorce became almost impossible for Christians in India because the law of divorce applicable to members of the community remained archaic and unreformed for a long time. Among the grounds recognised by the Indian Divorce Act, sexual delinquency became indispensable on the part of either the husband or the wife for obtaining divorce. It continued like that for a long time. In the meanwhile, different denominations of the Christian churches formed their own tribunals to decide whether divorce shall be granted on any specified ground. Divorce granted by such tribunals was treated for a long period as sufficient for the parties to the marriage and churches used to solemnise new marriage alliances with one of the spouses involved in such divorce.

The above position was recognised while the community and such practice was not faulted even by the courts for a long period. But a full bench of the Kerala High Court reconsidered the legal implications of the divorce granted by church tribunals. The full bench found that no party to the marriage can have a second marriage solemnised, if his or her spouse is alive, unless he succeeded in obtaining a decree of divorce from a court under the Indian Divorce Act. As a corollary it was laid down that by obtaining an order from the church tribunal the legal status of a husband

and wife could not be dissolved unless they succeeded in getting a court verdict. It was further decreed that any one undergoing the ceremony of a second marriage without such a decree and any one solemnising or assisting to solemnise such second marriage would be liable to the offence of bigamy. It was made clear that a church could, if so inclined, refuse to solemnize a second marriage until he obtained a verdict from the church tribunal, even if that person has secured a decree of divorce from a court. The judgment on behalf of the Full Bench was authored by me.

The above judgement created a flutter in the Christian community because till then the verdict made by the eparchical tribunal (Church Tribunal) was given absolute sanctity even for solemnizing a second marriage but the importance of such verdict was reduced to almost one of minor significance. That judgement was challenged in the Supreme Court as the leaders of the church felt that the High Court overturned something which they possessed by virtue of their divine authority. But the Supreme Court upheld our decision and thus the last word was said on the subject. I learned later from the advocate who argued in the Supreme Court that Justice N.P. Singh and Justice S.B. Majmudar (who heard the arguments in the case) was anxious to know the meaning of the word "sacrament". (This is because in the judgment of the Full Bench of the Kerala High Court I observed that "Christian marriage is a sacrament). The advocate told me that it was very difficult for him to explain the theological background and meaning of the word "sacrament" before two judges who were totally unfamiliar with such term. The judges later commended to the advocate that they need not bother much on that word and that the learned judge who authored the judgment of the Kerala High Court, (referring to me) being a Christian, would have understood it much better. For the judges of the Supreme Court it did not matter much, in the context of that case, that a Christian marriage was a sacrament or not. It is difficult to explain to the readers as to what is meant by "sacrament". Therefore I leave it without embarking on that theological subject.

22

Non-Brahmins as priests of temples

It was believed for long in the Hindu society that priests (poojaris) of the temples shall hail only from one community – Brahmins, and in Kerala they should belong to Nampoothiris (Malayala Brahmins). In fact, no one other than a Brahmin was accepted by a substantial section of the temple-going worshippers for performing ceremonies in the sanctum sanctorum of the temples. It was not possible for any non-Brahmin, however competent he might be, to become a priest in any temple. The above concept was given a jolt when the Constitution makers declared that the state shall not discriminate against any citizen on the ground only of religion, race or caste etc. and also that no citizen shall be ineligible for any office of the state on the grounds only of religion, race, caste etc. In spite of such specific provisions in the Constitution the custom that only a Brahmin could become a priest of the temple continued to be in vogue in the community.

But the Travancore Devaswam Board ventured to make a departure from the said tradition by appointing two gentlemen who belonged to backward communities. A writ petition was filed in the High Court of Kerala by an ardent devotee of the temple challenging such appointment on the premise that according to the customs and traditions of the Hindu community, a person other than a

Brahmin cannot hold the office of poojari. A single judge of the Kerala High Court admitted the writ petition and stayed the operation of the order of appointing persons from backward community as poojaris. But by the time the stay order was passed, the appointees had already taken charge of the office as poojari. When that development was brought to the notice of the single Judge he passed another order directing the appointees to demit the office with immediate effect. The writ petition was then referred to a two judge bench by keeping the orders passed by the single judge alive.

When the case was heard by a two judge bench constituted of Justices K.K. Usha and Balanarayana Marar, they differed from each other as to the conclusion. (I learnt that Justice Marar was inclined to uphold the orders of the single judge while Justice Usha took a different view). The case was then referred to a three Judge Bench, and it remained like that for a long time.

When I became Chief Justice (Officiating) of the Kerala High Court, I found out the cases remaining un-disposed by Full Bench. Hence I constituted a bench with me as the presiding Judge and Justices K.K. Usha and Shanmugham as co-judges. When we heard arguments in the case relating to the office of the priest of the temple we had no difficulty to conclude that the order of the single judge was unsustainable and hence we upheld the appointments made by the Devaswam Board. I wrote the judgement in which it was pointed out, among other things that "caste had been buried fathom down by the Constitution of India and what remains now is only a fossil for the students of social subjects to conduct researches". We declared in unreserved language that priesthood of a temple could not be denied to a person on the ground that he did not belong to Brahmin community.

I learnt later that the said judgement had a mixed reaction in the Hindu community. While a substantial section of it wholeheartedly welcomed the new innovation, the conservative members of the community, to whom the idea of a non-Brahmin performing ceremonies in the temple was abhorrent, raised their eye-brows. But the Supreme Court confirmed our judgement.

The said judgement was pronounced a few months prior to my appointment as judge of the Supreme Court. I later learnt that my judgement was cited by some people as an example of my approach to such questions which the conservative members of the community could not digest. But the former Law Minister of India (P. Sivasankar) who was the Governor of Kerala had quoted some sentences from my judgement, (extracted above) in a speech delivered by him at Hyderabad. I cannot conceive even for a moment as to how a different view is possible regarding any office of the state particularly an office linked to religious activities. A few years after the said judgment the issue again revived when a person connected to the Devesowm board aired his view that only Brahmins shall be appointed as poojaris of the temples. This view of that gentleman created a noisy debate in Kerala through the newspapers. Some of the newspapers reminded the readers of the sturdy reasoning advanced by me in the judgment of the full bench mentioned above. Fortunately the debate did not subsist for long.

23

Elected Panchayats were restored in Kerala

Local bodies are the basic frame work of a democratic republic. If representatives of the people can manage the local problems the functional efficacy would be much greater than the local bodies being managed by bureaucracy. There are more than one thousand Panchayats in the State of Kerala. . The life in Panchayats became more active when Panchayat committees formed through elections were allowed to govern the affairs of the local bodies. Elections were to be held at least once in five years for forming the governing body of the Panchayat. But unfortunately, the government of Kerala did not favour such elections even for a decade since 1974. In that context the demand for elected Panchayats became very strident. When the period of five years elapsed after holding elections in 1974 the government dissolved all panchayat committees and directed the local Tahsildar to take over the administration of the Panchayats. This situation continued for another five years. Public became agitated as elections to Panchayat committees were not held at all for ten years. When a new government assumed office in the state they declared, consistent with the promise made by the Left Democratic Front (LDF) that elections would be held to Panchayat committees as early as possible, that new elected Panchayat Committee would be formed within two months.

The new regime further declared that elections to the thousand Panchayats would be held in January 1988 with the age limit for voting reduced to 18 years. This necessitated a laborious work to prepare new voters list. It also compelled the state government to re-define the territorial limits of different wards of each Panchayat. But many persons felt aggrieved by the re-alignment of wards made by the LDF government. There was a provision in the Kerala Panchayat Act that anyone aggrieved by the delimitation of the ward could approach the government to redress the grievance. A flood of petitions were filed before the government from almost all the Panchayats. Government disposed of all such petitions very quickly.

Writ petitions were filed in the High Court challenging the orders of the government for re-defining the boundaries of each Panchayat. All these writ petitions were posted before me while sitting as single judge. In November 1987 many advocates who appeared for the petitioners pressed for staying the steps for elections till the disposal of each writ petition. I felt that if the writ petitions were not heard before the end of 1987, it would become impossible for the state government to issue necessary notification for holding elections to the Panchayat committees before the expiry of January 1988. Its consequence would be a fresh enumeration of the voters list as many more persons would qualify themselves to be voters by then. This again meant that Panchayat elections would further be postponed indefinitely. Each petitioner wanted his writ petition to be independently dealt with and a separate judgment to be passed because de-limitation in respect of at least one ward was involved in each writ petition. Each writ petition on the Panchayat elections, if to be heard and decided separately, it would take a very long time, perhaps many months.

K. Sudhakaran was the then Advocate General of Kerala. He was one of the resourceful Advocates General in the state, with a practical bend of mind, apart from his legal acumen. I have been benefited much by his practical approach to quite a number of cases which required such solution. While hearing arguments in the above writ petitions, he suggested a way out by quoting section 143 of the Kerala Panchayat Act. He contended that the said provision envisaged a second revision exercisable by the Government. He pleaded that all the writ petitions may be converted into revision petitions which could be heard and decided by the government. After bestowing the said contention, I felt it as a viable solution to tide over the great hurdle in holding the Panchayat elections within the time desired by the Government. The Advocate General also suggested that the Government would assign the services of one Mr. K.L.N. Rao, a senior Government Secretary for hearing all the writ petitions. The reputation of the said Secretary was such that none of the petitioners could say a word against him. To avoid all possible delay I adopted a novel measure. Agreeing with the contention of the Advocate General, I divided all the writ petitions into five divisions and fixed a particular day for each division for the purpose of enabling the government Secretary to hear arguments. I added that the advocate for the petitioner in each writ petition shall be treated as having taken notice for his client regarding the time and venue of hearing of the revision petition. All the days for the hearing of the writ petitions were so scheduled as to enable the Government to close arguments on the revision petitions by the end of December 1987. The Government Secretary completed the hearing within the scheduled time and passed orders in all the revision petitions. On the succeeding day the Government issued notification for holding elections to the Panchayats as well as the Municipalities to be held on 28th June 1988. Elections were held by and large peacefully, in all the local bodies and results were declared before the crowed assembled in front of each local body office. The elected persons assumed their office promptly. Thus the entire local bodies in Kerala came back to the democratic process after a long period of ten years. The print media praised the High Court for the speed and promptitude by which such a large number of writ petitions were usefully disposed of and enabled the Government to bring back the entire local bodies to democratic life.

24

Attempt to plunder public money with legal protection was averted

In India the governments, whether central or state, depend upon private agencies to execute public works including big projects. Such agencies are generally known as Contractors. It has been a common practice for Contractors to make claims for money on execution of the contract work. A good number of such claims were genuine, yet some of them were bogus. Some of the claims contained exaggerated figures. The system which continued in India for settling such claims was by referring the disputes to either a sole arbitrator or a panel of arbitrators. The system was governed earlier by the Arbitration Act 1940. This system had merits as well as demerits. The law was subsequently improved by a new Arbitration Act passed by the Parliament in 1988. The decisions taken by the arbitrator or panel of arbitrators were known as "awards". Such awards could be executed in the same manner as money decrees. Unless a government is very vigilant, the law of arbitration could be exploited by greedy contractors for knocking off huge public money. Here I propose to narrate an episode which happened when Arbitration Act 1940 was in force.

A contractor after executing a project work claimed a huge amount as damages from the Government of Kerala under three heads of claims. As the government was not willing to concede to such claim, the contractor moved for referring the claims to be decided by an arbitrator. Because one of the terms of the contract required the disputes to be so determined. Accordingly, the claims were referred to be decided by a Superintending Engineer as the Sole Arbitrator. An advocate for the government was appointed to defend the stand of the government that no amount was payable to the contractor over and above what was already paid. The contractor engaged his own advocate to argue before the arbitrator. The proceedings before the arbitrator continued for a long time. He finally passed three awards in favour of the contractor awarding a total amount nearing 13 crores of rupees.

The contractor filed petitions before the civil court to make the awards decrees of court. This is the legal procedure to be followed. However, the government filed petitions before the same court to set aside the awards on certain grounds. This is also permitted by law. But the government did not follow them up seriously. The civil court disposed of all the petitions as per a common judgement by which the entire amount awarded was made a common decree of the court.

If the government was not satisfied with any such decree it was open to the government to file appeal before the High Court. But the Government Pleader who appeared before the Arbitrator gave a legal opinion that the awards were fair and therefore no appeal was needed to be filed before the High Court. Sri. M.B. Kurup was the Advocate General then. He assigned the files to a Government Pleader to study the papers for examining whether appeals should be filed or not. The said Government Pleader also opined that no appeal need be filed. Normally, the government had to pay the entire amount covered by the decree to the contractor as they did not file any appeal. However, a Public Interest Litigation (PIL) writ petition was filed by somebody challenging the awards in the High Court, but a Division Bench of the High Court dismissed it on the ground that the decree became final as no appeal was preferred by the government.

As the way was cleared for the contractor to collect the money covered by the decree he moved the civil court to realise the decree amount from the government . It was then submitted on behalf of the government that two months time was necessary for depositing the entire amount. I learned later that the idea was to utilize a portion of the sum expected from the central government granted to the state government towards "plan outlay". The time sought for by the government was granted by the judges. The contractor was henceforth waiting for the expiry of two months for receiving the huge amount (about 13 crores of rupees with the interest accrued on the principal amount).

In the meanwhile S. Narayanan Potti (for short Mr. Potti) a doyen of the Bar was appointed as the Advocate General. Mr. Potti was then above the age of 80 years. He agreed to accept the post of Advocate General as the government was really thirsty to get the assistance of a very efficient advocate as many Government matters were in a bad shape. Mr. Potti was highly respected by all the leaders of the government. The judges had great confidence in his integrity as well as his forensic calibre. He had a galaxy of juniors trained under him including the celebrated Chief Justice Subramanian Potti. I still remember whatever case he conducted before me, he had performed his role with admirable quality and perfection. After Mr. Potti became the Advocate General he happened to peruse the records connected with the above arbitration awards. He felt very strongly that the awards were brought into existence by collusive efforts and fraudulent deals. But he noticed that the time for filing the appeals in the High Court had expired long ago. Yet, he ventured to file the appeals against all the three awards and along with them he filed applications to condone the long delay of about 1500 days.

Those appeals came up before a Division Bench consisting of myself and Justice N. Dinkar (he later became Chief Justice of Jharkand High Court and after retirement he was appointed Chairman of Kerala State Human Rights Commission). The plea for condoning the seemingly inordinate delay was vehemently opposed by Mr. M.A. George, advocate for the contractor. Mr. George was a connoisseur in the field of arbitration law. After taking his Law degree, he secured I.R.S. and was in service for some time, but he later resigned and started practice at Bombay concentrating on arbitration cases. After a few years of successful practice at Bombay, he shifted his office to Cochin, and within a short period he rose to high prominence in the High Court of Kerala. He was good in other branches of law also. In fact, I engaged him as the advocate in connection with a rent control matter in my family, when that case reached the High Court. He won the case for us, but he declined to accept the fees offered to him by my brothers. I had not become a judge of the High Court at that time and so I persuaded him to accept the fees. He again refused to accept it on the ground that his family too belonged to Kottayam and our parents had cordial relationship with each other. I record my gratitude to him.

Mr. S. Narayanan Potti, while arguing in support of the plea for condoning the long delay in filing the appeal, drew our attention to the general features of the award and required us to have a glimpse into the gamut of the whole exercise in which public money was about to be looted. I told Mr. George that we were inclined to condone the long delay as we felt that the High Court, being the guardian of public money, should have the opportunity to scrutinize the allegations made against the personnel involved in procuring the awards. Mr. George felt that there was no use in persisting with the opposition to condone the long delay. So he did not seriously pursue on that aspect, expecting that he would concentrate on the merits of the case. However, I wrote a detailed order for condoning the delay of 1500 days.

When the appeals were posted for hearing Mr. Potti started his arguments which continued for many days. Though we requested the aged advocate to sit down and argue, he opted to keep standing. He argued on very many details of every aspect of the case. Mr. George with his forceful forensic ability tried to dispel the image created in us by the arguments of the Advocate

General. Mr. George also argued for a number of days. I still remember how we saved time for completing the marathon arguments addressed by both sides. We offered to sit even on a public holiday. It was "Pongal" which was very important for Tamil people. Justice Dinkar (who hailed from Tamil Nadu) agreed to sit on that day also.

After we heard the arguments of both sides, I prepared a draft judgement and justice Dinkar gave his full concurrence to my reasoning and the conclusions. We set aside all the awards. Some of the observations made by us in the judgement are the following:

"Looking at the two impugned awards from the said legal angle, we are constrained to observe, even at the outset, that they reflect a sort of insatiable thirst to over pour a huge largesse on the contractor. A bias sprouted from a predisposed mind of the arbitrator is transparent in the two awards. The arbitrator's partiality towards the contractor is reflected at very many portions of the awards particularly when he blindly accepted many of the claims of the contractor even when such claims were multifoldedly higher than the agreed rates. The over-enthusiasm of the arbitrator in enriching the respondent had blindfolded him so tightly that even claims made up of patently mistaken dates were simply accepted by the arbitrator. Would the arbitrators have thought that all the above iniquities would escape the notice of others as the award was written in a volume ? Of course, credit must certainly go to the octogenarian Advocate General for winching up all such odious scum to the surface".

We concluded that "the awards involved in the appeals were vitiated by the misconduct of the arbitrator and thus appeals were allowed and the decrees based on the awards were set a side bell book and candle".

We immediately appointed Justice M.P. Menon (a retired judge of the High Court of Kerala) as the sole Arbitrator to pass a fresh award regarding the disputes between the contractor and the Government. I had a special reason to select Justice M.P. Menon for the said task. He was a judge of the highest calibre and was famous for his quick disposal. His academic career was spectacular. He was the gold medalist in one year's Bar Council examination. If all the qualities of M.P. Menon are to be penned down they might require a separate chapter. Justice M.P. Menon commenced and concluded his arbitration proceedings in a record time and passed a fresh award granting only relatively a small amount of Rs.11 lakhs to the contractor. The amount was collected by the contractor without demur.

If Narayanan Potti had not done what he did in such a commendable and admirable manner a huge amount of public money would have been plundered away from the public treasury through a legal channel. I felt quite happy that as guardians of public money the High Court could rise up and prevent misappropriation of such whopping amount from public fund.

I wish to record two more developments which took place relating to the above plunder attempt foiled by the forensic capabilities exhibited by Mr. Potti. One was the disclosure made by Mr. George a few months after the fresh award was passed. It took place when Mr. George visited me to pay his condolences to me on my bereavement (as my father passed away). During our conversation I asked Mr. George the following question to him.

I had a feeling that the real beneficiary of the awards would not have been the contractor. If you don't mind please tell me at least now, who was the real person behind the whole claim"

He smiled at me and kept silence for a while and then told me like this:

"My client would have got only a small portion of the amount covered by the original awards, if the money was collected the major portion of it would have gone to two important politicians".

He also disclosed the names of those two politicians. Both of them are alive today. However, I refrain from publishing the names of those persons for two reasons. One is, Mr. George is not alive now and hence I can not seek his permission to do so. Second is, without hearing the version of the persons concerned, it is not fair to make the names public.

The second development was that Potti sent a bill to the government for his remuneration. We all thought that he would have claimed at least Rs. 10 lakhs for the tenacious work done by him spreading over to several days together. But the amount claimed by him was only Rs. one lakh. The disquieting fact about that is, even for that small amount there was bureaucratic opposition. One day Mr. Potti called on me and showed me the sentences written by the law department on the file as to why Mr. Potti should not be given the amount claimed. The reasons stated by the department were obviously wrong and also unfair to the person who succeeded in securing a big victory for the government. I was pained reading such unfair grounds for not granting the amount claimed. Mr. Potti informed the government that no amount need be paid to him at all as fees. Yes, till he died, not even a pai was paid to him for the meritorious and tedious work done by him in saving a whopping sum which would have drained off from the public treasury.

I deem it appropriate, to mention in the above context, that a few years after Narayanan Potti passed away, the successor government was pleased to reconsider payment of remuneration to the work done by him in this case. The file was revived at the instances of M.K. Damodaran who became the Advocate General of Kerala by then. The government, though late, passed a favourable order for disbursing the amount claimed by Narayanan Potti. The payment was made to his widow albeit posthumously by M.K. Damaodaran himself on behalf of the government.

25

A Professor escaped from disaster

The new offence created by the Act of Parliament in 1986 called dowry death, prescribes very serious punishment for the offender. The substance of the offence is, if a wife dies within 7 years of marriage otherwise than under normal circumstances her husband and in-laws are vulnerable to serious punishment, if it is shown that the wife was subjected to harassment with the demand for dowry soon before her death. The punishment in such a cases can go up to imprisonment for life, but in no case the judge could impose a punishment less than imprisonment for 7 years. The offence was made still harsher by Parliament when the burden of proof is cast on the accused when it is established that the wife died unnatural death within 7 years of her marriage and also that she was subjected to harassment with a demand for dowry.

The above law was passed in the background of a spate of bride burning cases particularly in north India, though such cases were quite few and far between in Kerala. As a Supreme Court Judge, I had to deal with a lot of such cases, but I do not remember to have dealt with even two or three such cases as Judge of the High Court of Kerala. However, the facts in one such case are unerasable from my memory. In a nutshell those facts are the following:

A young man became the Reader of a professional college. He was designated as Professor. His wife was the Assistant Professor in another college. (Her name can be put as Saraswathy which was not her real name). They had a suckling child. When the spouses were living in the husband's parental house there were constant quarrels, sometimes between the husband and wife, but many time between Saraswathy and her mother-in-law. On the initiative of some other elder members of her family the couple moved their residence to the quarters allotted to the husband by the college authorities. After they shifted the residence, the skirmishes became much lesser during early days but with the arrival of the mother-in-law, her bad time revived. On one morning the wife went to her department and consumed a sudden killing poison and died instantaneously. But before consumed poison, she wrote six or seven letters in the postal inland form stating that she was harassed by her husband with the demand for dowry and she wished to end her life.

The trial court convicted the professor for the offence of dowry death and sentenced him to imprisonment for 7 years. He filed an appeal before the High Court against the conviction and sentence. The state of Kerala also filed an appeal urging that the punishment should have been imprisonment for life. Both appeals were heard together by a Division Bench headed by Justice S. Padmanabhan. During the course of arguments he expressed his strong view that the punishment should be enhanced to imprisonment for life. The said observation was naturally resented by P.V. Ayyappan (former Advocate General of Kerala and a famous criminal lawyer) who appeared for the accused. There were heated exchanges between him and Justice Padmanabhan regarding the above mentioned observation. At one stage P.V. Ayyappan informed the court that he had decided to relinquish his engagement as he did not wish to appear before a judge who made such a clear cut observation. Time was granted to him for making other arrangements for engaging a new advocate. In the meanwhile, Justice Padmanabhan himself felt that he should not continue to hear the arguments for the appeal. Hence he directed the registry of High Court to board that case before another bench. Thereafter, the appeals were posted before the bench consisting of me and Justice Manoharan.

The new counsel opened his arguments. At that time, we too felt that if the conviction was upheld for any reason whatsoever, the punishment should be enhanced to imprisonment for life on the peculiar facts of the case, we also expressed like that in open court, but no quarrel ensued upon it.

The accused had stated in writing that he had in fact received dowry from the deceased at the time of marriage. But he emphatically denied having demanded any more amount as dowry. He said in his defence that he never demanded any amount as dowry from his wife or her parents. When I came to know of the said defence, I asked the advocate about the advisability of admitting that he got some dowry at first. I over-heard the professor instructing the advocate not to disown the fact that he received dowry because it was a truth. That conduct of the accused gave us an inkling that the further case of the accused that he did not demand any dowry might also be true. But then why the lady wrote seven letters to different persons just before her death? We were anxious to know whether she had any mental illness. But the professor did not advance any case that she had any mental illness.

A number of diaries written by the lady was produced in evidence as they were used by the hand-writing expert to compare the handwriting on the letters written by her. We had no doubt that the letters were written by the lady herself. As the arguments continued till the end of the day, I told the court officer to send the entire records to my bungalow before resuming arguments on the succeeding day. I went through the records item by item. While perusing the diaries, one entry in a diary struck my attention. It read like this: "Met Dr. Sukumaran". When the arguments resumed next day I discussed it with Justice Manoharan about the said entry in the diary. We asked the advocate for the accused the details of "Dr. Sukumaran". He got instructions from the accused that Dr. Sukumaran was a psychiatrist practising at the local town of the lady.

We then ventured to summon Dr. Sukumaran to appear before the High Court with all the records, if any, relating to a patient by name Saraswathy. (Her address was also shown) Dr. Sukumaran appeared in the High Court pursuant to the summons and disclosed certain facts which were never brought on record prior thereto. According to Dr. Sukumaran, the accused was suffering from schizophrenia and that she had suicidal tendencies and she had become normal due to treatment but at any time her decease could revive. The doctor also said that she wanted this information to be kept out of her husband. The doctor did not disclose this professional communication of his patient to anyone else.

With the said disclosure made by the doctor the whole gamut of the case took a different turn. I then wanted to peruse the investigation file which the Public Prosecutor made available to us. On reading them I found out two important aspects concerning the case. One was that none of the witnesses had stated during investigation that there was any quarrel between the spouses over dowry at any time. Second was, on the morning of her death Saraswathy was very much irritated over a minor issue. i.e. before she woke up her child persistently cried for milk. Her mother-in-law rebuked both the parents of the child for not taking care it. The husband (accused) on hearing the rebuke blamed his wife for sleeping without caring the child. Hearing the hubbub Saraswathy woke up and overheard the tirade made by her husband and mother-in-law. In an irritated mood she rushed to the kitchen and boiled the milk. With the milk bottle in one hand and the child on her shoulder, and fuming with anger she walked towards the bed room to feed the child. She felt that she was also working in the same manner as her husband and if she happened to sleep due to fatigue her husband also had the responsibility to care the child as he was awake when the child cried for milk. While walking speedily she slipped down on the floor, the milk bottle was broken and her hand got injured. The child naturally intensified its cries. In the midst of all those turbulences she again boiled the milk and supplied to the child. During all these times her husband was just lying on the cot and was reading some books and was muttering blames on the wife. Saraswathy left the house without even taking breakfast and went to her college in a huff. Such vivid details were recorded by the investigating officer after questioning the inmates of the house.

I had a discussion with Justice Manoharan. If those were the real facts which took place on the morning, would it have been possible to revive her mental illness and to be afflicted by the suicidal proclivities. How could we depend on the letters of such a lady on account of three grave handicaps for the accused. Firstly, she was a mental patient and secondly she was in such an angry mood that she would thirst to take revenge on her nonchalant husband. The third handicap was that the accused was not able to cross-examine the author of the seven letters as she was not alive then. Those reasons were weighed by us with the total absence of any case for demand for dowry having been disclosed to the investigating officer. The resultant position was, we were not prepared to conclude that she was being harassed with the demand for dowry by solely depending on the letters written by the lady in a huff. We both agreed to acquit the professor. I authored the judgment of the bench and pronounced it acquitting the accused, in which I set out all our reasons with meticulous details as cogently as possible. Needless to say that our verdict was received with a mixed reaction. I learnt later that the Supreme Court declined to interfere with our verdict when the state moved for Special Leave before the apex court. Then and now neither me nor justice Manoharan never felt that our conclusion would have been wrong. On the contrary, we felt greatly relieved that we could avert a disaster befalling the Professor.

Look at the star of the professor. He would most probably have been punished with imprisonment for life or at least with imprisonment for seven years. His fate would have then been different, but for the snap discovery of the two words entered in one of the very many diaries.

That entry in the diary was a honeybee sent to us by the Almighty to guide us to avert disaster to a professor.

26

What is the right of litigants to occupy seats in court rooms ?

Such a question cropped up before me. Once a litigant who was very conscious and sensitive of his rights, occupied one of the chairs in the court room of a civil court of lower division. There were only a few chairs in the court hall, out of which only two or three were usable and the rest were in disrepair. The young litigant reached the court hall sufficiently early on the particular day and sat on a good chair in the front row. While the advocates (young and old) reached the court room, many of them had no vacant chairs to sit. The Judge, seeing the situation told the litigant to vacate the chair so that a senior advocate could occupy. But the petulant litigant protested and claimed that no one could unseat him in a court hall which was a public place. The Judge who was a daring youngster, ordered him to vacate the chair, but that too was disobeyed. He immediately initiated proceedings against the litigant by resorting to a special procedure and convicted him U/s. 228 of Indian Penal Code (intentional insult or interruption to public servant sitting in judicial proceeding). The Court imposed a punishment of Rs. 150/- and in default of payment he was directed to undergo imprisonment for a few days.

The captious litigant challenged the conviction in the High Court of Kerala. It reached before me as a single judge. I took the case as a rare academic subject. At the time of arguments the appellant was occupying a chair in the front row of the court room in the High Court, while many senior advocates were standing behind. Even the High Court could not provide adequate number of chairs to accommodate all the advocates present in the court room. However, I did not ask the appellant to vacate the seat for the senior advocates to sit, because I felt that without deciding on the right claimed by him, it was not judicially correct to ask him to vacate the seat for accommodating senior advocates who were on their legs.

Since a decision in the case could have created implications on the rights of members of the Bar, I gave notice to the Advocate General, the Director General of Prosecution and President of the Advocates Association. I heard them in detail, besides some other advocates who volunteered to argue the matter. On the one side of the question, there was equality of status enshrined in the Constitution of India. A court of law being a public institution, every one - whether the litigant conducts the case in person or his cause was espoused by an advocate – has the right to present the cause and there shall be no discrimination. On the other side, there was the special status of advocate in a court of law, being member of the Bar. The question raised in the case could not be answered without viewing the aforesaid profiles.

I considered the status of an advocate inside the court hall. I could get certain decisions touching the question as some practising advocates became litigants in the same court. On all such occasions the court insisted on the advocates to disrobe themselves while addressing arguments as litigants. I dealt with decisions in English and Indian courts on the subject and declared that in a court room members of the Bar have certain privileges being officers of the court, and even among the members of Bar certain special privileges have been conferred some among them holding special position and ranking. I then observed that when members of the Bar were to stand inside the court room due to lack of seating facilities, members of the public, even if they were litigants in the same court, could not claim any right to occupy the seating facilities available inside the court. In the judgement delivered by me I said thus:

"A court room cannot be allowed to become a noisy crowding place. It is neither a casino nor a causerie chamber. It is apposite to remind all concerned the words of Francis Bacon that "the place of justice is a hallowed place". Decorum must prevail inside the court room and for that there must be rules of discipline to be observed albeit implied. Justice can best be administered when legal proceedings are conducted with decorum and certain degree of formality. Sartorial elegance or costume decorum is insisted on in the court room for maintaining the dignity of court proceedings. If the rule relating to costume insistence is relaxed, it is not unlikely that the trappings of the court room may be mutilated".

I reminded that advocate is an officer of the court and quoted from the Rules of the Bar Council of India that "an advocate shall, at all times, comport himself in a manner befitting his status as an officer of the court – a privileged member of the community". I held that members of the Bar have certain privileges in a court room, being officers of the court. When they are to stand due to lack of seating facilities, members of the public, even if they are litigants in the same court, cannot claim any right to occupy such facilities available inside the court, in preference to the members of the Bar. I also said that it is open to the presiding officer of the court to direct any member of the public, including a litigant, to vacate for accommodating members of the Bar. I concluded that the above must be regarded as a rule of practice to be followed in the court hall for the upkeep of discipline and decorum of court proceedings. I did not concede to the prayer for showing further leniency to the appellant as I felt that the cussedness unabashedly and persistently displayed by the petitioner in open court warranted the steps adopted by the lower court. I confirmed the punishment and dismissed the appeal.

The above judgement was almost "sui generis" (which means the only one of its kind) perhaps because no other litigant would have so far dared to defy the court order for vacating the seat for the advocates to occupy. Even if a litigant disobeyed, any such court order, no judicial officer would have chosen to proceed against a contumacious litigant, as was done in this case. Hence such an occasion as the above case provided would never have occurred earlier and it is unlikely to occur in future. The said judgement is reported in 1993 (Vol. 3) Kerala Law Times, page 342 with the title "Jose Vs. Nandakumar". It is also reported in 1997 All India Reports (Kerala) at page 243.

27

Re-writing a judgment

Judgments were made in Kerala High Court either by dictating in open court at the close of arguments or by reserving for judgment on completion of arguments in which case dictation was done by the judge at his residence. The interval between reserving and pronouncing judgments could be very short for some judges, but could be long for some other judges and perhaps unduly long for others. Judgments dictated in open court were treated as pronounced, though signature of the judge would be affixed only after carrying out all typographical corrections in the transcribed draft. The other category of judgments would be signed by the judge as soon as they are pronounced. In either case, once signature of the judge was affixed, it would not (and should not) be changed, or even corrected. Of course, the court has power to amend or review the judgment for which a formal procedure is prescribed. Any judge who rewrites the signed judgment (except as indicated above) would be guilty of misconduct. However, if a judgment pronounced by dictation in open court requires marginal changes the judge is required to repost the case for "spoken to". Barring this, changing the whole judgment is not permissible. Could there be any exception to this?

In a writ petition the advocate of a bus owner addressed arguments challenging the order passed by State Transport Appellate Tribunal. I was sitting a single judge then. The Government advocate argued in support of the order under challenge. During the course of arguments I put many questions to the counsel for the petitioner, as I used to do in almost all cases. While answering one of the questions the advocate ventured to remind me that I did not know much about the law relating to motor vehicles. He would have meant that my questions were too silly as no judge having some knowledge in that branch of law would put such questions. I felt that he was insinuating me particularly because I too had conducted quite a large number of cases relating to motor vehicles when I was practising as an advocate. I kept silent at the riposte hurled but those remarks oscillated in my mind. When arguments were concluded, I called the stenographer and dictated the judgement in open court dismissing the writ petition.

On the same day I pronounced judgments in a few more writ petitions by giving oral dictation in open court. The draft judgements of all such dictated matters were brought home for my reading, so that necessary corrections could be carried out. Then a thought passed through my mind that I would have been hurt by the insinuation hurled by the counsel and that conduct perhaps would have caused the dismissal of the writ petition. Then I decided not to read the draft of the said judgement, instead I read and corrected only the remaining judgements.

After a few days I took up the draft judgement in the aforementioned case and read it along with its case papers. I then realised that my conclusion was wrong. I decided not to affix my signature on the judgement. I informed the advocate on both sides that the said writ petition would be posted again as I wished to hear arguments afresh. After hearing the arguments over again I became convinced that the plea of the advocate deserved acceptance. The new judgement was given by dictation in open court and the relief prayed for in the writ petition was granted.

Was I right in adopting such a course ? There could be two different views. But I believe then and now, had I not adopted the said course of re-hearing the arguments afresh, I could have been held guilty of unjudicial disposition and the canker formed in my judicial conscience would have remained un-erased. It was my practice to submit account to the ultimate dispenser of justice before going to bed. My inner mind (conscience) indicated to me that the first judgement could have been influenced by the insinuation willy-nilly hurled by the counsel in open court. But when the new judgement was pronounced I heaved a sigh of relief.

It is a reality that temperamental reactions of individual judges might play a decisive role in judgment making. The High Courts, during early years of functioning in this country, had constituted only benches of not less than two judges to hear each case. This was to minimize the scope of faulty judgments due to individual predilections, temperamental prejudices and conceptual bias. The system of single judge hearing cases in the High Court was adopted in later years to cope up with the fast swelling of dockets in High Courts. At the same time, it has to be noted that a bench of two judges need not necessarily pronounce faultless judgments. I heard complaints from many advocates that quite often senior judge of the bench used to overshadow the thinking process of the junior judge and in many cases the opinion of the senior judge would constitute the judgment of the division bench as the junior judge meekly yielded to the views of the senior judge. Fali S. Nariman, one of the most eminent advocates of the Supreme Court of India recently made a suggestion in a speech that the Supreme Court must have the practice of each bench having a strength of minimum three judges to hear and decide every case. He pointed out that being the last resort of a litigant, the decision of the Supreme Court should not be the outcome of give and take between two judges for achieving a unanimous opinion in order to avert the ordeal of reposting and rehearing of the case. If it is a bench of three judges the majority opinion would automatically become judgment without individual judges sacrificing in his own opinion. No doubt what F.S. Nariman said is the ideal. If so, it should be the system in the High Courts also. But then, what about the ever-increasing dockets in the High Courts and in the Supreme Court. If a solution can be found out, then the above ideal system can be resorted to it.

28

King of Saudi Arabia as defendant

This episode happened in the sub court falling under the jurisdiction of the Kerala High Court. Justice Jaganatha Rao was the Chief Justice then. He was brought from the High of Court of Andhra Pradesh. He always had a scholarly approach to legal questions. Though I was one of the senior judges of High Court by that time, I could get only a formal relationship with him. Later he became Chief Justice of the High Court of Delhi on the persuasion of the then Chief Justice of India (Justice M.N. Venkitachelliah). He told me later that he suffered a lot as Chief Justice of Delhi High Court as some of the senior judges of that High Court made his official career miserable. Whenever I met him he used to recollect his days in the Kerala High Court with great sense of happiness. He thought his elevation as judge of the Supreme Court was quite imminent and under that legitimate expectation he put up with all the difficulties created by some of his senior colleagues of the Delhi High Court. But his elevation to the Supreme Court was much delayed due to inexplicable reasons. Of course, he reached there subsequent to my elevation and thereafter we developed close friendship.

The episode in which King of Saudi Arabia became defendant arose in a suit filed by one plaintiff in the sub court, Trichur. Mr.

Barkat Ali was the sub judge of that court. He unwittingly passed an order issuing summons to the King of Saudi Arabia in that civil suit filed claiming a large amount of compensation from the defendants. There were many defendants in the suit and King of Saudi Arabia was only one of them.

When summons reached Saudi Arabia, a furore was created as the monarch of the Arab Kingdom took it very seriously. The government of India was informed by the Saudi Arabian government that the King was being proceeded against by a Judge in Kerala. The Indian government conveyed it to the Chief Secretary of Kerala and apprised him of the serious diplomatic consequences which might ensue. The Chief Secretary was directed to bring the matter to the notice of the High Court. He informed the Registrar of the High Court and requested him to bring it to the notice of the Chief Justice of Kerala.

The then Chief Justice (Justice Jaganatha Rao) on being told about the action adopted by the Sub Judge of Trichur convened a full court meeting (it is a meeting attended by all judges of the High Court for deciding administrative matters). The subject above quoted was also put on the agenda of the meeting. When the discussion started the Chief Justice said about the serious repercussions which emanated from the fauxpas committed by the Sub Judge and expressed his view that something should be done to allay the misgivings of the Arab country with whom the Government of India had very cordial relationship. Many of the judges took the stand that the Sub Judge should be proceeded against for not complying with the provisions contained in Section 86 (i) of the Code of Civil Procedure (CPC). As per the said section "no foreign state may be sued in any court except with the consent of the central government certified in writing by a secretary to that government". That ban was made applicable to the ruler of the foreign states as well.

A number of judges of the High Court felt that unless some action was taken against the sub judge to mitigate the strong feeling of resentment of the Saudi Arabian Government they might even repatriate all Keralites working in Saudi Arabia, if not all the Indians living in that country. But I pointed out that the Sub Judge acted in exercise of his judicial power and that could not be called in question on the administrative side, even if all the judges held a different view about it. The High Court judges were aware of it, but an unexpected snag cropped up in the same meeting. The next item on the agenda of the meeting was to prepare a panel of Sub Judges for promotion to the cadre of District Judge. Seniority-wise sub judge Barkat Ali should normally have been on the top of the panel. When this was pointed out by the Registrar of the High Court, many judges felt that the situation would turn bad if the High Court would promote such a Sub Judge to the cadre of District Judge all on a sudden. They argued that even if no disciplinary action was taken against the Sub Judge for issuing summons to the monarch of Saudi Arabia on the premise that his order was on the judicial side, any decision at this very juncture to promote him would be misunderstood and hence become counter productive, though the timing of the promotion was only coincidental. But we only knew that it was coincidental, whereas, the Saudi Arabian government might interpret this as an intentional act of the High Court to admire the subject, according to those judges. I persisted with my plea that we should not take into account the judicial order passed by the Sub Judge while considering his promotion prospects. In spite of my importunes, majority of the judges decided to keep him out of the panel for promotion until he gave an explanation in the matter.

I was very restless thereafter. As I felt that the decision excluding him from promotion, although it was only a temporary measure, would be enough to cause great anguish to the Sub Judge and demoralize him if not tarnishing his name. In the night I woke up from sleep and with some intuition in my mind browsed through the case law under section 86 of the CPC. To my great relief I came across a decision of the Bombay High Court holding that the ban under section 86(i) could be waived by the foreign ruler as the same was made only for his protection and that an order issuing summons to a foreign ruler by itself was not illegal. I felt a ray of light was shown to me for saving an innocent Sub Judge from undeserved disciplinary proceedings and its consequent ignominy befalling him. Early morning I called my stenographer over the phone and he reached my house soon. I dictated to him a detailed note and a forwarding letter containing a request to the Chief Justice quoting the above mentioned decision of the Bombay High Court and I pointed out that what the Sub Judge did was supported by the decision of the Bombay High Court and that was enough to protect a subordinate judicial officer. I further pointed out that excluding him from the panel of promotees on the ground of issuing summons to the King of Saudi Arabia would amount to an illegal act on the part of the High Court in its administrative powers.

Chief Justice Jagnatha Rao after reading the note prepared by me felt that the proposed action should be kept in abeyance as otherwise the High Court could be guilty of adopting wrong proceeding against an innocent judicial officer. Thus the action against Barkat Ali, though earlier decided by the High Court, turned into a damp squib.

The most interesting part of the above episode was that Barkat Ali never knew anything about it even a long time thereafter. When I recollected what I have done in the above case I derived a lot of mental satisfaction. On the next day Mr. Justice Pareed Pillai, who was then a senior judge of the High Court sent a letter to me in which he said: "you fought like a valiant soldier in defence of a cause concerning one subordinate officer, and those who opposed you first, were convinced later that they were wrong and you were correct". Barkat Ali was duly promoted and he is now working as a senior District Judge with or without knowing how narrowly he escaped from being by-passed by his juniors.

29

As a senior judge of the High Court

As one of the first five senior most judges of the High Court I was included in the Administrative Committee when Justice Jaganatha Rao (J.N. Rao J, for short) was the Chief Justice on being transferred from Andhra Pradesh High Court. He was considered to be a scholarly judge. As he was eager to be elevated to the Supreme Court of India (like any other judge) he did not take any risk in any matter. He wished to utilise the opportunity of the visit of CJI (Justice Venkitachelliah) by requesting him to lay the foundation stone of the new massive building of the High Court. J.N. Rao J, included me in the Building committee. I was not in favour of locating the new building of the High Court near the old building because that locality already became very congested and the traffic very unwieldy. So I persuaded the other members of the building committee to have the new building constructed on the vast land (where the present International stadium at Cochin stands). When Justice Malimath was the Chief Justice he too strongly favoured the new High Court building constructed at the above vast land. But the then Chief Minister (Mr. K. Karunakaran) had a different plan. He wished that land to be utilised for the new International stadium. J.N. Rao J knew the above desire of the

Chief Minister and hence he did not want to displease the executive head. Then I suggested that the new High court could be constructed at a sprawling land elsewhere. When the news of the CJI's visit reached Justice J.N. Rao hurriedly got a plan drawn up for the new High Court building. The location was fixed at the place where the present new High Court building stands. In a coulourful function CJI Venkitachellaiah laid the foundation stone.

It was during the above period Justice Venkitachellaiah implemented his pet scheme of one third judges of the every High Court to be transferred to different High Courts. He felt that such a measure was necessary for arresting the sagging name of different High Courts. Though his targets were some of the High Courts in the North, he included all the High Courts within the said scheme in order to give it a uniform colour. Every Chief Justice of the High Court was asked to recommend the names for such transfers. Justice J. N. Rao recommended four judges of the Kerala High Court out of which two were transferred (Justice P. Krishnamoorthy to Karnataka High Court and Justice L. Manoharan to Bombay High Court). But J.N. Rao,J. was transferred as Chief Justice of Delhi High Court instead of the Supreme Court. Due to certain permutations and combinations he could reach the Supreme Court only after I became judge of the Supreme court. In fact, my personal relationship with Justice Jaganatha Rao became very close after we both became colleagues in the Supreme Court. I remember him as a pious and suave judge with high degree of legal acumen.

Justice Sujatha Manohar was appointed as Chief Justice of Kerala High Court on being transferred from the Bombay High Court where also she was the Chief Justice for a short period. We had very cordial relationship. She maintained a high degree of judicial rectitude and at the same time she had the mind and hospitality of a good housewife. Her husband (Mr. Manohar) became close to me and the couple were our family friends. Justice Sujatha had innate artistic talents. Her official bungalow at Ernakulam was studded with her paintings and other trinkets made by her. When she looked at the plan for the new High Court building she became thoroughly disgusted, so she brought down the Chief Architect and wanted the plan to be revised. The Chief Architect expressed certain difficulties to do so. Nevertheless, on her insistence, they made some alterations to give the present appearance of the High Court building (a look at the original plan had the shape of a big five star hotel). Justice Sujatha had only a short stint as Chief Justice of Kerala. But she created a very good impression as a strong and dedicated Chief Justice. She was elevated to the Supreme Court. When I too was elevated later my wife and I could revive very cordial relationship with Justice Sujatha and her husband Mr. Vasant Manohar.

Justice M.M. Pareed Pillai was appointed as the Acting Chief Justice of Kerala High Court after Sujatha Manohar was elevated to the Supreme Court. Within a few months Justice Pareed Pillai was made the permanent Chief Justice of Kerala High Court which appointment even he did not expect for two reasons. Justice U.L. Bhat a Kerala Judge was appointed as Chief Justice of the Gauhati High Court and later as Chief Justice of the Madhya Pradesh High Court. He was to continue as the Chief Justice until he attained the age of 62. But Justice Pareed Pillai was due to retire on superanuation before the retirement of his senior (Justice U.L. Bhat). As per the normal rule only one judge from one High Court could become the Chief Justice at the same time and his next in rank could be appointed only after the former ceased to hold the office. There were only a very few exceptions to the said normal rule. Justice Pareed Pillai fell within the purview of those fortunate scarce exceptions. Second reason was that during the last twenty five years no judge could normally become Chief Justice of the same High Court wherein he was initially appointed as a Judge. Deviation from the said normal rule happened only in the case of two or three judges and Justice Pareed Pillai was fortunate in being within that limited category as well.

Justice Pareed Pillai was a very upright judge. He was scrupulously honest and was strictly adhering to judicial discipline and rectitude. He was very zealous in maintaining his secular credentials and did not budge an inch in interpreting any legal principle from that angle. An earlier incident which happened when he was District Judge of Tellicheri bore testimony of his judicial aloofness. That incident happened when the Chief Justice of India (Justice M.H. Beg) was invited to deliver a lecture at Tellicheri during some time in 1978. A dinner was hosted by the managing director of a renowned industry of Kannoor town in honour of the visiting Chief Justice of India. The host invited, among others, the Chief Justice and some senior judges of Kerala High Court to attend the dinner along with the Chief Justice of India. He also invited District Judge Pareed Pillai and his colleagues. The dinner was held at Kannoor which is situated only a few miles away from Tellicheri. The dinner was attended by Chief Justice of India, Chief Justice of Kerala as well as some other judges of the High Court of Kerala who were also specially invited. But District Judge Pareed Pillai refused to attend the same as there were litigations pending in the courts concerning the industrial establishment run by the person who hosted the dinner. Next day some newspapers in Kerala flashed the news admiring the District Judge and his colleagues for keeping away from the dinner hosted by a local tycoon and criticised the Chief Justice and his companion judges of the High Court for falling into an invitation to the dinner hosted by a litigant. But the said news flash, instead of earning kudos for the District Judge, invited trouble for him, of course, on certain other pretext. Though ultimately he got out of those troubles, he knew well that the real cause was the newspaper report about his refusal to attend the dinner which the Chief Justice attended.

When Justice Pareed Pillai was Chief Justice of the Kerala High Court I was the next senior most judge in rank and Justice K. Sreedharan was immediate next to me. We three formed the "collegium" which could recommend persons as judges of the High Court. I can record with satisfaction that we discharged our functions free from any external influence. Though merit was our prime concern, we were forced to consider the necessity of affording representations to different communities in Kerala which were either inadequately represented or were not represented at all on the bench of the High Court. There are two schools of thought in this regard. One propounded that merit and excellence alone should be the criteria in selecting persons for the constitutional post of judge of the High Court. The other school advocated for some relaxation of that rule in order to give representation to different communities in constitutional bodies as the state is a mosaic of many communities. I cannot hold that one of those schools of thought is absolutely correct and the other absolutely wrong because I heard arguments for and against both the approaches. Nonetheless, I was inclined to adopt a middle course in the matter without sacrificing merit and excellence altogether.

During the same period we conducted a strenuous test to select six advocates to be recruited as district judges directly from the Bar. There were about 400 applications for the vacancies pursuant to a notification issued for that purpose. As the test was by oral interview, we short listed the applications to one half of that number. A collegium of five judges (Chief Justice Pareed Pillai, myself, Justices Sreedharan, K.G. Balakrishnan and T.V. Ramakrishnan) sat together from morning till evening for seven or eight consecutive days for selecting persons from among the short listed applicants. According to the rules we had to select the first person on the basis of merit alone and the next person on the communal reservation policy. But the candidate, in order to get selected was to secure a minimum percentage of marks in the oral interview to qualify themselves for the post. Though the sanction was to select only six persons, we found it necessary to increase the number to seven for accommodating the communal reservation policy. Thus we prepared a list of seven advocates and sent it to the government for appointment. The government also found the list reflecting judicial statesmanship and hence the appointments were made without any delay at all. All the appointees are now holding office at different stations and I must say that as per the reports they are performing well.

30

As Chief Justice (Officiating)

On the retirement of Chief Justice Pareed Pillai on attaining 62 years, the President of India appointed me as Officiating Chief Justice of Kerala High Court on 18.9.1995. In fact, I should have been appointed as permanent Chief Justice of the Kerala High Court or any other High Court in October 1995 having become the senior most judge of the Kerala High Court on the retirement of Chief Justice U.L. Bhat. So I had legitimate expectation to hear the news of my appointment as Chief Justice. But it did not come through. However, since there was no difference in the functional duties between the Officiating Chief Justice and a confirmed Chief Justice of the High Court, I discharged the functions as Chief Justice unmindful of the delay in being confirmed as such. All that I did not do then was to make recommendations to the vacancies of judges of the High Court lest the Law Ministry might return them for consideration by the new Chief Justice.

During this period Chief Justice of India (Justice Ahmedi) reached Trivandrum for inaugurating the Silver Jubilee celebrations of the Law Academy. I presided over the function and delivered presidential address. The Principal of Law Academy, while welcoming the guests, referred to my continuing as Officiating Chief Justice and requested the CJI to confirm me in that office. After the meeting, in a private conversation, CJI asked me whether I was willing to be appointed as Chief Justice of Orrissa High Court.

I said I am willing to be appointed as Chief Justice of any High Court except Sikkim and Jammu and Kashmir due to security reasons. But nothing happened. Much later, when I became the colleague of Justice Ahmedi he disclosed to me that I was first considered for Chief Justiceship of the High Court of Punjab and Haryana and later as Chief Justice of Gujarat High Court. He also disclosed to me that since the collegiums of the Supreme Court considered me as worthy to be elevated to the Supreme Court, CJI did not want me to undergo the difficulties of shifting of residence twice. Hence I continued as Officiating Chief Justice of Kerala High Court for good period of seven months.

One small, but worth mentioning, episode which happened during the tenure when I officiated as Chief Justice, was this:- The President of India (Sankar Dayal Sharma) made a visit to Kerala. He was scheduled to arrive at Cochin airport at 12 noon on a particular day. Chief Secretary of the state informed the Registrar of the High Court that as per the protocol precedents Rashtrapathi should be received at the airport by the Governor, the Chief Minister and the Chief Justice. But as the scheduled time of arrival of the President was 12 noon, I thought it improper to leave the court during sitting hours. So I told the Registrar to convey to the Chief Secretary of my inability to be present at the airport. The President after arrival at the airport proceeded to the government guest house at Ernakulam and took rest during the remaining hours. When the court sitting was over I called on the President during evening. I started my talk pleading to pardon me for not being present at the airport as I was holding court sitting then. Rashtrapathi expressed his appreciation that I chose to remain to discharge judicial functions instead of going to the airport for a protocol work. I was much relieved to hear those words from the head of the nation. I was inspired to do so as one of my great predecessors (Chief Justice P.T. Raman Nair) did like that once when the then President arrived at Cochin airport. I never appreciated judicial officers calling on visiting judges (either of High Court or of Supreme Court) during court hours. In fact, I discouraged it with all my might. But I heard from judicial officers that some judges (of the High Court as well as Supreme Court) expressing resentment in not seeing subordinate judicial officers at places of their arrival. I am sorry that persons occupying such high offices are even now inclined to give greater priority to such ego satisfaction under the pretext of protocol adherence. This must be curbed, if need be, with statutory prescription.

P. Sivasankar was appointed Governor of Kerala by the latter half of 1995. As per the convention the oath of the new Governor was to be administered by the Chief Justice. I was informed of it and an invitation was extended to me and my wife to stay in Raj Bhavan on the previous night to have dinner with the Governor designate. Sivasankar and his wife reached Raj Bhavan on the eve of the swearing in ceremony. The dinner time gave us a good opportunity to communicate our respective ideas and ideals as between each other. He was earlier Union Minister for Law when Indira Gandhi was Prime Minister. He was one of the most powerful and capable Law Ministers in India. He was first appointed as a judge of the High Court of Andra Pradesh but he did not agree to be confirmed later due to certain personal reasons. He had vast experiences as an advocate, as a Judge and as an efficient parliamentarian, besides sagacity as a politician and administrator. His appointment as Governor of Kerala was welcomed by all, particularly the legal fraternity. He was quiet informal and simple in his dealings and behaviour which enabled him to be liked by every one. Even on the firs day of becoming governor of Kerala he distinguished himself by his simple dress. He came to the podium of the Durbar Hall (where the swearing in ceremony was arranged) wearing a half shirt and dhoti with just one Khadi shawl hanging on the shoulder. Everybody observed this difference as all were accustomed with the sight of Governors in national coat and pants. He became the most popular governor of Kerala and at the same time he was counted as an effective governor of the state. Even on the first occasion he impressed me as a personality to be reckoned with. He used to read the decisions reported in law journals. He once told me that he had read my judgements and particularly the judgment holding that any Hindu is entitled to become priest of a temple, Brahmin or non-Brahmin. He expressed his unreserved admiration for proclaiming the secular content of the Constitution through that judgement. We had a number of occasions to meet and exchange our views and eventually I became one of his admirers. I felt that his services should be utilised more in the administrative forums rather than gubernatorial offices. In fact, I conveyed to some of the members of Parliament who are my personal friends not to allow his capabilities to go unutilised.

On the Republic day of 1996 I hoisted the national flag at the function arranged for that purpose in the sprawling compound of the High Court in the presence of a large gathering including advocates and judges past and present. I delivered the conventional Republic Day message in which I referred to the work done by the Kerala judiciary during the preceding year. After my speech was over, some of the judges (particularly those transferred from Madras High Court) profusely admired me for some of the exceptional achievements registered in different fields of judicial administration.

31

Pangs of elevation

On 25th January 1996 Justice A.M. Ahmedi, Chief Justice of India called me over phone and told me to be ready to leave Kerala to occupy a higher post. I thought that I was to go as Chief Justice of some other High Court and hence I requested him to indicate the High Court of which I was to become the Chief Justice. He then told me: "It is some thing better". He also asked me to direct my immediate next judge to call on him next day. Then I had a hunch from his talk that it was not a case of merely appointing me as Chief Justice of some other High Court but quite possibly I was to become a judge of the Supreme Court of India. What else could be something better than Chief Justice of a High C? I called Justice K. Sreedharan and conveyed this to him and requested him to proceed to New Delhi on the next day itself. He had some personal difficulty to rush up on account of some health problem which he developed a couple of weeks ago. Though he became improved considerably, I insisted on him to take his wife also to New Delhi. Mrs. Sreedharan was a medical doctor of outstanding merit. So I thought it safer that she accompanied her husband during the journey to and fro Delhi. Next day the couple proceeded to New Delhi by plane. They came back from New Delhi within two days and he disclosed to me that CJI asked him whether he had any objection to become Chief Justice of the High Court of Punjab and Haryana and that he immediately replied in the affirmative. Justice Sreedharan also disclosed to me that Chief Justice of India sounded to him that I was tipped to be a judge of the Supreme Court of India. He then conveyed a note of warning administered by the CJI that the above informations should be kept confidential. We both kept the above information confidential with the only exception that we disclosed the news to our spouses. For ten days thereafter, we had no other news about any further development.

On the 5th of February 1996 I got a telephone call during lunch recess from the Governor of Kerala (P. Sivasankar) who was then staying in the Kerala House, New Delhi. He conveyed to me a disquieting information that my name for elevation to the Supreme Court of India was dropped. I thought that it was due to some mistake that he passed such a wrong information to me. Hence I told him that the fact was just the other way around as the Chief Justice of India himself informed me in unmistakable terms that I could expect the order of appointment as Judge of the Supreme Court at any time. When I mentioned to him that it was only on previous 25th January that the Chief Justice of India gave me the above hint, the Governor disclosed that he got the new information just then "directly from the horse's mouth". He also disclosed to me that the Chief Justice of India really wanted to recommend my name but he was prevailed upon by certain others to refrain from doing so. Governor Sivasankar conveyed that those others who interceded against my elevation caricatured me as not worthy to be made a judge of the Supreme Court. The Governor was able to find out the persons who possibly could have given a wrong information about me to the CJI. I need not say that the above information passed on to me by the Governor really upset me. It was not because I was not elevated to the Supreme Court, but after being told in clear terms that a decision had been taken by the collegium, they later decided to rescind it because of adverse reports reaching the collegium of the Supreme Court. I felt very bad. I cut short my sitting on the day and returned home early with a heavy heart. I shared my pangs with my wife and tried to reduce the mental tribulation. I never imagined, when I started my career as an advocate, that I would ever become a Judge of the High Court of Kerala. Nor did I dream that I would ever reach the

Supreme Court of India as a judge. Still I reached the position of a High Court Judge much ahead of the time calculated by many and I could also function as officiating Chief Justice of the High Court of Kerala for a fairly good period. If God could lift me up to such heights, learn how to count the blessings and not to brood over what has not been conferred. Hence, why should I be disturbed in not being elevated to the Supreme Court? This is one way of looking at it. In this way I controlled my mind and resumed my work with all the vitality as before.

Here I have to mention the name of one person Fr. T.V. Thomas, he was the vicar of my parish at Trichur as well as at Calicut. He had studied theology at the Connecticut university in U.S.A. He was a man of prayer. After he retired from active service he settled down at Cochin. We maintained very good personal relationship. He visited me at a time I was brooding over the information passed on to me by the Governor of Kerala that the decision to elevate me to the Supreme Court was shelved. I shared my disturbed mind with him. He assured me of his prayers for abating the distress tormenting my mind. The dialogue I had with Fr. Thomas relieved me of the strain which vexed my mind. His words gave me enough confidence that the Lord who is my shepherd is a good shepherd and if I was taken by Him to the still waters and was led through the green pastures the valley of dark could be the way to the abode of God.

A couple of days later a seminar was held at Hyderabad. It was inaugurated by Justice A.M. Ahmedi, the Chief Justice of India and presided over by Sri. P. Sivasankar, the Governor of Kerala. He was once a leading advocate and also a judge of the High Court of Andhra Pradesh and hence he was held very high by the legal fraternity. In his presidential address the Governor quoted a sentence from my judgement in the case relating to appointment of non-Brahmins as priests of the temple. The sentence quoted was this: "Caste had been buried fathom down by the Constitution of India and what remains is only a fossil for future students of social subjects to make research". The Chief

Justice of India was very much fascinated by the Governor's speech particularly the above extracted sentence. When he conveyed his appreciation to the Governor the latter disclosed to the CJI that the above sentence was collected by him from a judgment delivered by the officiating Chief Justice of Kerala High Court (the Governor had the habit of reading most of the judgments published by the Kerala Law Times. He would have read my judgment in the above case in the course of such reading).

A few days thereafter, a meeting was held at Trivandrum in connection with the silver jubilee celebrations of the Kerala Law Academy. Justice A.M. Ahmedi, the Chief Justice of India delivered the inaugural address. Governor of Kerala was to preside over the function. But at the final stage, he expressed his inconveniences to do so and suggested to the Academy people to persuade me to preside over the function. I readily accepted the offer. (later I learnt from P. Sivasankar that he resiled from his earlier consent to preside over the function only for the purpose of facilitating me to have an opportunity to impress upon the visiting CJI. The Governor had occasion to hear my speeches and he developed a confidence that my speech could create a good impression in the mind of the CJI). The jubilee function was well attended and well conducted. I had prepared my presidential address well in advance. When I delivered it the entire audience was seen keenly following every bit of what I said. I noticed the CJI very attentively observing how I spoke then. I have good reasons to presume that my speech had impressed the CJI. Justice P. Subramanian Potti was also one of the speakers. He was earlier Chief Justice of Gujarat High Court on being transferred from Kerala. During that time Justice Ahmedi was the next senior most Judge of the High Court of Gujarat. Justice Potti, after his retirement set up practice as a senior advocate of the Supreme Court. Hence It was only natural that Justice Ahmedi would have given due weight to the opinions and assessment of Justice Potti regarding judges of the Kerala High Court. After the jubilee function of the Law Academy was over and while staying in the Raj Bhavan, Trivandrum the CJI wished to see Subramanian Potti. This desire of the CJI was communicated to Mr. Potti and hence he called on the former at Raj Bhavan. They were closeted together for some time. Later I understood that the CJI made enquiries about me during his talk with Mr. Potti. I have no doubt that Justice Potti would have given a high impression about me. In fact, Justice Potti held such a high impression not only on account of my performance as District Judge but he had enough sources to collect information of how I performed as Judge of the High Court.

The above episodes became a turning point. I learned from knowledgeable circles that after returning to New Delhi, Chief Justice Ahmedi contacted five former Chief Justices of Kerala High Court who were then available in New Delhi and ascertained their impression about me. Thereafter, the Chief Justice of India decided to recommend me for elevation to the Supreme Court of India.

On 16th March 1996 at 10 p.m. I had a call from the Chief Justice of India. He told me like this. "Now pack up and be ready to leave Kerala". I requested him to tell me at least then as to which High Court I was to go as Chief Justice. He answered that "you are not going to any High Court, you are going to join me as my colleague, but do not give any publicity to it as any thing can happen again between the cup and the lip". Next day I got a fax message from Rashtrapathi Bhavan, New Delhi, stating that "President of India has been pleased to appoint you as a judge of the Supreme Court of India".

32

Farewell from High Court

A formal order appointing me as judge of the Supreme Court of India was issued by the President of India. I had only a very short time to join the new assignment. Hectic engagements followed including farewell functions. There was a customary farewell reference by the "full court" which was attended by all judges in their official costume and a huge gathering of advocates in their official dress. The senior most judge of the High Court (Justice K. Sreedharan) spoke bidding farewell to me. It was followed by speeches made by the President of Advocates Association and Advocate General of Kerala. Though it was usual practice for the speakers of such farewell functions to eulogise the departing judge, S. Narayanan Potti the Advocate General was unusually long in addressing the farewell peroration. I asked him later "why you spoke at such great length". His answer was touching. "It should have been lengthier but there was time constraint, so I made it short". It is appropriate to extract the following excerpts from the speech made by the octogenarian Advocate General who was venerated by one and all on both sides of the profession, bench and the bar.

"On the occasion of your elevation to this court, I remember late Sri. P.V. Ayyappan, the then Advocate General asserting that you were capable of doing tremendous work in this Court, thus affording effective relief to the "over-burdened backlog of this

Court". These words were prophetic. In the last Republic Day Celebrations you mentioned about the disposal of cases, both in the High Court as well as in the Subordinate Courts of this State during the period of your tenure as the Acting Chief Justice, which showed a record. Sri. Ayyappan further indicated that your equipment and your knowledge of men and matters will enable you to discharge the duties of your office with rare distinction so that his successor standing in his place could, without a prick of conscience, proclaim that you had acquitted yourself creditably. Again, these words were prophetic and I, as his successor standing in the very same court, can proudly declare with a clear conscience that you have exceeded our expectations.

Your legal erudition, your desire to dispense 'even-handled justice', your sterling qualities of head and heart, had endeared you to the members of the Bar and the staff and the subordinate judiciary. You can unhesitatingly assure yourself that your performance as a Judge of this Court and then as the Chief Justice has been a record of which any man can be proud. It is a fact accepted by all in this country, by which I mean not in Kerala only but the entire nation, that this Court is the best in India, and in that you did have the co-operation and assistance of equally talented Judges who have each proved himself to be possessed of all the qualities required in a Judge. In your written speech on the occasion of your elevation to the Bench you mentioned the legend of the Queen of Sheba and the judgement of the great King Solomon distinguishing between a bouquet of natural flowers and another with man-made flowers. King Solomon was guided by a bee on the bouquet of natural flowers. You prayed for the blessings from Almighty to help you in keeping the pledge which you have made on your entry into this Court. In your decisions in choosing between the right and the wrong, between truth and falsehood, between the good and the bad, you have been guided by Almighty God by showing the bee in the correct bouquet. You have a long stint in the Apex Court to which you are now justly and rightfully elevated and I believe that with your sense of dedication and your uprightness you will be guided by Almighty God in showing you the bee in the right place".

Sri. S. Gopakumaran Nair, the President of the Kerala High Court Advocates Association said the following, inter alia, in his speech.

"We might have seen more brilliant judges. We might have also seen more fine persons among judges. But, only very rarely we had come across with a well balanced combination of a brilliant judge, a reasonable citizen and a fine person as we now see in His Lordship Justice K.T. Thomas. One of the most remarkable characteristics of Justice Thomas, which I have noticed as a lawyer, is his identification with the legal profession. He is even now more proud of re-calling his reminiscence as a lawyer than as a judge. For any successful man it requires great effort, humility and nobility to constantly remind himself about his past, the trials, tribulations and the agonies he had passed through. It is more so in the case of a judge because of the detachment that calls for from our surroundings and the power that is vested with. I have seen in my Lord Justice K.T. Thomas this rare quality of remembering his past and identifying with the Bar. Another notable feature of His Lordship's judicial personality is His Lordship's affinity towards junior Advocates".

In my reply I thanked all my colleagues, members of the Registry of the High Court and my personal staff besides the galaxy of advocates for all what they did to make my career as a judge to the utmost satisfaction of all concerned. I may extract the following excerpts of the reply speech here:

"It is my greatest fortune that I received overwhelming support from you, the advocates. May I add with humility and with a sense of gratitude that this support I got from the Bar wherever I sat as Judge right from 1977 onwards. There was not a single occasion when any one of you became offensive to me. I used to feel that you had a special regard for me. I am exceptionally lucky that even my reproachments were treated by junior advocates as parental rebukes intended only to get the best out of them. If I could make any contribution to the wealth of case-law it is due to the meritorious feed back which I received in abundant measure from the Bar, juniors as well as seniors. The fame which Kerala High Court has secured is mostly the reflection of the conduct and performance of the members of the Bar of this Court. I regard it as precious to have been assisted by the nonagenarian Kunhirama Menon who has now become a legend in the legal profession. Our Advocate General S. Narayanan Potti is leader of the Bar not merely ex-officio, he is not only primus interpares, but he is prima primate as well. It is time consuming to mention the names of all the doyens of this Bar, so I skip that endeavour".

"Friends, from here I am proceeding to a totally different place where I am an utter stranger though the subject of my work is the same. From the land of green, whose fauna and flora are resplendent, from the land of torrential rains, lakes and rivers I am going to a place of extreme heat and cold. I have to move from far in the south to the farthest in the north. From a state's legal capital to the nations constitutional capital. From the High Court of a small state to the apex court of the highest jurisdiction in the vast republic. From this new town of Eranakulam situated on the bank of backwaters where Vembanad lake meets with the Arabian Sea, I proceed to the very ancient Metropolis of Delhi situated on the bank of Yamuna river where antiquity meets with modernity. I have the comforting factor that frontiers of my area of work would cover this beautiful land of mine which cradled and fondled me and brought me up to this level".

While bidding goodbye to you all, the deepest desire in me is not that I may be remembered as a judge with any juristic acumen or legalistic faculty, but only as one who discharged his judicial function with utmost rectitude and integrity. I thank you for bearing with me all these years and particularly now".

On the day I left Ernakulam to Delhi a large gathering of advocates and judges besides a good number of judicial officers (despite that being a working day) turned up at the airport to bid me adieu. Justice K. Bhaskaran (former Chief Justice of Kerala

High Court on whose recommendation I became judge of the High Court) travelled down with his gracious wife from Calicut to Cochin airport, and a few advocates representing my parent Bar also came down to bid me farewell. A guard of honour ceremony was arranged by the state with the armed constabulary at the airport accompanied by the customary military bugle blow. My wife and I bade good-bye to all. At 10 30 a.m. the aircraft with us inside took off from the Cochin airport and thus my judicial career in Kerala came to an end once and for all.

33

Becoming Judge of the Supreme Court of India

My wife and I reached Palam airport at Delhi on the afternoon on 27.3.1996. Mr. P.S. Divakaran Registrar of Kerala High Court and Mr. Jayaprakash, my private secretary had also accompanied me to Delhi by the same flight. We were received by the Registrar General of the Supreme Court and his colleagues Registrars. They first introduced Ms. Meera Hemant who had been appointed by the CJI as my principal private secretary. My wife and I were accommodated during the initial days in the VIP suite of the Kerala House, New Delhi. A number of visitors called on me to congratulate me on being appointed as judge of the Supreme Court of India. On the same evening my wife and I visited Mr. Justice A.M. Ahmedi the Chief Justice of India and his wife at the official bungalow of the CJI (5 Kershnamenon Marg). Both of them received us with curtsey and hospitality. On the following day we visited the next two senior most judges (Mr. Justice Kuldip Singh and Mr. Justice J.S. Verma). I did so not only because of a convention till then followed by the new judges, but because those three judges together, as a collegium, unanimously decided to recommend me as judge of the Supreme Court.

During the conversation with Justice J.S. Verma he told me that at the time of his elevation to Supreme Court he too visited the senior most two judges only after he was sworn in as judge of the Supreme Court. Why he mentioned this to me needs some elaboration. When my elevation to the Supreme Court was in the offing, some of my senior colleagues advised me that I should cultivate personal acquaintance with the two senior most judges of the Supreme Court, besides the CJI, because it was the collegium comprising of those three judges had to make the recommendation for my elevation. I told my friends that I had to see the Chief Justice of India for official purposes, but not the next two senior most judges with whom I had no scope for any official discussion. Even some of my senior colleagues argued with me in order to persuade me to call on the two senior most judges of the Supreme Court without which, they expressed the apprehension, that my name could not be cleared by them due to lack of familiarity. But I firmly remained on my stand that I should not do so, otherwise my visiting them could be interpreted at least by them as an anticipatory strategy to canvass for my elevation. I am glad that I could reach the Supreme Court without even seeing those two senior most judges before my elevation. But I am more glad that those two senior most judges not only concurred with the CJI for recommending me, but later expressed their admiration of my conduct in not calling on them earlier.

The visits helped me to have personal acquaintance with the three senior most judges even before assuming office. We then went to see the magnificent Supreme Court building as I had not seen its inside earlier. The building was constructed in the shape of a pair of scales in the balance. The design was thoughtfully and meaningfully made by the architect, apart from providing the majesty of its appearance. We both went through the corridors and had a glimpse of the sprawling court hall of the Chief justice of India besides some other court halls. By then Supreme Court of India has been acclaimed as the most powerful judicial institution in the world. Some of the provisions of the Constitution of India were so enacted as to make the apex court the most throbbing and effective judicial institution in order to uphold the commanding position of the Indian Constitution as the paramount power. I knew that I was to be a judge of that great Supreme Court during the following long period of six years, if Almighty had willed me to be alive and agile.

I was sworn in as judge of the Supreme Court of India at 10.30 a.m. on 29.3.1996 in the Chief Justice's court hall along with Justice S.P. Kurdukar who was Chief Justice of the Punjab and Haryana High Court. The oath was administered to us by the Chief Justice of India (Mr. Justice A.M. Ahmedi) Though the function was short it was solemn and was attended by the spouses of the new judges and a few friends besides a large gathering of advocates.

Babu Paul who was the Chief Secretary of the State of Kerala was one of the persons present in the court hall witnessing the function. It is interesting to mention here of a wish expressed by him many years ago when I was a practising lawyer at Kottayam. We used to have morning walks together and during one of such walks he made a casual remark that he was desirous of attending a function in which I would be sworn in as a judge. When he said so, I took it only as his wishful thinking and I just laughed it away. A few years later when I was sworn in as judge of the High Court of Kerala, Babu Paul was unable to be present at the function. Being Chairman of the Cochin Port Trust he had to go to Delhi on that day. After returning to Cochin he expressed his wish that God would give him another opportunity to fulfill his desire to be present at the function of my swearing in. What he then meant might be that Chief Justiceship of a High Court was almost certain counting my seniority range. But little did I imagine then that the swearing in ceremony would be in the Supreme Court. As he wished he was able to be present during my oath taking ceremony. He was a very sentimental person by nature and hence he could not contain his emotion while witnessing the ceremony. He took out the kerchief and plugged his mouth. Later he told me, when he did so, he noticed one of the judges staring at him seriously as though

Babu might be trying to bite out the trigger of a grenade. Those were days when terrorism started in Delhi and the terrorists were employing explosive weapons like grenade. Later Babu Paul disclosed to others, during a tea reception accorded to the new judges in the lounge of the Supreme Court soon after the swearing in function, that one of the judges stared at him. In the tea function the relatives and friends of the new judges had also been invited. They all had a hearty laugh. Then Babu Paul told them that he was counted as a terrorist who managed to sneak into the court hall.

All the judges of the Supreme Court hosted a customary dinner to welcome the new judges in the dining hall of the Supreme Court building. We utilised the opportunity to get acquainted with our colleague judges and their spouses. Justice A.M. Ahmedi, in a mood of bonhomie, cracked a satire that the dinner was given on the principle that the largest amount of work could be extracted from the judge only after feeding him up to the brim.

On the first day evening I made two visits which I considered memorable. The first was to "Gandhi Smirthi", the place where Mahatma Gandhi was assassinated. It was a sort of pilgrimage to me. There was none greater than him who lived in the 20th century. The date of assassination of Gandhiji (30th January) was since then observed as "Martyr's Day". As my birthday happened to fall on 30th January, I made it a point to pay homage to 'Gandhi Smrithi' on the morning of every 30th of January as long as I lived in Delhi. The last prayer meeting scheduled for Mahatma Gandhi on the day of his assassination was delayed by a few minutes as he and Sardar Vallabhai Patel (the first Deputy Prime Minister of India) was closeted in the adjoining Birla Mandir for some serious conversation. When Gandhiji noted from his "Ingersoll" pocket watch that he was late by a few minutes, he hurriedly left Sardar Patel and walked fast towards the podium set apart for his squatting during the prayer meeting. When he neared the podium Nathuram Godse confronted him, gave him a "pranam" and fired the gun which pierced the heart of Mahatma and the blood oozed down on the ground. All the spots on which Gandhiji's feet touched on his way to the podium and the spots were the last drops of his blood fell, have been specially marked and solemnly preserved at Gandhiji smrithi. The "Ingersoll pocket watch" and the chapels he wore, the pen he used, the cot he lied on and such other small things intimately connected with Gandhiji's day-to-day life are also preserved there.

Next I visited the residence of Justice H.R. Khanna who had acquired legendary attainment on account of the historic dissenting judgment delivered by him in the habeas-corpus case during the infamous emergency (when four other judges in "ADM Jabelpur case" held that nobody had the right to question the detention of a citizen during emergency, Justice Khanna took a bold and candid stand that no citizen could be arrested even during emergency without proper grounds and the court could consider whether the ground of detention was valid or not). Justice Khanna was very happy seeing me and encouraged me saying that his was also a similar ladder in reaching the Supreme Court. (He started his judicial career as a District and Sessions Judge directly recruited from the Bar and finally reached the apex court of India). He is now leading a quite retired life. Though, he was superceded by Prime Minister Indira Gandhi in the appointment as Chief Justice of India, his performance as judge of the Supreme Court became so memorable and admirable that he was specially honoured by the Supreme Court Bar during the Golden Jubilee celebrations of the Supreme Court. Among all the retired judges of the Supreme Court, Justice H.R. Khanna remained head and shoulders above the rest.

34

Ostracised bungalow to reside in and a scholarly companion to walk with

After joining the Supreme Court I stayed in "the Kerala House" for nearly two months as there was delay in allotting official bungalow to me. There was a time when Supreme Court judges had to wait for long to get allotment of official bungalows in New Delhi. During those days only one bungalow was allotted to the Supreme Court and that was earmarked for the Chief Justice of India. Other judges had to wait in the queue along with all other public men like ministers, members of parliament and government secretaries and the allotment was made on a priority basis by the Housing Department of the Central Government. Often, govt. Secretaries and politicians including Cabinet Ministers would get such allotment ahead of the Judges. However, the situation came to a satisfactory end when the Supreme Court directed the Central Government to set apart 24 bungalows situated in New Delhi for residence of Judges of Supreme Court. Though sufficient number of houses were set apart, pursuant to the said direction there was still delay for the judges to actually occupy the allotted houses on account of other causes.

When I joined the Supreme Court there were only two bungalows which remained vacant. Justice Kurdukar who was senior to me occupied one of them. The other one was at 15 Tuglak Road, but no judge dared to occupy it as it was considered a haunted house frequented by ghosts, and it was pronounced to be an ostracised bungalow. The story which gained currency was that two former judges who occupied that bungalow had undergone a lot of miseries and tribulations. One of them died in a car accident and the other had to face impeachment proceedings initiated by the Parliament. I did not believe in any such bigoted concepts nor in any mystic beliefs (though I am a believer in God) and hence I decided to exercise my option in favour of that bungalow. As it remained unoccupied for more than a decade, it was a dilapidated house by then. The sprawling premises and its compound were thickly grown with grass weeds and bushes. Even those who had no faith in ghosts or haunted houses hesitated to occupy that bungalow due to its dilapidated condition. I visited the house with my wife and found that if proper repairs and maintenance were given it could be turned into a beautiful bungalow. Hence I wrote to the CJI to allot it to me.

My driver spoke to my wife in Hindi (she could speak Hindi much better than me) that I should be persuaded to decline to occupy that house because of its ghost infested condition. My personal staff including the driver were supposed to reside in the staff quarters attached to the bungalow all of which were situated in the same compound. The staff were fearful as they had to stay with their family in such quarters. But such intercessions did not change my decision to occupy the osctracised bungalow. The CJI Justice A.M. Ahammadi, on reading my letter requesting for allotment of this house disclosed to me that he was glad at least one judge had expressed readiness to occupy it as he was about to surrender that house to the government for substituting it with another house since no judge dared to occupy it for ten years. When the news of my agreeing to occupy 15 Tuglak Road went around, many of my colleague judges called me and cautioned me against it, but I did not yield to it. My reply to them was that even if any calamity were to visit me while staying in the bungalow I would only take it as Godsent, but I would never blame the mortar and the brick of that bungalow. Apart from that, I was certain that all the bungalows situated in New Delhi, being as old as hundred years, would have witnessed some or the other miseries affecting the inmates therein. At any rate, I was firm that I would reside in that ostracised bungalow.

The C.P.W.D. which was the authorised agency to repair and keep the official bungalows in good condition, took three months to refurbish that bungalow. As the summer vacation intervened in the meanwhile, my stay in Kerala House could be reduced considerably. Ms. Meera Hemant, the Asst. Registrar of the Supreme Court was appointed as my private secretary. I wish to say a word about her. She was a smart and energetic lady. Her husband Mr. Hemant was an officer of the UCO Bank, her daughter Karishma is a brilliant girl with literary and artistic talents and her son Chandan an exuberant boy. She was very sincere in her work and absolutely loyal to me and my wife. Looking back, I feel fortunate in having had a private secretary who did all her might to make my career as judge of the Supreme Court effective. She was supervising the work done by CPWD to refurbish 15 Tuglak Road during summer vacation and hence the house was made ready for our occupation when we returned to New Delhi in July 1996 after summer vacation.

I must record here that my wife and I resided in that bungalow quite happily for four years. During that period the wedding of my youngest son was conducted for which a reception was arranged at this bungalow. No ghost visited the house during our stay and I was able to discharge my functions as effectively as was expected. All my personal staff stayed in the quarters attached to the bungalow very happily. On one night a minor tremor occurred all over Delhi and suburbs. Some of my personal staff thought, when their utensils were shaking, that it was due to the visitation of the ghost. They rushed to my bungalow in panic and conveyed to me that they experienced the visit of the ghost. As I was certain that the trembling in the houses was the result of a tremor, I smiled at those who ran to me and told them that all the companions of the ghost had gone to all the houses of the New Delhi during that night. On next morning we all read the news that a tremor had occurred in New Delhi during the previous night. Those staff of mine who rushed to me in the night felt ridiculed of the reaction. All of them had a very comfortably living in the staff quarters during those four years. In fact, when we later moved into a bigger bungalow (on my becoming a senior judge) my driver and other staff were sad to leave 15 Tuglak Road as they too had happy and enjoyable stay therein. That bungalow was next occupied by Justice K.G. Balakrishnan who also resided therein quite comfortably for more than three years when he moved into a senior judge's bungalow. (Mr. Justice K.G. Balakrishnan is being appointed as the Chief Justice of India and he has to move into the official bungalow earmarked for the CJI) 15 Tuglak Road is now being occupied by Justice Mathur of the Supreme Court. Thus the ostracised 15 Tuglak Road bungalow became perfectly residentiable.

Before and after becoming a judge, I used to undertake regular morning walks. It was a matter of joy and it was more joyous when there was a companion to walk with. There are very good walkways in New Delhi. Lodhi Garden, at all times, was bristling with walkers, no matter morning or evening, winter or summer. It is almost like the Hyde Park in London, but the antiquity is more pronounced with Lodhi Gardens.

Once I met Justice S.B. Majmudar of the Supreme Court walking on the road, I buttonholed him and thenceforth we became companion walkers. He was punctual in his daily walk. I never missed getting his phone call exactly at 6.15 every morning with the query "Shall I start ?" Then we both set out from our bungalows and met together in five minutes time and continued our walk along six different routes chosen by him for six different days in a week. I skipped Sundays as I had to reach the church on the morning for worship, but Justice Majmudar used to walk even on Sundays, though alone.

At first Justice Majmudar was a judge of the Gujarat High Court and later became Chief Justice of the High Court of Andhra Pradesh from where he was moved as Chief Justice of Karnataka High Court. He was elevated to the Supreme Court about a year prior to my appointment in the Supreme Court. He became a widower about 25 years ago and was well looked after by his children during his loneliness. He was one of the beloved of the Bar due to his courteous behaviour and patient hearing. He was a scholarly judge particularly in civil and constitutional law. The Bar had great confidence in his integrity and unbiased judicial approach.

Apart from walking together I had travelled with him to places outside New Delhi. My wife and I visited Nepal in the company of Justice Majmudar. We together visited many important places in the Himalayan Kingdom. We saw the palace of Nepal King Mahendra who reigned then. It was very unfortunate that a few years later King Mahendra and his queen were assassinated by their own son. The young royal fledgling who turned berserk finished the lives of all the members of the dynasty who were living in the palace then, in that shooting spree. Kathmandu, the capital of Nepal, has its own beauty with a special architectural uniqueness of buildings and pagodas. Nepal is the only country where the entire population consists of Hindus. Pasupathinath temple, the most famous shrine of Nepal, is situated at Kathmandu. The statue of a huge cow is the cynosure of the temple and its deity is Lord Shiva. We three visited the temple and Justice Majmudar offered his worship therein. With all its majesty the temple was kept untidy. The temples in Kerala are far tidier and better maintained than those in the north including Nepal. The commercial streets of Katmandu were very crowded and the business was very hectic. It is claimed that the city is almost like Hong Kong. Indian rupee had greater value in Nepal and hence shopping was far less burdensome for us. While returning from Kathmandu we waited at the airport and noticed that the security arrangements were far more lax than the airports in India. Little did we foresee then that the Thaliban terrorists would utilise Kathmandu airport for hijacking the Indian Airlines aircraft which carried a full load of passengers. They took the aircraft and passengers to Kandahar, the capital of Afghanistan and after days and nights of horrifying and harrowing experiences for the passengers and the crew the terrorists succeeded in wangling much gains in return for releasing the innocent passengers. One of the airhostesses attached to the flight wrote a book narrating the entire episode from the point of her entering the aircraft at Kathmandu till she was set free at Kandahar along with the passengers. The vicissitudes of the changing hopes and fears of the innocent passengers have been well portrayed in the book.

Justice Majumdar rendered many judgments in the Supreme Court. After his retirement he declined to accept the assignments offered to him by the Union Government as he wanted to go back to his home city of Ahmedabad. We visited him at Ahmedabad subsequently and found him enjoying life in the company of his children and grand children. It was my good fortune to have had the chance to associate with him. I feel I became richer in thoughts and knowledge on account my association with Mr. Justice S.B. Majmudar.

35

Sittings in the early days of judgeship in the Supreme Court

My first sitting in the Supreme Court was with Justice Kuldip Singh who was the senior most judge next to the CJI. His bench was known as green bench on account of a series of orders which he made against environmental pollution. Due to my inexperience in the Supreme Court I found it difficulty to catch up with him. By evening a huge bundle of special leave petitions (compendiously called SLPs) and other files were brought to my room in the Kerala House where I was staying. Though I went on reading the files, I could read only three or four files by 10.30 p.m. I was told that every judge of the Supreme Court was supposed to familiarise with all the files posted to the next day but I could only go through a fringe of the huge docket scheduled for the next day. Then I felt that I was not the suitable person to be elevated to the Supreme Court as I could not cope up with the work. Next morning I confided to Justice H.N. Hansaria (he too was a District Judge recruited from the Bar and eventually became Chief Justice of the Orissa High Court before his elevation to the apex court) that the huge volume of the listed cases for the succeeding day was too heavy for me to bear with. Justice Hansaria took pity on me and offered to help by giving me some tit-bits regarding the methods for completing the home work. He told me how he managed the problem when he was a new entrant in the Supreme Court. However, I got into the groove within a few days, and the huge piles of files fixed for each day became manageable to me.

After a short stint of sitting with Justice Kuldip Singh the CJI constituted a regular bench for me by posting me in a bench headed by Justice M.M. Punchi (who later became the Chief Justice of India). He was a dignified Judge who was one of the most popular judges among the members of the Bar with his courteous behaviour. I have observed him as a quick grasping judge who overlooked technicalities for advancing substantial justice to the litigants. I sat with him on the bench for a long period and that enabled us to develop a very close friendship. He had a commendable command over English language and it was a pleasure to hear him giving oral dictation of judgements and orders on the bench. But he seldom reserved cases for judgements to be authored by himself either due to lethargy or want of time. Hence his bench-mates got many opportunities to write judgements. Thus I could author judgements in a large number of cases while I sat with him.

One of the cases which deserves special mention was the case of P.V. Narasimha Rao, former Prime Minister of India. He was the accused in a criminal case and naturally it evoked a lot of sensation as the media gave good coverage to the case. For him Prime Ministership came as a windfall on account of the assassination of Rajiv Gandhi. In the following general elections his party (The Congress - I) did not secure absolute majority though it became the largest party in Lok Sabha. When the question of leadership of the legislature party was mooted, P.V. Narasimha Rao emerged as a dark horse and he was invited by the President to form the government. He successfully managed to complete five years as Prime Minister in office, but he was accused of engineering defections from other political parties for the purpose of continuing in power. In the subsequent general elections his party was virtually routed and the successor government at the centre did not protect him from the prosecutions launched against him in certain criminal cases. It was his misfortune that he became very unpopular by then though there were many plus points in his rule among which some were very longstanding. Mention must be made about the steps he has taken for reviving the financial position of the central government which had reached a pathetic situation during the period when his predecessor (K. Chandrasekhar) was in office. The fist step P.V. Narasimha Rao did as Prmie Minister was to appoint one of the ablest technocrats/ economists of this country Mr. Manmohan Singh who was once governor of Reserve Bank of India. Prime Minister Rao and his able Finance Minister really transformed the Indian financial condition and thereby saved the country. They started a new era of liberalization on the industrial and commercial fronts. Many people felt that the awakening of the economic field was almost like a miracle brought out by the magic wand swished by Manmohan Singh with the full support of Prime Minister Narasimha Rao. But it is quite unfortunate that in the last period of his Prime Ministership he adopted certain political steps in order to come back to power after the next general elections. Such steps landed him in great trouble and became costly for him in the general elections. When the new government was formed the role of Narasimha Rao got transposed into the criminal courts of Delhi. As he was in the hit list of the terrorists, special protection had to be provided to him and even otherwise he was entitled to have special protection as a former Prime Minster.

The venue of the trial of his criminal cases was normally in one of the court rooms of the Tis Hazari court complex. It was one of the most over crowded court complexes in India. A huge crowd of people used to visit the complex every day either as litigants or as witnesses or as spectators. The police felt that a change of venue was advisable for affording Narasimha Rao effective protection, particularly because of his vulnerability to the blitz of the terrorists. Hence the police moved the High Court of Delhi to transfer his case to some other venue. But the Delhi High Court, on its administrative side, took a decision to reject the petition. The police (The Special Protection Force) then moved the Supreme Court with a special leave petition to have the said case shifted to a different venue. The SLP came up for arguments before a bench consisting of Justice M.M. Punchi and me. Tis Hazari Bar Association moved an application seeking permission to intervene in the matter. I asked the counsel for the Bar Association why a

Bar Association showed such interest in a particular case being tried in a particular court. There was no satisfactory answer to the said query. After hearing the arguments Justice M.M. Punchi authored the judgement of our bench. We directed that the case involving Narasimha Rao shall be tried in a court hall specially made in "Vigyan Bhavan" for special reasons of security arrangements.

I remember that the said judgement was criticized by the print media. When I visited the Delhi Law University to deliver a lecture some students hurled questions at me regarding the correctness of our judgement. Judges are not expected to defend their own judgements outside court. However, I felt that if I failed to answer the questions hurled at me, the students would form an impression that the judgement was without reasoning. I asked them whether any one of them had read the judgement and as expected they answered in the negative. I told them that every judgement contained reasons by which the judges reached the conclusions and that it would be unfair to criticise any judgement without even reading them. I offered to answer any further questions put to me after reading the judgement. This would have satisfied the audience and hence no further questions were asked.

36

The travails of a non-resident husband

One case which needs special mention here is Satheesh Mehra Vs. Delhi Administration. It was a battle between a husband and wife who had fallen out with each other. The couple had good affluence and hence they could reach the Supreme Court even at the early stage of litigation. The case was argued before us (Justice M.M. Punchi and myself) by the petitioner himself and a young advocate argued for the respondent (wife of the petitioner) The petitioner husband was alleged to have raped his 3½ year old daughter. The complaint against him was filed by his wife.

The couple and their two little daughters were living in New York. The husband had business in U.S.A. and a good amount saved by him was deposited in a bank in India in the joint names of his wife and himself. The estrangement between the couple started after the children were born. The exact cause of their falling out with each other was not disclosed to us. When their relationship reached a point of no return she flew back to India with her daughters. Within a few months of such return she lodged the complaint with Delhi police alleging that her husband had raped her second daughter. The husband then came down to India and filed a writ petition before Delhi High Court for quashing the said complaint. But the High Court dismissed his writ petition and directed the police to proceed with investigation of the case. Then he approached the Supreme Court with a special leave petition. The case was first heard by a bench of which Justice Punchi was a member. They directed the police to complete investigation and submit final report. However the Supreme Court kept the matter pending. Within a short time the police completed investigation and laid charge sheet indicting the husband for the offence of rape. At that stage the appeal came up for final hearing. Though the husband had no legal training his arguments were impressive, of course with a personal touch in his submissions. It was usual for a party arguing himself to overlook norms of submissions in court which advocates stick to. But we observed that this petitioner submitted his arguments without offending such norms in any manner. The advocate who argued for the respondent was formerly in the police department after securing high rank in the IPS. But he chose legal practice after resigning his job as IPS officer. Though he was not an experienced advocate his arguments were also quite impressive. We gave both sides a patient hearing.

When arguments were completed we were convinced beyond a speck of doubt that the allegations made by the wife against her husband were concocted and motivated, her intentions were to ruin the husband and his business career as the thirst to seek vengeance against him was seemingly bubbling up in her mind. We both felt that the prosecution is an abuse of the process of the court. Yet, for reclaiming a broken family we suggested to both sides that the disputes between them should be settled amicably out of court. His wife agreed to it on three conditions. First was that the husband should not contest her case for divorce,(which she had filed separately) second was that he should allow her to withdraw the huge amount of money deposited in the bank in their joint names and the third was, he should withdraw his claim before the civil court for custody of the children. The husband conceded to the first two conditions, but opposed the third one. According to him, if his children were allowed to be in the custody of his wife he had reasons to fear that she would use them for wreaking vengeance against other people also and the future of his children also would thus be ruined by her.

We noticed how the husband ended up his peroration inside the court. He sat down and while wiping off the drops of perspiration from his forehead with his hand kerchief he said: "if my wife persists with her last condition, I would choose to remain in India and fight the case to the finish, but I would not allow my little children to be in the custody of such a dangerous woman".

We could have disposed of the matter directing the trial court to consider all the contentions and reach its own conclusion. But we knew that in doing so the husband whom we found to be totally innocent might have to undergo enormous tribulations and would be compelled to remain in India until the whole trial was concluded. As per the legal system which prevailed in India, a trial would be completed only after the lapse of three years, if not more. It meant that the husband should have been away from his business in U.S.A. and he would suffer a lot and might even collapse his business. Allowing the trial to run its full course in this case would result in manifest miscarriage of justice, that was what we concluded. We felt that this was a fit case in which the apex court should do justice without waiting for all the formalities of a trial to be completed.

Under law, a pre trial discharge of the accused in a case involving offence triable by Sessions Court, is permissible only if the court finds that the case presented by the prosecution was so weak or groundless as to render the trial a futile exercise. For the above purpose it was thought, during those days, that the court could look into the records produced by the prosecution alone. In the present case we were satisfied that the prosecution was launched only with the object of making vengeance against the husband as we could see certain documents produced by the husband. One such document showed that the same wife lodged a complaint with New York police alleging that her young child was raped by a teacher of the school wherein the kid studied in that city. The New York police after investigation had found the allegation to be false. Another document produced by the husband showed that the wife had preferred an earlier complaint with the

US police alleging that her husband had raped the little child on a prior occasion. This was also investigated into by the US police and found to be false. A third document produced by the husband showed that a US court allowed the husband to have the custody of the children particularly in the light of bogus complaints launched by the mother. We decided to expand the scope of law by permitting the courts to look into the records produced by the defence also at the early stage itself in order to find out whether the trial would be wholly misconceived or that there are grounds fatally affecting the prosecution.

I wrote the judgement of the bench wherein I dealt with the law on the point and finally quashed all the prosecution proceedings against the husband. Justice Punchi, without any reservation, signed the judgement. Later I read from certain publications that the said judgement of ours was scathingly attacked by some women organisations. However, we remained unruffled as we had the utmost satisfaction that complete justice was given through our judgement. This decision was reported as Satheesh Mehra Vs. Delhi Administration 1996 (9) SCC 766.

The dictum laid down by us in the above case stood in good stead for a long time. Many advocates usefully employed the principle laid down in the aforementioned decision for closing prosecution even before commencement of the trial. However, another bench of the Supreme Court, in another case, expressed the opinion that the ratio laid down in Satheesh Mehra Vs. Delhi Administration should be reconsidered. After my retirement from Supreme Court the legal principle laid down by us in Satheesh Mehra was reconsidered by a larger bench of five judges. They held that for pre-empting a trial, the court could only look into the records produced by the prosecution and that it was a premature stage for permitting the accused to produce the documents.

37

Eleven Judge bench and minority rights

The Indian Constitution conferred special rights on the minorities in the matter of establishing and administering educational institutions of their choice. Such rights are enshrined in Article 30. A direction is contained in the same Article that the state shall not discriminate any educational institution for granting aid on the ground that it is under the management of a minority. At the same time, Article 29 (2) inhibits against denial of admission to any citizen in any educational institution receiving aid out of state funds on the grounds only of religion, race, caste, language or any of them. The basis of minority envisaged in that Article is either religion or language. When the Constitution was made, the makers had in mind some of the best educational institutions in India which were founded by zealous educationalists of religious denomination, particularly Christian missionaries. When Article 30 was framed and passed, the constitution makers had in mind that such institutions shall be protected from state interference. But the Education Bill passed by the State of Kerala in 1958 when it was under Communist rule, contained provisions to control the powers of management of the schools. This evoked protests from managements of all private schools irrespective of religion. They succeeded in creating a big stir throughout the state which lasted for a long period. Those who organized the agitation impressed upon the people that the provisions in the new education bill were aimed at indoctrinating the young minds with communist philosophy. The propaganda of the school managements became very effective because the agitation became stronger and stronger on each day. The government of Kerala forwarded the Bill for obtaining the assent of the President of India. In the light of growing agitation in Kerala the Union Cabinet advised the President of India to seek the advisory opinion of the Supreme Court of India regarding the constitutional validity of that Bill. A seven judge bench of the Supreme Court gave its opinion in 1958 itself in which they said that the minorities had almost absolute right to administer the educational institutions established by them and that the only restriction which could be imposed on them was regarding the curriculum or the qualifications of the teachers besides maintenance of hygiene, discipline etc. This opinion of the seven judge bench became the sheet-anchor of many of the subsequent decisions of the Supreme Court regarding the minority rights envisaged in Article 30 of the Constitution. At the same time, the said judicial opinion became the foundation for some decisions concerning professional colleges which claimed protection of minority rights for collecting capitation fees from the students admitted therein. A two judge bench of the Supreme Court expressed very seriously against the practice of receiving capitation fees. Subsequently, another five judge bench of the Supreme Court formulated a scheme for admitting students in the professional colleges run by private agencies. It is called 'the scheme in Unnikrishnan case'. Some of the minority professional colleges did not reconcile with the said scheme. One of them, TMA Pai Foundation, moved the Supreme Court for reconsideration of the said scheme. Certain other managements also followed it.

In the above background a larger bench of seven judges was constituted by Chief Justice A.M. Ahamadi in 1996 to reconsider the validity of the scheme evolved by the previous five judge bench regarding payment of capitation fee in professional colleges. I was included in the seven judge bench headed by CJI, A.M. Ahamadi. After hearing arguments for some time, we felt that we should have the freedom to reconsider even the decision rendered by the first seven judge bench regarding the Kerala Educational Bill. So we enlarged our bench to nine. The enlarged bench heard arguments for some time and then we felt that the strength of the bench should be still larger because an earlier bench of nine judges had followed the dictum evolved in the judgment concerning the Kerala Education Bill and that should not block our way to interpret Article 30 afresh. Thus we decided to constitute a bench of eleven judges.

Chief Justice A.M. Ahamadi felt that he would not be able to continue to hear arguments if he sat on the eleven judge bench because he had only a few more days left for superannuation. Hence, he recused himself from hearing that case. The next senior most judge Justice J.S. Verma was not included but his next senior judge (Justice M.M. Punchi) was included in it and hence the new bench was headed by him. I was one in the new eleven judge bench.

The new bench was constituted by Chief Justice A.M. Ahamadi with such sagacity as to give it a representative look. Judges from different parts of the country belonging to different sections of the society inclusive of religious and linguistic minorities in India were included in that bench. Though Justice J.S. Verma was the next senior most judge of the Supreme court of India, and would, in all probability, be the next CJI, his non-inclusion on the very large bench for hearing a momentous issue was not understood by us. But I have a feeling that justice J.S. Verma had his reservation about his non-inclusion.

A large number of senior advocates of the Supreme Court were arrayed before us to present the arguments for the management of various educational institutions including those which claimed minority rights. Fali S. Nariman, one of the most outstanding lawyers, having excellent court manners led the arguments for the managements of minority institutions. All the senior advocates addressed arguments on different facets of the main issue. It took a number of days to complete the arguments for one side. Equally brilliant advocates including the Attorney General appeared on the other side. We could reach almost the final stage of hearing arguments. All that remained was to hear Ashok Desai, the Attorney General for India. At that stage Justice A.M. Ahamadi retired as Chief Justice of India and in that place Justice J.S. Verma was appointed.

Justice J.S. Verma on assuming the office changed the roaster of judges for the ensuing week. He formed a new constitution bench of five judges including himself for hearing some other case. It consisted of himself and four others, one of them belonged to the bench which heard partly the minority rights case. Consequently our bench could not proceed with the minority rights case next week. Again another constitution bench was formed for hearing yet another case by including one from our bench. It went on like that for a few months during which the bench hearing minority rights case remained in limbo. In the meanwhile Justice K. Ramaswamy (who was one of the members of the eleven judge bench) attained the age of superanuation and retired. Consequently the bench which heard the minority rights case almost fully stood dissolved once and for all.

It was unfortunate that many days of precious judicial time became wasted apart from the huge amounts shelled out by litigants for engaging senior advocates to argue the matter. If the eleven judge bench could continue to function for two more days, the whole exercise would have been completed. What a great loss of public money as well as avoidable suffering for private litigants at enormous measure !. I do not want to say anything more about that unfortunate episode.

After about ten months Justice M.M. Punchi became Chief Justice of India, but he did not reconstitute the eleven judge bench until he himself retired within an year. He was succeeded by Justice A.S. Anand as Chief Justice who held the office for nearly three years, but he too did not constitute a bench for hearing that matter though he himself was a member of the dissolved bench. In fact,

I had a great desire to have the eleven judge bench reconstituted either during the tenure of Justice M.M. Punchi or during the much longer tenure of Dr. Justice A.S. Anand as Chief Justice of India. My reasons were two for developing such a desire. The first was, most of the judges who heard arguments addressed before the dissolved bench of eleven judges continued to be in service and hence it would be of advantage for us and the advocates. Second was, my experience as a member of a religious minority community having seen directly how many of the educational institutions were functioning (or mal-functioning) in this most literate state (Kerala), would be of much use in evolving a decision on the contentious issues relating to minority rights. In fact, Justice S.B. Majmudar who was then the senior most judge of the Supreme Court talked to the two successive CJIs, of the necessity to re-constitute the eleven judge bench before I retired from the Supreme Court. But due to one reason or the other, neither could Justice Punchi nor could Dr. Justice Anand reconstitute the same. With my retirement from the Supreme Court none of the original eleven judge bench was in office as all of them retired prior to me.

When Justice B.N. Kirpal became Chief Justice of India, having only a short tenure of a few months, the large bench of eleven judges was reconstituted for hearing the ticklish issues concerning minority rights. All the members of the reconstituted eleven judge bench could hear arguments afresh. The new bench was able to get the arguments completed in a shorter period. Chief Justice B.N. Kirpal delivered the main judgment for the bench answering some of the important issues concerning the rights of minorities for establishing and administering professional educational institutions in this country. A few other judges wrote supporting or dissenting judgments. However, the majority opinion was in agreement with the judgment authored by the Chief Justice B.N. Kirpal. This judgment, during later years, became a momentous one. This came to be known as the decision in "TMA Pai Foundation case". Even then the problems relating to admissions to professional colleges have not been solved and new issues started cropping up thereafter.

One more Constitution bench of five judges had to be created by the successor Chief Justice to deal with certain issues which cropped up as by-products of the decision of TMA Pai Foundation case. The judgment produced by this five judge bench came to be known as the decision in "Inamdar case". As per the said decision two committees were to be formed in each state. One committee was intended to finalise the fixation of the fees in different unaided private professional colleges. The other committee was to oversee the transparency and fairness of admission process adopted by such colleges. When committees were to be formed in the state of Kerala, the Chief Justice of the High Court of Kerala (Mr. Justice Jawaharlal Gupta, one of the ablest and upright Chief Justices in any High Court in India) proposed my name as the Chairman of both committees. The Chief Minister of Kerala (A.K. Antony) persuaded me to accept the Chairmanship of both committees and I accepted the offer on two conditions. First was that I would not receive any salary. Second was that the headquarters of the committees should be located in my hometown. The Chief Minister was pleased to accede to those conditions. As I propose to write later on my experiences as Chairman of those committees, I wish to leave that subject presently. It appears that the Constitution of India has created a perennial problem by evolving Articles 29 and 30, the embers of which would continue to burn.

The period during which Justice J.S. Verma was the Chief Justice of India the prestige of the Supreme Court had soared up high on account of his handling of what is known as "Hawala cases". Many big guns including some leading politicians of the day were implicated consequently as accused in criminal cases involving corruption charges. I have learnt from the media that the confidence of the people in the Supreme Court during that period was quite high. Justice J.S. Verma was a darling of the media. But after his retirement, it was unfortunate, that some dark clouds billowed around the handling of the Hawala cases. However, due to the timely intervention made by the Supreme Court Bar Association those dark clouds were not allowed to create thunder and lightening. In course of time they faded out.

38

Sitting with the Chief Justice of India

Though I sat with all the Chief Justices of India who held the office during my tenure in the Supreme Court, I had the opportunity to sit with Chief Justice Punchi for the longest period. It would be interesting to narrate some of the events which preceded his appointment as CJI.

After the infamous supercession of senior-most judges for appointment as CJI during the reign of Prime Minister Indira Gandhi in nineteenseventees, Indian Chief Justiceship had never become a national problem. Thereafter the senior-most pusne judge of the Supreme Court invariably succeeded the retiring CJI. So normally there was nothing unexpected in the senior most judge being appointed as the Chief Justice of India. But when the turn for Justice M.M. Punchi to become the CJI, arose there was a period of suspense on account of certain developments which happened during that period.

Justice M.M. Punchi, though he was the senior most Judge of the Supreme Court when Justice J.S. Verma was the Chief Justice of India, had his own reasons to apprehend that he might be superceded. The accepted practice was that the incumbent CJI would send up his recommendation regarding his successor well ahead of time to enable the government to proceed with the work of appointing the successor Chief Justice. In the case of Justice M.M. Punchi, a lot of suspense and drama were created because the incumbent CJI did not send up his recommendation well in advance. There was a lobby in Punjab and Haryana as well as in Delhi which campaigned against appointing Justice Punchi as the CJI. In fact, that lobby made a serious effort to forestall his appointment. Information of the move to supercede Justice Punchi was sensed by the Supreme Court Bar Association. Then most of the members made a counter campaign in favour of Justice Punchi who was very popular judge among the members of the Bar. The junior members of the Bar, by and large, liked him because of his courteous behaviour in court and the spirit of accommodation shown by him to all the fledglings at the bar. The Supreme Court Bar Association thereupon passed a resolution with a massive majority expressing their anxiety that the proclamation appointing Justice Punchi as the CJI was not issued. However, Justice J.S. Verma continued to keep his next judge on tender-hook by declining to send up the recommendation. The Prime Minister then was I.K. Gujaral. He knew both J.S. Verma and M.M. Punchi well. The Prime Minister requested Justice Verma to send his recommendation without any further delay. The lobby which tried to stall the appointment of Punchi as CJI accelerated their campaign, and they met a few members of the Parliament to bring a motion of impeachment against Justice Punchi. But they failed to get the minimum number required to move such a resolution in Parliament. There was real suspense among the Judges as well as members of the Bar on account of the unexplained delay on the part of Justice Verma in sending up his recommendation. In fact, Justice Punchi confided his feelings of anguish to some of his colleagues, and I was one of them.

I do not know how the problem was finally solved. The notification showing that President of India appointed Justice M.M. Punchi as CJI was issued from Rastrapathibhavan only two days before the retirement of Justice Verma.

I was included in the combination of judges of the bench headed by Chief Justice Punchi during his tenure as Chief Justice of India, except perhaps on very rare occasions. Among the cases which I could hear while sitting with the Chief Justice of India, some of them are of topical interest and I could recollect them with vivid details. However, I prefer to mention only two of those cases as they stand out prominently, one of them related to the wages for prisoners in India and the other related to the ticklish and perennial problem of Indian politics, namely, defection of legislatures. Presently I deal with the judgment authored by me regarding the wages of prisoners. This was heard by the bench comprised of Chief Justice M.M. Punchi , myself and Justice D.P. Wadhwa. As the judgment authored by me was fully concurred by the Chief Justice. the same became the judgment of the Court. Justice Wadhwa wrote a separate judgment which might appear to be a dissenting one, but by and large, it was in agreement with the main judgment.

For two reasons that judgment is very close to my heart. I am tempted to regard it as the most human rights touched verdict passed by me. First reason is that it concerned a set of people kept behind the bars whose wailings could not be heard by us sitting inside the four walls of the court. Second is, after pronouncing the judgment authored by me, I heard a tribute paid to the quality of that judgment. In a private function attended by a large number of judges (both sitting and retired) the tribute came out from Justice V.S. Malimath who was formerly Chief Justice of Karnataka High Court as well as Kerala High Court. He said thus to the hearing of those who were present:- "yesterday I read the judgment of the Supreme Court regarding the wages of the prisoners. I venture to say that this judgment had reached the standard by which the Supreme Court pronounced judgments in the early years". He profusely complimented me with admiring words for the style, language, reasoning and the human rights approach glittered in that judgment. Being the author of the judgment, when I heard it emanating from an eminent judge like him who was my own Chief Justice for nearly six years in the Kerala High Court, I felt considerably gratified.

Reforms and wages for prisoners

Jail reform was a subject to which scant regard was bestowed by many state governments. This appears ironical because most of the ministers in the early years of the post constitution period were politicians who suffered prison life varying from short term to long term during the freedom struggle. But the pace of reforms made in prison administration was very insignificant. In my knowledge, V.R. Krishna Iyer was the only exception. He was a minister in charge of prisons in Kerala state cabinet for a short period of two years during the latter part of 1950's. It was he who introduced many experiments for reforming the prisons. Thereafter till now no other minister could make more reforms in that human rights area.

Among the judges of the post constitution years nobody had done as much service towards jail reforms as Justice P. Subramonian Potti had done. When he was a judge of the Kerala High Court and later a Chief Justice of Gujarat High Court, he well utilised opportunities to deliver judgments which became beacon lights in judicial pronouncements providing guidelines for jail reforms. The Gujarat government filed an appeal before the Supreme Court against his judgment by which he directed the state government to increase wages for prisoners leaps and bounds. The National Human Rights Commission (N.H.R.C) got impleaded in the appeal and engaged a senior advocate to present their views in the matter. The questions posed before us were mainly three. The first was, whether prisoners could be compelled to do hard labour during their detention period. Second is, if it is part of punishment, are they entitled to wages for such work. The third is, if they are entitled to wages, what is the rate at which they should be paid.

During arguments, we came across some startling facts and figures. All the jails in India had become over crowded with prisoners. Most of the jails were designed and built to accommodate only one third of the actual inmates interred therein now. More than half of the prisoners in the jails are those who wait for the trial in their cases to reach termination. As they were not granted bail, they were to remain in jail. They are called "under-trial prisoners". The other category of prisoners are those who are convicted and sentenced to imprisonment by the verdicts of criminal courts. They are called "convict prisoners". But they are far less in number when compared with the under-trial prisoners. There is no dispute that no under-trial prisoner can be asked to do skilled or unskilled labour so long as he continued to be such. Both categories were mingled together in the same cell in almost all jails. They were segregated from each other only in one or two central prisons in the country. The living conditions in most of the prisons in India were really pitiable. Most of the jails looked like dungeons. The inmates therein were to live a life worse than caged animals.

As the under trial prisoners could not be asked to do any work it is a lamentable feature of our criminal justice system that the unconvicted prisoners have to remain for many months and even years inside the jail without being found guilty of any offence. The number of such prisoners far exceeded the convict prisoners. Some of them had remained in jail even for longer period than they would have been sentenced to any period of imprisonment even if they were convicted by the court. In a republic, where life and liberty of a citizen are protected by the constitution, it is an irony that persons who were not found guilty had to remain in jail for such long period. The main reason why there are many under-trial prisoners in Indian jails is attributable to the long delay on the part of criminal justice system for concluding the trials. In spite of many experiments made and provisions enacted, the delay became one of the curses hovering around Indian criminal justice system.

A preliminary objection was raised in the appeal on behalf of Gujarat government based on Article 23 of the Constitution. By that Article "forced labour" is prohibited. The only exception is that compulsory service can be imposed if it is for public purpose. Indian Penal Code recognized two types of imprisonment. One is called "rigorous imprisonment" which means that the prisoner must do hard labour. The other is called "simple imprisonment" where he need not do any work at all. When the Constitution came into force IPC was already in force. If any provision of the IPC is inconsistent with the fundamental rights enshrined in the Constitution such provision would become automatically void. So we had to consider whether jail authorities could impose labour on any prisoner whether hard or light, skilled or unskilled. In order to understand the scope of the prohibition contained in Article 23, we perused the debates which took place in the constituent assembly while formulating that article. We then came across certain interesting aspects. Some members of the constituent assembly had cited corresponding provisions in the constitution of certain other countries where similar prohibition has been incorporated and pointed out that one exception was given in all such constitution by providing that "labour can be imposed on a person as part of punishment". On that basis a plea was made for including a similar exception in Article 23 also. But Dr. Ambedker who was the propounder of many provisions concerning social advancements pointed out that if any public purpose could be achieved by extracting compulsory labour from any person that would be sufficient exception to the prohibition contained in Article 23.

In the judgment authored by me for the bench I dealt with this aspect whether any public purpose would be served by imposing hard labour. The old notions of punishment were required to be replaced by new thinking. Today imposition of punishment should be mainly for the purpose of reforming the convict and not to torture him. The ancient theory that the object of punishment is "retribution" became a primitive thinking. The philosophy that punishment is meant to deter others from committing similar offences has also become outmoded now. Of course element of deterrence carries a little weight in the punishment. But the major aim of a punishment should be to reform the convicted person. You punish your child with the only desire that he should be reformed. A good republic could impose punishment on its citizens mainly with that motive. I quoted in the judgment the sayings of certain modern criminologists. One of them said like this: "The standard to measure the level of civilization of a nation is not by counting the percentage of modern equipment and facilities acquired by its citizens but how well you care your prisoners in jails". No one is a born criminal. He is made so by circumstances. I quoted the words of Jesus Christ in my judgment. (Gospel according to Mathew Chapter 25 verse 43) "when I was in prison you did not visit me". Valmiki was a notorious murderer, but he was so much reformed that he became the most celebrated poet and author in India. Ramayana was written by him. I pointed out in my judgment that many among the prisoners could be reformed into worthy citizens and hence the public policy should be to take steps for reforming every prisoner. By allowing prisoners to do skilled or unskilled work inside the jail on payment of wages would keep their body and mind engaged. That would be a good tonic for developing their personality. That apart, such labour would give the prisoner a purpose for his life in the jail, something to look forward. Reformation of offenders is certainly a public purpose to be achieved. Hence I justified imposition of labour on the prisoners provided reasonable wages could be paid to them for such labour.

The next question was how much should be the wages to be paid to the prisoner for the work done by him while undergoing imprisonment. We thought, why should not he be paid at the same rate as another workman outside the jail was paid for similar work. At any rate, I suggested that the wages paid to the prisoner should be based on the rate prescribed under the Minimum Wages Act. However I pointed out that the cost incurred by the government for providing food and clothes to the prisoner should be deducted from such wages.

An argument was raised, if a prisoner could earn while undergoing punishment as though he was employed outside the jail, would it not provide incentive to the unemployed youth to become offenders so that they could also get into jails as convict prisoners and earn wages. This argument, according to us, has no merit because the deepest urge for every human being is to have his basic right of liberty. We came across sufficient data to prove this reality, and they were set out in the judgment to support that reasoning.

Lastly we said in our judgment that 1/3rd of the wages earned by a prisoner shall be sent to his wife and children and another 1/3rd shall be credited to his account as a saving to help him to rehabilitate himself on becoming a free man. The remaining 1/3rd can be set apart to provide compensation to the victims of the offences for which the prisoner was punished and imprisoned. We directed the state governments to make suitable law for taking the last mentioned 1/3rd portion because the wages earned by a person being his earned property that could be appropriated by the government only if there is a law for that purpose.

The judgment authored by me was fully concurred with by CJI (M.M. Punchi). But Justice Wadhwa, the other judge on the bench, disagreed with me regarding the theory of objectives of punishment. He wrote a dissenting judgment. Nonetheless, he too was in favour of paying wages to the prisoners for the work done by him at the same rates as suggested in our judgment. After pronouncement of the said judgment we ordered all the state governments to implement the directions contained therein by appointing a commission to work out the rate of wages payable to the prisoners, the expenses to be deducted there from etc.. Notices were issued to all state governments to submit report to the Supreme Court regarding the implementation of the directions. We also directed the state governments to make interim provisions for paying revised rate of wages to the prisoners until final shape was worked out. Even after the retirement of Justice M.M. Punchi and Justice Wadhwa the above case continued to be posted before the bench which I headed for more than two years as I wanted to see that the state governments complied with the directions for making adequate provisions to pay wages to the prisoners.

Tihar Jail in Delhi was considered to be a very notorious prison house, though it was one of the largest in the world. (About

200 acres) Inmates of Tihar Jail were then considered to be hardcore criminals and their behaviour inside the jail was unbearable even to the jail authorities. Stories of how the prisoners in Tihar Jail behaved were published in newspapers and magazines. The condition continued like that for a long time until a new lady police officer (Kiren Bedi) was posted as D.G.P. of Tihar jail. She has now become a celebrity on account of the tremendous reforms brought about in Tihar Jail. Such reforms not only improved the condition of life of every prisoner, but their mental attitude had attained remarkable transformation. This was brought about by Kiren Bedi in a period of five years. These reforms earned two creditable laurels, one for Tihar Jail itself and the other for Kiren Bedi. She was adjudged as the recipient of one of the most coveted awards "Magsase Award" for the yeomen services rendered in the filed of jail reforms. "The TIME" magazine published from New York contained an article under the title "Tihar – A Haven of Prisoners". When I read the article in the TIME magazine I felt the urge to visit Tihar Jail and to see for myself as to the changes brought about in the prison. By then Kiren Bedi had been shifted to another field and one Mr. Aggarwal succeeded her as D.G.P. At my request he called on me and he made arrangements for our visiting Tihar Jail without disclosing my identity as a sitting Judge of the Supreme Court of India. My wife and I went there. Mr. V.K. Madhavan Kutty (an awardee of "Padma Shree" who is a renowned social activist of Delhi) was also present when we visited Tihar Jail.

There were actually six different jails within the complex of 200 acres and each jail contained nearly 2000 persons. We were invited to visit the jail on a special day when there was a combined assembly called "Mahapanchayat". The top ranking jail officers were seated on a podium and all the inmates of these jails in Tihar were seated under a shamiana erected in the park, inside the complex. None of the inmates nor even the officers of the jail except Mr. Aggarwal (D.G.P) and his next junior officer realised our identity and hence we could hear the deliberations carried on in that assembly. That was the day when the inmates were to speak out their grievances and experiences and even praises for the officers. At the end of the meeting all the inmates (it was a huge crowd of nearly 10,000 prisoners) stood up and they all sang the Hindi song "He, malik, the re bande hum" (Oh God, we too are your children) The song was composed for an ancient Hindi film depicting jail life of convicts.

I must mention here that we could see the perfect cleanliness insisted on in the culinary sections of the jail as we were taken to those parts. Each jail consisted of huge kitchen sections and each kitchen consisted of different rooms for making different food stuffs to be supplied to the prisoners. Some of the life convicts were trained to make food articles. We were asked to change our foot wears and we had to put on the slip-ons supplied at the door step of each jail. Special head cover was also given to us. Chappathi was seen made in a highly refined manner with clean apparatus and utensils.

The areas outside the prison cells were converted into beautiful gardens. The place where the prisoners were making biscuits and manure were also visited by us. During Kiren Bedi's time, biscuits and manure produced at Tihar Jail became export commodities and were sold in foreign markets and very handsome profit was earned and that amount was put in the prisoners' welfare fund. We were also taken to the special halls within which the prisoners were performing Yoga and Vipanyas (a particular form of spiritual meditation). Places of worship were also separately provided and all of them were kept in spotless tidiness.

I learnt that there was a time whenever any prisoner left the jail either on completion of his punishment term or by reason of any remission granted to him the remaining prisoners used to wait for his return to the jail very soon by indulging himself in some offences. If he could get back to the jail he was received with uproarious welcome slogans by the other inmates. But by the time I visited Tihar Jail I learnt the change which took place in their attitude. If any prisoner happened to go back to the jail once again his former colleagues languishing in jail used to lament saying "Why Tihar experiment could not change you and why did you commit another offence. We are sorry to see you here again". I was told that this mental transformation of the convicts was the greatest achievement of Kiren Bedi through certain spiritual exercises.

After returning home I expressed a desire to meet Kiren Bedi who became celebrity for igniting the sea changes in that one time dreaded prison house. When she heard that I expressed such desire she promptly reciprocated to it and called on me. When I told her of the article which the TIME magazine published, she was very anxious to read it as she did not know about it earlier. She then supplied a book authored by her which is titled "It is always possible". It contains the vivid narration of all steps taken by her for transforming the notorious jail into an ashram of prisoners. After reading that book I was convinced that she was rightly adjudged the recipient of the coveted international award.

Defection of legislatures in Uttar Pradesh Assembly

During those days the political scenario in the state of U.P. was very murky. Kalyan Singh was leader of the B.J.P. legislative party in the U.P. and hence he was the Chief Minister also. The Governor of U.P. was then Romesh Bhandari who was considered very close to Mulayam Singh Yadav, who was then Union Minister for Defence. He was actively involved in UP politics and was once the Chief Minister for the state. He was anxious to become Chief Minister of the state again. One day a news broke out that Governor Romesh Bandari dismissed the government headed by Kalyan Singh and installed one Jagadambika Pal as the Chief Minister. He headed a splinter group defected from BJP. The legislature party of which Mulayam Singh Yadav was the leader gave support to Jagadambika Pal.

The Speaker of the U.P. Assembly was then one Tripathy who was a senior advocate of the Allahabad Bar. The Speaker did not accept the position that Jagadambika Pal had the support of majority of the members of the legislative assembly. But Governor Romesh Bandari asserted that he was satisfied about Jagadambika Pal having majority support. Kalyan Singh claimed that he was continuing as Chief Minister since he did not lose majority support of the MLAs while Jagadambika Pal asserted that he was the legally appointed Chief Minister. It was in that background Kalyan Singh moved the Supreme Court for a declaration that he continued to enjoy the majority support of the legislative assembly.

The appeal was boarded before a bench of 3 Judges headed by Chief Justice Punchi. Justice S.C. Aggarwal and me were the other members of the bench. I wish to point out that Supreme Court never had occasion to deal with such a strange case. After hearing the arguments of some of the senior advocates who appeared for both sides in the packed court room, we decided to give a direction to the Speaker to examine at the floor of the Assembly whether Kalyan Singh or Jagadambika Pal commanded majority. That direction was very happily complied with by the Speaker of the Assembly because he wanted to prove that the Governor was wrong. In our order we suggested to the Speaker to conduct the test in the assembly through a "composite voting" i.e. he should ascertain the M.L.As who supported Kalyan Singh and Jagadambika Pal in the same voting. The Speaker promptly reported to the Supreme Court that the test was conducted and that he found Kalyan Singh commanding a decisive majority in the Assembly. Thereupon Governor Romesh Bandari resigned as he could not continue in office in spite of the support of Mulayam Singh Yadav. The next Governor who succeeded him declared that Kalyan Singh would continue to be the Chief Minister.

There was strong criticism in the press that the Supreme Court had transgressed the limits by issuing such a direction to the Speaker of the Assembly. It is true that the Constitution inhibited the supreme Court and the High Court from interfering with the affairs of the House whether Legislature or Parliament. But nobody has raised such objection before us when we dealt with the matter in the court. After we passed the direction, even the Speaker did not express any dissent over it. On the contrary, the Speaker willingly complied with the direction. Perhaps, the direction reached him very conveniently to over come the imbroglio created by the action of the Governor.

The above episode gave rise to a very unusual situation. There were 13 MLAs among those who voted for Kalyan Singh who initially belonged to a party called BSP headed by Ms. Mayavathy (who later became Chief Minister of UP). BSP had a strength of more than 65 M. L. As in the U.P. Assembly. When 13 of them defected to the B.J.P, they were required to be disqualified as MLAs in accordance with the provisions of the Tenth Schedule of the Constitution. Speaker of the Assembly was the final authority to declare such MLAs to be disqualified and the decision of the Speaker shall be final and could not be called in question in any court. This was the provision in that Tenth Schedule. However, the defectors could escape from disqualification if the defected MLAs constituted more than 1/3rd of the total strength of MLAs of that political party in which case it would be called a split (As per a recent Constitutional Amendment, anybody defecting from the legislative party would forfeit his MLAship irrespective of any more MLAs joining him in floor crossing. No "split" is recognised now).

Mayavathy persisted with her demand that Speaker of the assembly should take a decision on her petition, but the Speaker went on postponing it. However, he could not continue the strategy of avoiding the decision too long because the Supreme Court directed the Speaker not to count the votes of the 13 defected MLAs for determining whether Kalyan Singh had majority support. In such a situation it became a matter of compulsion for the Speaker to decide the petition filed by Mayavathy. Therefore, he heard arguments and passed his order holding that the 13 MLAs of BSP were not disqualified at all because more than 1/3rd of the BSP legislative party had defected. To reach that arithmetical formulation the Speaker accepted the stand of Kalyan Singh that another 12 MLAs also had defected earlier along with the present

13 MLAs and the former set of 12 MLAs had gone back to the parent party very soon. The decision of the speaker became beneficial to Kalyan Singh to continue as Chief Minister.

Mayavathy filed an appeal before the Supreme Court through a Special Leave Petition against the said decision of the Speaker. Even though the decision of the Speaker was final according to the Tenth Schedule of the Constitution, the Supreme Court had held earlier in another case (wherein the Constitutional validity of the Tenth Schedule was challenged) that an appeal could still be entertained by the Supreme Court if special leave is granted but the Supreme Court has jurisdiction to interfere with the decision of the Speaker only if the decision is contrary to the provisions of the Constitution or is mala-fide or perverse or violative of the principles of natural justice.

The appeal filed by Mayavathy was heard by a three judge bench (Justice M.M. Punchi, the CJI myself and Justice Srinivasan). Arguments were addressed by some of the senior advocates which lasted for a few days. From the questions put to the advocates and the observations made by the judges during the course of arguments an impression was created that I was inclined to interfere with the decision of the Speaker while Justice Srinivasan would dismiss the appeal and Justice Punchi might in all probabilities agree with my stance. After completion of arguments, CJI suggested to Justice Srinivasan to prepare a draft judgment for the bench. But knowing that I could not agree with his line of thinking, I prepared my draft judgment. Justice Srinivasan without going into the merits of the factual position took a firm stand that the Speaker's decision was final. But I adopted the stand that no authority under the Constitution has the right to flout the provisions of the Constitution by resorting to a finding on facts which was glaringly unreasonable or perverse. I said that when the legislature party of BSP had 67 members, the number 13 could not form 1/3rd by any mathematical calculations. I pointed out and highlighted that the finding of the Speaker that a few more MLAs had also defected along with the present 13 MLAs initially, was perverse as each one of those MLAs had filed affidavit before the Speaker asserting that at no time did any one of them defect to any other party and that the Speaker deliberately did not act on those affidavits. I observed in strong language that if the reasoning of the Speaker was treated as probable, it would strike a death knell to the very philosophy enshrined in the Tenth Schedule of the Constitution.

The case was posted for pronouncement of our verdict on the afternoon of the last day of Justice Punchi's judgeship. The court hall was fully packed to hear the verdict. After Justice Srinivasan read out his judgement I started reading mine. Everybody waited in suspense to hear the view of the Chief Justice, being the remaining judge to pronounce his opinion. Chief Justice Punchi read out his opinion thus:-

"In view of the cleavage of the opinions expressed by my two learned brethren I deem it fit that the matter should be heard by a larger bench".

After pronouncement of the individual verdicts the bench was dissolved and we the three judges retired to the chambers of the CJI as usual. But we never talked about what we pronounced in that case. However, the view of the CJI that the matter should be heard by a larger bench was not the opinion of the bench of the three judges because only one among us said so. It became a debate outside the court as to the fate of the appeal. As the bench was dissolved soon after the pronouncement of the verdict and Justice M.M. Punchi retired from his service on that evening the appeal was to be posted to another day for hearing again. The successor CJI (Justice Dr. A.S. Anand) told me that a peculiar situation had been created by the split verdict and hence the matter could not be posted before a larger bench. The case remained in the docket for a long time and ultimately it became infructuous by lapse of time.

A similar situation arose later when the Governor of Jharkhand state appointed Shibu Soren as Chief Minister. His rival claimant staged a demonstration parading 41 MLAs of the state before Rastrapathi (41 MLAs would be sufficient to make a majority in that Assembly). When the matter was brought to the Supreme Court a three judge bench suggested that the Speaker of Jharkhand Assembly would conduct a 'composite vote testing' on the floor of the Assembly. As the Speaker was not happy to obey the orders of the Supreme Court a furore was created in the Lok Sabha. Somnath Chatterji, the Speaker of the Lok Sabha (who himself was a renowned advocate) expressed his dissent over the direction issued by the Supreme Court on a matter pending in the legislative Assembly. But in the case of Kalyan Singh Vs. Jagadambika Pal, the Speaker of UP Assembly was very happy to carry out the direction of the Supreme Court. Hence the imbroglio could be resolved without any hitch between the Parliament / Assembly and the Supreme Court of India.

39

Rajiv Gandhi assassination case

This was really the most sensational murder case tried in the Supreme Court during my period. Not only because the murdered person was a former Prime Minister of India, or because of the wide spectrum of activities involved in the case before and after the assassination of Rajiv Gandhi but the record number of accused convicted and sentenced in the case and the speed by which the trial and punishment were completed gave this case a special place in the criminal law history in this country. Twenty six persons were made accused by the CBI which investigated the case. The trial was conducted by a special judge appointed under "Terrorist And Disruptive Activities" Act (TADA) and after a marathon trial the special judge not only convicted all the twenty six accused, but sentenced all of them to death penalty. As the appeal could be heard only by the Supreme Court against a judgment of the TADA court, all the convicted persons filed appeals in the Supreme Court. A special bench was constituted headed by me with Justice Wadhwa and Justice Mohd. Quadri to hear arguments in that case. We heard arguments of different advocates who appeared in the case for many days covering a long period of four months. After arguments were over the papers were sent to my residence. It consisted of piles of records. The office room in my bungalow became crammed with racks of records of that case.

The draft judgement was completed by me within 21 days. My bench-mates also wrote separate judgements and we were able to pronounce the judgement within one month from the date of completion of arguments. This was a record in the matter of disposal of cases in the Supreme Court. The Registrar General of the Supreme Court expressed his amazement saying that all the officers of the registry expected the judgment to be pronounced only after a minimum period of one year because of the unusually large number of hearing days and the voluminous documents involved. As the case and its judgments evoked much public interest, I wish to state the facts of the case in brief.

Rajiv Gandhi, a former Prime Minister of India was assassinated on 21.5.1991 at a place called Sriperumbudur in Tamil Nadu. The assassin was an adolescent girl named Dhanu who was made into a human bomb and she got herself exploded at 10.19 p.m. at very close proximity to the visiting former Prime Minister. In a trice, the life of Rajiv Gandhi was snuffed out and his body was smashed into smithereens. As for the assassin nothing except a few pieces of charred limbs and her sundered head were left behind. In the explosion lives of 18 others also got extinguished.

The genesis can be traced to a movement which burgeoned in Sri Lanka for ventilating the grievances of the people of Tamil origin and for making certain demands for the Tamil speaking people of the island. Under the leadership of one Veluppillai Piribhakaran (some times it is spelled as Prabhakaran), a militant organization called "Liberation Tigers of Tamil Eelam" ('LTTE' as it was known) was formed. When the movement became belligerent the Government of Sri Lanka adopted sterner measures to curb their activities. Eventually a series of confrontations took place between the Government of Sri Lanka and the activists of LTTE.

When the Sri lankan Government found it difficult to meet the situation by themselves, it sought assistance from the Government of India for tackling the problem. This was reciprocated by the Government of India. Some parleys took place between the diplomats of both the nations in 1987. The President of Sri Lanka (Jayawardane) and the Prime Minister of India (Rajiv Gandhi) met together at New Delhi and Veluppillai Prabhakaran was also invited to be involved. An accord was signed by the aforesaid three persons by which the Indian Government agreed, inter alia, to form a cadre called Indian Peace-Keeping Force (IPKF for short). One of the tasks assigned to the Force was to disarm LTTE militants. Pursuant to the terms of the accord the Government of India dispatched a large number of IPKF personnel to Sri Lanka. While discharging their duties, IPKF committed many excesses which became an inhuman conduct towards the followers of LTTE. Consequently hostility developed in the minds of LTTE cadre towards IPK Force.

Skirmishes became rampant between the members of IPK Force and LTTE activists. In October 1987, a vessel carrying 17 LTTE functionaries was intercepted by the Sri lankan navy while patrolling on the high seas and the passengers were held captives. Leaders of LTTE made a bid to save them by appealing to the Indian Government to intervene, but there was no response. 12 out of 17 captives committed suicide by consuming potassium cyanide.

K. Chandrasekhar was chosen as Prime Minister of India by the Rashtrapathi on the assurance that the Congress Parliamentary party would support him, but before Chandrasekhar could face the Lok Sabha, the Congress Parliamentary party withdrew support for some reason or the other. At this juncture, the President of India dissolved the Lok Sabha and called for fresh elections. The President of India issued a notification for fresh general election. All the political parties swing into frenetic activities. Rajiv Gandhi started campaigning for the Congress (I) Party. He made his view public when a correspondent of Amrita Bazar Patrika interviewed him which was published in a magazine. According to him, the government of India stands towards Sri Lankan problems during his primeministership was justified and is liable to be resumed. In the election manifesto published by Congress (I) for the ensuing general elections, the party reiterated its commitment to send IPKF soldiers again to Sri Lanka. This policy of Rajiv Gandhi was a nightmare to the LTTE. They felt that Rajiv Gandhi had a good prospect of winning the election and if so, he would surely become Prime Minister again, in which case LTTE would again be in peril.

A criminal conspiracy was hatched and developed by the hard-core LTTE cadre. The main objects of the conspiracy were: to carry out acts of terrorism and disruptive activities in Tamil Nadu and other places in India during the course of which to assassinate Rajiv Gandhi and others. Among the conspirators nobody else seems to

have played a greater role than what Sivarasan had done. He was the kingpin of the conspiracy. HeSivarasan reached India sometime in December 1990 and in collaboration with some others who arrived earlier he chalked out a plan. Sivarasan came to know that Rajiv Gandhi would address a meeting at Sriperumbudur in Tamil Nadu on 21.5.1991. Sivarasan was determined to see that this opportunity should not be missed on any account. He ascertained all about Sriperumbudur from Nalini (A-1) and then only he told Nalini that the target was Rajiv Gandhi.

When Rajiv Gandhi arrived at the meeting place, Nalini and Suba got out of the enclosure and moved a little far away. Dhanu, who became the human bomb, stood in the front row with garland. None of the police suspected that girl to be the would-be-killer of the visiting former P.M. There were a few other girls also standing in the front row. Rajiv Gandhi went near a little girl called Kokila for receiving a poem written by that child in praise of Rajiv Gandhi. Perhaps prior permission would have granted to that girl for doing so. He would have either received the poem or was about to receive the same, and at that moment the hideous battery switch was clawed by the assassin herself. Suddenly the pawn bomb got herself blown up as the incendiary device exploded with a deadening sound. All human lives within a certain radius were smashed to shreds. The head of a female, without its forso, was seen flinging up in the air and rolling down. In a twinkle, 18 human lives were turned into fragments of flesh among which was included the former Prime Minister of India - Rajiv Gandhi and his personal security men, besides Dhanu. Many others who sustained injuries in the explosion, however, survived.

On 24.5.1991 the newspapers published a photograph of Dhanu holding a garland at Sriperumbudur in the company of a few other females waiting for the arrival of Rajiv Gandhi. On seeing the photograph Pottu Omman sent a wireless query to Sivarasan whether Dhanu was identifiable in the photo. What answer he received to that query had not been brought out. Initially the hands of some other terrorist organizations were suspected in the assassination of Rajiv Gandhi. Perhaps, Sivarasan and his henchmen would have heaved a sigh of relief at first as the needle of suspicion was not turned to them in the beginning. Sivarasan, Suba, Nalini, her husband Murugan and mother Padma proceeded to Tirupati to offer thanksgiving worship to the Lord and they returned to Madras on the next day. Sivarasan thereafter moved from place to place and Suba was shifted to different houses.

By middle of June, photographs of Nalini and Suba appeared in the newspapers. Sivarasan kept Pottu Omman informed of the developments in India through wireless transmissions. They and some other conspirators went to Karnataka state and they lived incognito somewhere in the suburb of Bangalore.

The police got some scent regarding the hide-out of the culprits and they rushed to that house. Sivarasan and Suba, and some other LTTE activists, who too were hiding in the same house, ended their lives by committing suicide. The remaining accused were arrested on different days at different places.

The special Judge, after a marathon trial, convicted all the 26 accused of all the main offences charged against each of them. He sentenced all of them to the extreme penalty under law.

Whenever any person was sentenced to death such sentence was not executed until it was confirmed by the High Court of the state. This is the legal provision now also. Normally an appeal from the judgement of a Sessions Court would be filed only before the High Court. But the law under TADA provided that appeal from the judgement of the Special Court created under TADA could be heard only by the Supreme Court. Hence, the Madras High Court, in this case, did not have any jurisdiction to hear the appeal of any one of the 26 convicted persons. Nor did that High Court have any authority to consider whether death sentence passed on those accused could be confirmed or not. Therefore, all those convicted persons filed appeals in the Supreme Court directly.

Different advocates appeared for different convicted persons for those appeals. All of them argued their part very well. The CBI engaged Mr. Altaf Ahammad (Additional Solicitor General of India) to argue the appeal on behalf of CBI. We felt that Altaf Ahammad would have taken considerable pains to get a complete grip over every item of the massive evidence and also the intricate legal points involved in the case. He was assisted by the Advocate who conducted the prosecution before the Special Court. As I mentioned earlier, advocates who argued the appeals in Rajiv Gandhi assassination case had consumed the largest number of working hours of the Supreme Court in any particular case.

After completion of arguments, I felt that Justice Wadhva and Justice Quadri were holding a contrary view regarding the utility of confession made by an accused to a police officer (TADA contained a special provision making the confession of the accused given to a police officer as admissible in evidence. Under the general law such confession is not only inadmissible in evidence but it is completely tabooed). So we three judges had one or two sittings in our residence to sort out the differences and to arrive among ourselves at a unanimous decision regarding the legal position concerning the confession made by an accused to a police officer. But the other two judges stuck to the position that such confession could be used against the accused like any other evidence. However, I could not reconcile with such a legal proposition. This sharp difference of opinion on the above legal point has reflected in the separate judgments delivered by each one of us.

All the three judges concluded that only seven out of twenty six accused could be convicted for the offence of murder and criminal conspiracy and all the remaining nineteen accused are liable to be set at liberty. The convicted persons were Nalini, her husband Murugan, one Santhan, one Robert, Payas, one Jayakumar, one Revi Chandran and one Arivu. There was unanimity between the three judges on the aspect that all of them were to be held guilty. But regarding the sentence to be imposed on them, we the judges differed between ourselves. We all agreed that Robert Payas, Jayakumar and Revi Chandran were to be sentenced to imprisonment for life. Dealing with the rest of the convicted accused I said thus:-

The conspirators in the Rajiv Gandhi assassination can be vivisected into four broad categories. First, those who formed the hardcore nucleus which took the decision to assassinate Rajiv Gandhi. Second, those who induced others to join the ring and played active as well as supervisory roles in the conspiracy. Third, those who joined the conspiracy by inducement whether through indoctrination or otherwise. Fourth those among the conspirators who participated in the actual commission of murder.

I pointed out that persons who fell within the first category were not brought to trial. They were Piriphakaran, Pottuommen, Akila, Sivarasan and Santhan. I expressed my view that all the other convicted persons except the lady (Nalini) belonged to the second category.

They were not merely carrying out the orders of the first category personnel but they made others to work according to their directions in order to achieve the target. The role played by them was prominently direct and active. They were in the leadership layer among the conspirators. We were not able to find out anything extenuating as for the said three persons in their activities for implementation of the decisions of the cabal. So I confirmed the sentence as for those three persons. Justice Wadhwa and Justice Qadri agreed with the above conclusion.

Regarding Nalini, I took the stand that though she belonged to the fourth category, she was led into the conspiracy by playing on her feminine sentiments. She became an obedient participant without doing any dominating role. She was persistently brain-washed by Murugan who became her husband and then the father of her child. Suba and Thanu would certainly have etched a woeful picture to Nalini regarding the atrocities committed by IPKF on women and girls of Tamil origin in Sri Lanka. By such indoctrinating exercises she would have honestly believed in the virtue of offering her help to the task undertaken by the conspirators. Considering the fact that she belonged to the weaker sex and her helplessness in escaping from the cobweb of Sivarasan and company, the mere fact that she became obedient to all the instructions of Sivarasan, need not be used for treating her conduct as amounting to "rarest of the rare cases".

There was yet another consideration which weighed with me. She was mother of a little female child who would not have even experienced maternal cling as that little one was born in captivity. As we have confirmed the death sentence passed on the father of that small child an effort to save its mother from gallows would not militate against criminal justice and thus an innocent child could be saved from imposed orphan hood. I therefore directed that she should be sentenced only to imprisonment for life. Thus in my judgment Nalini was saved from the death penalty.

But Justice Wadhwa and Justice Quadri in their separate judgments differed from me and took the view that Nalini was also liable to be sentenced to the death penalty. Thus by a majority view the death sentence passed on Nalini was confirmed in spite of my strong dissent.

A few days later, an application was filed on behalf of Nalini for review of the death sentence passed on her. That review application was dismissed because Justice Wadhwa and Justice Quadri said that when the majority of the judges confirmed death sentence on her there was no "error apparent on the face of the record" (error apparent on the face of the record is normally the sole basis for reviewing any order or judgment of a court). But I dissented from that stand in regard to the review application filed by Nalini under Article 142 of the Constitution. I adopted a novel reasoning like this:- "In a bench of three Judges when one judge decided that the accused cannot be sentenced to death penalty and two judges held the other view, it was necessary to show that the lesser alternative was not unquestionably foreclosed. (The constitutional validity of death sentence in the penal law of India was upheld by the Supreme Court twenty years ago on the basis of a reasoning that death sentence could be awarded only in "rarest of rare cases in which the lesser alternative is unquestionably foreclosed"). Here again, I pointed out that the death sentence passed on Nalini was confirmed because majority of the judges (though it was only by a wafer thin majority) held that she was liable to be put to death. According to me, death sentence would have been unconstitutional being ultravires to Article 21 of the Constitution. Unless death sentence is restricted to the tiniest percentage of rarest of rare cases, which should pass equally another sturdy test that "the lesser alternative is unquestionably foreclosed". I pointed out that when one judge out of three felt that the lesser alternative (life imprisonment) is a sufficient sentence for Nalini, how can it be said that the lesser alternative is "unquestionably foreclosed". So I expressed the view that the review application for Nalini should be allowed and she should be awarded only imprisonment for life, as otherwise the death sentence imposed on her would be unconstitutional. Here again the view of the two judges on the review application that the death sentence passed on Nalini did not warrant any review by the Supreme Court, became the verdict of the court being the majority view. The media inside and outside India flashed the judgement and highlighted the dissenting view of mine regarding Nalini.

Perhaps Nalini was not destined to be hanged by neck. In a mercy petition submitted before the President of India the widow of Rajiv Gandhi (Sonia Gandhi) had requested to the President of India to reduce her sentence to life imprisonment. I was told that Sonia Gandhi was much persuaded by the reasoning contained in the dissenting judgment that Nalini may be saved from the gallows. Finally, the constitutional authority passed orders commuting the death sentence passed on Nalini to one of life imprisonment. The act of grace and compassion of the widow of Rajiv Gandhi saved the life of Nalini from death and the life of her child from orphan-hood.

Before closing this matter, I feel obliged to mention about the performance of my private secretary (Mr. Anand Bist). His dedication to my work was so commendable that there was not a single occasion when I had to correct him. The enormous dictation work in the Rajiv Gandhi case was taken down by him on many days even by sitting late in the night and all the modifications and additions which I would have thought of making were promptly carried out by him. Many of the judgments in other cases which I dictated at my residence were taken down by him in such a manner as to evince my unreserved admiration. Even the other secretarial work assigned to him were very well performed by him. I regard him as a role-model secretary to a Supreme Court Judge.

40

The fall of a Rajasthani bride from the top floor of a multi-storied building

The victim of this episode was a young lady (Kamala Devi) hailing from a lower middle class family in Rajasthan. From the narration in the evidence this young lady would have been very pretty. A young business man hailing from the State of Rajasthan and doing business at Madras (now Chennai) desired to have that young girl as his wife. Her father was not able to provide much dowry to the husband as he could not afford it. However, the business man, enamored of the charm of the young girl, was willing to forego a bulky dowry. The marriage between him and this young girl was solemnised at the bride's town/village in Rajasthan. The couple, after marriage, proceeded to Madras for their new life. His younger brother collaborated in the business and they formed a partnership firm. The business prospered very much. They all lived together on the top floor of a multi storied building situated on Thulasinga Mudali Street at Madras.

Within a year the bride gave birth to a child and in another year she became pregnant again. By now her husband and brother began to brood over a thought that, had the marriage been from a wealthy family they could have obtained a good amount of money as dowry which could have been invested in their business. This thinking eventually snowballed into wicked ideas and finally the two brothers orchestrated a plan to liquidate Kamala Devi once and for all. They got two of their employees in the business to assist them in this task.

On the mid night of 9.7.1987 when the residents of the locality were sleeping Kamala Devi was dropped from the top floor of the building and she died instantaneously with her skull smashed. During the early days of this episode Kamala Devi's fall was considered by the police as well as the local people as a case of suicide or an accidental fall. When Kamala Devi died her husband was at Singapore on a business tour. When the news was conveyed to him he stayed on for some more days in Singapore. However, when he returned to Madras, his reaction on the death of his young wife was very cool. This conduct of the husband created suspicion in the mind of the neighbours. At any rate, the parents of Kamala Devi did not believe the story of either suicide or possible accidental fall of their daughter. They conveyed to the police their strong suspicion in the matter. Finally the police after a full fledged investigation concluded that Kamala Devi was actually killed for which her husband and brother and their two employees conspired together. The police arrested all the four accused and charge sheeted them with the following story:

The younger brother used to take alcoholic drinks often. This was disliked by the sister-in-law. She told this to her husband who in turn rebuked him. From then on wards the younger brother was ill-disposed to his sister-in-law. This animosity grew wilder in due course of time. Once her husband confided to her younger brother that marriage with another girl from a wealthy family would have helped them to garner a good amount as dowry for investing in the business. While thinking of a way out, the two brothers decided to remove Kamala Devi once and for all to pave the way for the husband to contract a new marriage. They chalked out a plan for achieving the purpose. Pursuant to it, the husband went on a tour to Singapore to make it appear that he had no role in the death of his wife. On the crucial night the other three accused went to the apartment where Kamala Devi was sleeping with her child. They first gagged her mouth with a cloth and when she woke up she instinctively resisted the physical attack made on her. She was over powered, her neck and mouth were pressed up. Then all the three persons lifted her up and was dragged to the balcony. She gripped on the parapet frieze, but the grip was too fragile and they pushed her down from such a height.

During evidence one of the accused was tendered with a pardon and he became an "approver". He gave evidence regarding the entire episode as an accomplice (the word accomplice means one who had participated in the crime along with other main offenders). The Sessions Court acquitted the husband of Kamala Devi, but convicted the other two persons and sentenced them to death. The Sessions Court relied on the evidence of the accomplice. The division bench of the High Court of Madras acquitted both the accused on the ground that the evidence of an accomplice is unworthy of credit and more so, because it did not receive sufficient corroboration from other sources. The judges of the High Court, however, entertained strong suspicion about the involvement of the accused in the death of Kamala Devi. This could be gathered from the following observations made by them in their judgement.

"Even though there is a lurking doubt in our mind as to the involvement of one or more of the accused in this crime, they cannot be punished on such a doubt however strong it might be. Following the high traditions of criminal jurisprudence in our country, we are not inclined to send the accused to gallows on mere suspicion and on the evidence of the approver (the accomplice) whose evidence stands uncorroborated".

The State of Tamil Nadu filed an appeal before the Supreme Court. A two Judge bench consisting of Justice M. K. Mukerji and myself heard arguments in the appeal. Justice M. K. Mukerji was one of the best criminal law judges of the Supreme Court at all times. He was very quick to grasp the facts of the case, he had an amazing grip on the legal aspects of the criminal law and nobody doubted his integrity. I sat with him for quite some time and during which period we were able to dispose of a large number of criminal cases. After hearing arguments in this case Justice Mukerji suggested to me that the judgement might be authored by me. We decided to set aside the verdict of the High Court and restored the judgement of the Sessions Court. We have chosen to believe the evidence of the "approver" although he was an accomplice and we have picked out four other items of evidence as supporting the testimony of the approver.

The importance of this judgement was that the Supreme Court widened the scope of Sec. 157 of the Evidence Act in a considerable manner. As per that section any former statement made by a witness relating to a fact deposed to by him, "at or about the time when the fact took place" can also be used to corroborate the testimony of that witness. We pointed out that there could be a narrow interpretation for the words, as also there could be a broader view. We adopted the broader view that if such statement was made within a reasonable proximity of time, it could be used to corroborate his own testimony. We found support for the said interpretation from the observations made by Justice Vivian Bose in a judgement of 1952. Justice Vivian Bose was a stalwart in the field of criminal law during the infantile period of our constitutional history. He too had given a wider interpretation to Sec. 157 of the Evidence Act. We said that the acquittal passed by the Madras High Court did result in a miscarriage of justice as it allowed the two perpetrators of a dastardly crime committed against a helpless young pregnant house wife (who was sleeping in her own apartment with her little baby during the absence of her husband) to go scot-free. However, we did not impose death sentence on the accused, instead they were sentenced to imprisonment for life, on account of "the distance of time and the intervention of an order of acquittal in between".

41

The Extortionists of Bow Bazar in Calcutta

Mir Mohammad Omar was the leader of a six member gangster group which reigned in Bow Bazar area of Calcutta (renamed as Kolkota) during the first half of nineteen eighties. Extortion was their style of functioning for making huge wealth. Whoever rose in any business within the vicinity of that Bazar had to pay ransom to the members of this gang for sparing him from the tentacles of their brutalities. Many businessmen in and around that area feared the members of the gang and they lived in suspense apprehending that anyone among them would be the next victim of their extortion activities. It appeared, even from the government did not do anything to crush such extortionist activities, or the someone in the government would also have been hand in glove with the main gangsters. Whatever that be, Bow Bazar was under the spell of fear of the extortionists and Mir Mohammad Omar ruled the roost.

The present case related to the tragic end of one Mahesh, a young bachelor who was an upcoming entrepreneur of the city. He was residing with his elder sister in an apartment situated near Bow Bazar. On one evening in October 1984 a person belonging to the gangsters group of Omar (which will be referred to as 'Omar Group') demanded Mahesh to pay half a lac of rupees, if he was anxious to get himself exculpated from the gangsterism of Omar group. Somehow, Mahesh could not reconcile himself to this browbeating tactics. He did not want to surrender to the bully. So he refused to part with money which the gangsters demanded. They haggled with Mahesh and lowered the ransom amount, but still Mahesh did not capitulate to the terms dictated by them.

On the night of 4.11.1984 the gangsters broke open the door of the apartment where Mahesh and his sister lived. Mahesh had not returned home by then and so the intruders passed a message to him through his sister that they would again visit the apartment to get Mahesh. When he returned home his sister narrated all what happened. He felt unsafe to remain there and so he left the apartment and reached the house of his friend Abdul Aziz who gave him asylum during the night.

After midnight one fruit-seller reached that house and passed a message that Omar was waiting outside to see Mahesh. On getting this information Mahesh stealthily escaped from that house and finally reached the residence of one Mohd Sayeed and sought refuge therein. At about 3 A.M. Omar and his companions succeeded in getting a sniffing of this hideout and sprinted to that place. Four of them sneaked inside and made a prowl for Mahesh and traced him out and he was dragged out of the room, and brought before Omar who then yelled at him, Rascal, "you escaped earlier, now let me see how you would escape again". Mahesh was taken captive and all the gangsters left the scene with the booty in the direct sight of the house owner.

In the course of towing away the prey the headman, Omar showered lathi blows on him saying "I will beat and kill you like a pig". They took Mahesh away from the ken of the residents of that area. Thereafter, Mahesh was not seen alive either by his kith and kin or friends. Next day Mahesh's sister gave a short account of the abduction episode to her nephew and deputed him to make enquiries. In the course of the enquiries he came across the mangled body of Mahesh lying in the mortuary of a hospital.

The above incidence captured a big flash in the media. There was an outcry from people around that such pillages took place with the indirect support offered by the police. This movement collected momentum day-by-day and the police was compelled to resort to strong and swift steps to apprehend the killers. Within a few days the police nabbed the six member gangster group including Omar. After completing investigation they were charge-sheeted for abduction and murder. The Sessions Court finally found that Mahesh was abducted by those six persons, but the judge observed that there was no evidence to show who murdered Mahesh. So the accused were convicted only for the offence of abduction (Sec. 364 IPC) and they were sentenced to imprisonment for 10 years.

Though the convicted persons surrendered to jail they got their sentence suspended after a few days when they filed appeal before the Calcutta High Court. The state of West Bengal filed another appeal against the acquittal of the accused of the murder charge. Ultimately a division bench of the Calcutta High Court dismissed both appeals. The disquieting feature of the High Court judgment was that the judges reduced the sentence to the period of imprisonment which the accused had already undergone. In fact, they had undergone imprisonment only for a few days because the sentence was, in the meanwhile, suspended by the High Court. In other words, for such a heinous crime the offenders escaped punishment for all practical purposes.

The state of West Bengal filed an appeal before the Supreme Court against the judgment of the Calcutta High Court. That appeal came up for arguments before a bench which consisted of me and Justice R.P. Sethi. Sri. K.T.S. Tulsi, a former Solicitor General of India argued for the state. After he narrated the facts of the case, I made the observation in open court, if we agreed with the finding that Mahesh was abducted by these accused, we would be compelled to presume that the murder was committed by the abductors themselves and in such event It was for the abductors to explain how else the victim was murdered. I also pointed out that the Sessions Court and the High Court uniformly found that the accused were guilty of abduction. So we suggested that arguments of the advocates who appeared for the accused should be confined to rebut that presumption. K.T.S. Tulsi felt that his task was considerably reduced because the finding regarding abduction had by then become unassailably final. Mr. Tulsi was formerly Solicitor General of India. I would rank him as one of the best criminal lawyers of the Supreme Court Bar. He hailed from Punjab and he would have conducted a lot of criminal cases in the trial courts and before the High Court before shifting his practice to the Supreme Court. He is one of the few advocates of the Supreme Court sought after by clients to argue before different High Courts in sensational criminal cases. With such rich experience in the criminal law, it was an easy task for the judges to make him understand the legal implications of finding of facts.

Sidhartha Sankar Ray (a former Chief Minister of West Bengal and Governor of Punjab) was a senior advocate of the Supreme Court. He argued for one or two of the accused in this case. P.S. Mishra, senior Advocate of the Supreme Court (who was formerly the Chief Justice of Andra Predesh High Court and later Calcutta High Court) argued for some of the accused. We pointed out to the advocates that unless they succeeded in saving the accused from the charge of abduction under Sec.364 of the Penal Code, it would be an uphill task for them to escape even from the charge of murder. Sidhartha Sankar Ray realised the difficult situation and he did not proceed with his arguments further. But P.S. Misra made frantic efforts to convince us that such a leap forward in favour of the prosecution could not be taken. During the course of arguments, I put a query in the form of an illustration to him like this:-

"If a child was abducted in the presence of others by a group of kidnappers and later the murdered body of the child was recovered from elsewhere, why a presumption, that the child was killed by those abductors, could not be drawn ?".

P.S. Misra requested us to grant him a day's time to give reply to the said query. Hence the case was adjourned to another day for further arguments. In the meanwhile, there arose an unexpected episode. A child was abducted by a notorious gangster group of Meerut (UP state) in the presence of his father when the boy just stepped out his car in front of the gate of the school compound. The gangsters made a sleuth to communicate with the father and bargained for ransom. The bargaining, perhaps, would have failed and next morning dead body of the boy was recovered from the field abutting the Delhi - Lucknow National High way. All the newspapers of Delhi carried this story as a sensational news flash on the succeeding Monday. Arguments of P.S. Misra were to be resumed on the next Tuesday. Misra had also read that news and became baffled. So he submitted before us, when the case came up for arguments again, that he did not want to join issue with us on the query put by us. We did not know how the above incident involving the boy had occurred right at that appropriate context itself.

I authored the judgement in Mahesh's case. We set-aside the acquittal order and convicted all the six for the offence of murder and sentenced them to life imprisonment. In reaching the said conclusion we adverted to a legal proposition on the factual situation. We accepted the finding arrived at by both courts (Sessions Court and High Court) that Mahesh was abducted by all the accused and was taken out of the sight of the witnesses and the murdered body of Mahesh was found lying in the mortuary of the hospital on the succeeding day. The abductors could not give any explanation as to what happened to Mahesh after he was abducted by them. We concluded that Mahesh was murdered by the abductors themselves. This case opened new vista regarding the burden of proof in criminal cases.

The pristine rule that the burden of proof is on the prosecution to prove the guilt of the accused should not be taken as a fossilized doctrine as though it admits of no process of intelligent reasoning. The doctrine of presumption is not alien to the above rule. On the other hand, if the traditional rule relating to burden of proof of the prosecution is allowed to be wrapped in pedantic coverage, many offenders in serious offences would be the major beneficiaries, and the society would be the causality.

To reach the said conclusion, we utilised the legal principle embodied in Sec. 106 of the Indian Evidence Act which reads as follows:-

"When any fact is especially within the knowledge of any person, the burden of proving that fact, is upon him".

The case ended as above but something more happened later on. A sitting judge of the Supreme Court after having read the newspaper which flashed our judgement, told me that a lot of scandals were in the air after the judgment was passed by the Calcutta High Court in the above case. A couple of months later I had to travel in a flight from Calcutta to Delhi. A senior advocate practising in Calcutta High Court was sitting next to me in the flight. He recognized me very soon and introduced himself to me. We had a pleasant chat. During which he told me like this:- "Sir, we all read your judgment in the Omar case and it was a matter of great relief to the lovers of justice that the Supreme Court corrected an absolutely unjust and wrong verdict of the High Court". He said something more which I do not wish to write here. Though, I did not show special inquisitiveness to get more details of the remarks passed by the senior advocate of Calcutta High Court. His remarks remained in my mind, lingering for a long time.

42

A treasure hunt

This relates to the case of how the greed for wealth could lead men to the extreme limit of human destruction. Sometimes, value of gold could eclipse value of human beings. Desire to become rich overnight without effort would blindfold human beings and transform them as demons.

Once, a gold ring was disinterred from the land of one Guruji, when the surface was tilled for cultivation. Some of his friends believed (and Guruji was also made to believe) that somewhere in the land a cauldron of treasure was lying deep down. A handful of greedy inhabitants of the locality made frantic searches to locate the treasure. They consulted a person called Damu Gopinath who was specializing in occult practices. He advised them to sacrifice five little children and to pour their blood on the land in order to get the hidden treasure winch to the fore. As the irrepressible greed for wealth could not be quenched by the land owner and his companions they further consulted Damu Gopinath (Damu for short) as to the details of the ceremony to be performed for the infantile sacrifices. Damu choreographed an agenda of rituals to be performed. Four persons decided among themselves to carry out the programme, so that they could become wealthy overnight. As per the scheme so calibrated by the propounders, the first child to be sacrificed should be a female whose blood should be colleted in a pot by cutting her vagina cross-shaped and that the rituals should be performed with that blood. Next was the blood of a boy who should be the only child of its parents. Like that they finalised the scheme for abducting and sacrificing all the five children one by one at appreciable interval between one and the other.

The events narrated in this case have the silhouette of a crime thriller. Mystery hovered around Chanda Village in Newasa Taluk (Ahmadnagar District in Maharashtra) over the sudden disappearance of children one after the other. Horror struck the minds of the villagers when cadavers of the children were recovered one after another from a canal which flowed through Newasa.

The episodes started on 4.3.1992 when a little girl named Meera (one of the four children of their father Ramdas) was missing from her house. The elders of the family made hectic searches and caused announcements to be broadcast regarding the disappearance of the child. Next day a complaint was lodged with the police. On the third day her dead body was recovered from a canal flowing through the locality. Among the injuries noted by the doctor on the dead body, two injuries were so peculiar that the mystery deepened further. The doctor who conducted the autopsy described the injury as a "triangular wound on the perineal region just posterior to the vaginal opening".

On 9.2.1994 a five year old kid by name Devidas was found missing. A complaint was lodged with the police on the succeeding day and three days later the dead body of Devidas was found floating in the canal at Dedgaon in Newasa Taluk. He had an injury on the back of his head and his penis was seen chopped off.

On 13.2.1995 another male child named Deepak (who was studying in the second standard) was found missing from his house. His father Suresh deputed his uncle to lodge complaint with the police. Three days later some people spotted the dead body of Deepak floating in the same canal. Penis of that child was also seen chopped off, besides the lobes of his ears sliced off.

While the above events had rocked the locality a seemingly eventless incident took place. A five-year old boy named Sagar became endeared to one of the accused Balu Joshi whom the boy used to address "Balu Mama". On two occasions Balu Mama tried to allure Sagar by offering sweets to him and took him to some distance but on both occasions Sagar wriggled out from his grip and ran off. The boy told his father about it but he did not take it serious.

Almost one year elapsed thereafter and the treasure-hunters wanted to try once again to get Sagar. On 10.2.1995, Balu Joshi went to the school where that boy was studying and he took the boy to some distance by offering sweets, somehow Sagar did not bite the bait and he ran away from Balu Mama. The boy reported this to his father who took it seriously. He informed the police of the attempt made on his son. Though the police registered a crime there was only slow progress as they could not get any clue in the matter.

Disappearance of Deepak created a big sensation in the locality and the police were compelled to take sterner steps to trace out the abductors. They succeeded in catching Damu Gopinath and thereafter they could reach all the remaining conspirators. The police could elicited confessions from the all the accused, but none of such confessions was admissible in evidence. However, Damu expressed willingness to confess before a magistrate, hence he was produced before a judicial Magistrate who recorded detailed confessional statement made by him containing all the vivid details of the events. He revealed in his confession that after bathing the child, his earlobes and penis were pealed off. They collected the blood oozed from those injuries and a heavy blow was inflicted on his head. He died instantaneously. His dead body was carried on a motor cycle and was dropped in the canal. Such details were disclosed by Damu before the judicial magistrate.

During the trial of the case in the Sessions Court Damu retracted his confession. According to him the confession was concocted by the police and put it in his mouth for narrating before the judicial magistrate. However, the Sessions Judge accepted the confessions as true and voluntary. He also accepted the evidence relating to the other circumstances brought against all the accused. The Sessions Judge convicted all the four accused and sentenced them to death penalty. There was great media coverage of the verdict passed by the Sessions Judge. Some of the parents of the slain children heaved a sigh of relief that at least condign punishment was awarded by the judiciary of the land on the killers of their little children. The sentence of death could be carried out only if it was confirmed by the High Court, according to the law. The convicted persons filed appeals before the High Court of Bombay. A Division bench of the Aurangabad bench of the Bombay High Court heard both the confirmation proceedings and the appeals together. The Division Bench rejected the confession recorded by the judicial magistrate as tainted by vitiating factors. Without the confession, the case as a whole, became considerably weakened. Consequently, the Aurangabad bench of the High Court acquitted all the accused. There was rampant protest against the High Court verdict. Such protests were voiced not only by the media but by the jurists and social activists.

In the above backdrop this case reached the Supreme Court. In the meanwhile, one more handicap visited the case. Damu died when the appeal was pending in the Supreme Court. According to law, the criminal proceedings shall stand closed as against an accused person on his death. The confession made by Damu could be used only against him, and none else, as substantive evidence, that too, if Damu were alive. So his death gave the remaining accused much advantage. However, there was a limited usage of that confession as against the remaining accused in the case. But such use was again hurdled because one of the conditions of such use is that the maker of the confession should also be a co-accused in the criminal case to enable his confession to be used as against the other accused even for the very limited purpose. Nonetheless, we were impressed by the testimony of Sagar (the boy who succeeded to escape from the abductors). The High Court did not attach any weight to the evidence of the boy for the reason that he was only aged six when he was abducted. But we in the Supreme Court, did not find any reason for sidelining the evidence of such a crucial witness on the mere ground that he is a child.

In spite of the above handicaps we could reverse the order of acquittal passed by the High Court. We convicted all the remaining three accused. In the judgment which I authored, formidable reasons were shown for believing the evidence of the boy who escaped, (Sagar).

Importance of this case in criminal law was that the Supreme Court found utility of the confession made by a dead accused. This was mainly due to the fact that the accused were charged with the offence of criminal conspiracy also, among other offences. We expanded the scope of Section 10 of the Indian Evidence Act and ventured to make use of the confession of Damu, though he died, in order to reach a conclusion that there was a criminal conspiracy as between all the four accused to make child sacrifice to trace out the treasure. Unless we have done so, it would not have been possible for the Supreme Court to convict those who murdered the children for acquiring wealth overnight. In fact, we derived great satisfaction in that we could salvage criminal justice in a difficult and seemingly helpless situation. The law we propounded for that purpose was the first of its kind. I am happy that through later decision rendered by other benches of the Supreme Court the aforesaid law has been affirmed as for other cases.

However, we were not able to impose death penalty on the accused. We gave the following reasons for choosing the lesser alternative of life imprisonment on the remaining culprits.

"Now, we have to make up our mind regarding the sentence to be imposed on the three accused. Learned counsel for the state pleaded for restoration of the same sentence which the trial court has imposed, i.e., death penalty. The question is whether this case can be regarded as rarest of rare cases in which the lesser alternative is unquestionably foreclosed. Looking at the horrendous acts committed by the accused, it can doubtlessly be said that this is an extremely rare case. Nonetheless, a factor which looms large in this case is that the accused genuinely believed that a hidden treasure trove could be winched to the surface by infantile sacrifices ceremonially performed. It is germane to note that none of the children was abducted or killed for ransom or for committing robbery. It was due to utter ignorance that these accused became so gullible to such superstitious thinking. Of course, such thinking was also motivated by greed for gold. Even so, we persuade ourselves to choose the normal punishment prescribed for murder as for these accused. Accordingly, while restoring the sentence passed by the trial court in respect of other counts of offences, we order that the accused shall undergo imprisonment for life".

Though the Supreme Court averted a miscarriage of justice by setting a side the acquittal of the treasure hunters who sacrificed little children, one of the leading English dailies next day carried the following headlines in a prominent manner. "Supreme Court saves murderers of innocent children from death penalty". It was unfortunate that the public who read the news particularly the above caption, would have felt that the Supreme Court went to the rescue of those notorious killers of infants, though as a matter of fact, it was the Supreme Court which convicted them and put them behind the prison walls for the rest of their life dissenting from the verdict of acquittal passed by the High Court.

43

Regarding treatment of witnesses

While practising as a lawyer, I felt concerned seeing the plight of many witnesses summoned to appear in courts. Witnesses are, by and large, strangers to the litigations in almost all cases, but they are compelled to go to the court because of the summons issued to them. In many a case, the witnesses have to travel from far distant places, but the courts are generally unsympathetic to the tribulations of such witnesses and hence the courts do not give any priority to them who are summoned to help the court with their testimony. In spite of vast improvement achieved in information technology, the governments did not thus far introduce the system of video conferencing for collecting evidence from witnesses. So they struggle very hard to reach the court on the time fixed in the summons. As no seats are provided for them in side the court hall they all have to stand outside the court, looking through the window, hoping for the call to mount the witness stand, and very often the call does not emanate, but at the end of the day they are told to be present either on the succeeding day or another day fixed by the court. Like that the witnesses go on attending the court. The fortunate among them get a call to face the questions put to them by the advocates which may be relevant and sometimes irrelevant also.

When I was a judge of the High Court, I came across a typical case in which the officer of a plantation situated in the hill district of Wayanad (Kerala) was summoned to appear in a court located at a far distant place. The only purpose for summoning him as a witness was to identify some of the domestic articles involved in a theft case. The said officer went to Calicut being the nearest railway station from his office. It required 5 to 6 hours journey by car. He booked a ticket from Calicut up to the place where the court (which summoned him) was situated. It involved overnight train journey. On reaching the destination he took a room in a hotel and after refreshing himself he presented before the court at the scheduled time. He remained on the court veranda until his case was called. A court peon approached him and informed that his case was adjourned to another day and he was free to go back. He was thoroughly exasperated. Any way, on reaching the railway station he booked the ticket for his return journey. On reaching Calicut he again booked the ticket for his onward journey for the next posting day and went back to his plantation by car. This tedious process was repeated on the next posting day and again on the further succeeding posting day also. When he was told on the third posting day that his case was again adjourned, he complained to the Magistrate of the enormous sufferings which he underwent just for honoring the summons of the court. The magistrate consoled him saying that such plights were inevitable for witnesses. On the fourth occasion he was examined by putting only three formal questions to him and then he was discharged. Later he sent a petition to the High Court narrating all the above. I do not know what the High Court did on that petition. The above episode is given here as a typical example of how witnesses were being tortured.

Though different Law Commissions made recommendations for improving the plight of witnesses summoned by the courts the situations remained unchanged. When I was a trial judge, I realised that the courts have a significant role to play for lessening the tribulations of witnesses. All what required was a mindset and a philosophy that the witnesses is summoned to help the court and hence he should be treated with utmost care and dignity. But it is a distressing feature of the Indian judicial scenario that many of the judges/ magistrates consider witnesses as objects of displaying judicial power and authority. The predicament of witnesses is of no concern to such judges/magistrates.

As a judge of the High Court, I had adopted many measures to improve this archaic system on the administrative side of the High Court and in training classes I exhorted judicial trainees to do everything possible to ameliorate the tribulations of the witnesses. I am unable to record here as to whether such exhortations had resulted in improving the system.

When I got an opportunity in the Supreme Court to deal with such situation, we laid down certain propositions. It happened in the background wherein a witness had to appear on eight occasions in a trial court (from 9th November 1994 to 25th September 1995), but for one reason or the other he was not examined on any of those occasions. Finally when the witness was absent on a particular day the judge became angry and closed the evidence without examining him. When the matter reached in the Supreme Court, I said the following in the judgment.

"Witnesses tremble on getting summons from courts in India, not because they fear examination or cross examination in courts but because of the fear that they might not be examined at all for several days and on all such days they would be nailed to the precincts of the Courts awaiting their chance of being examined. The witnesses, per force, keep aside their avocation and go to the courts and wait and wait for hours to be told at the end of the day to come again and wait and wait like that. This is the infelicitous scenario in many of the Courts in India so far as witnesses are concerned. It is high time that trial courts should regard witnesses as guests invited (through summons) for helping such courts with their testimony for reaching judicial findings. But the malady is that the predicament of the witnesses is worse than the litigants themselves"

"What a pity when a sessions court was engaged in adjourning and again adjourning the case at long intervals in spite of the presence of eyewitnesses willing to be examined fully.

"We make it abundantly clear that if a witness is present in court he must be examined on that day. The court must know that most of the witnesses could attend the court only at heavy cost to them, after keeping aside their own avocation. Certainly they incur suffering and loss of income. The meager amount of Bata (allowance) even if paid to him is a poor solace for the financial loss incurred by him. It is a sad plight in the trial courts that witnesses who are called through summons or other processes stand at the doorstep from morning till evening only to be told at the end of the day that the case is adjourned to another day. This primitive practice must be reformed by presiding officers of the trial courts and it can be reformed by every one provided the presiding officer concerned has a commitment to duty. No sadistic pleasure in seeing how other persons summoned by him as witnesses are stranded on account of the dimension of his judicial powers can be a persuading factor for grating such adjournments lavishly, that too in a casual manner".

We quoted Sec. 309(1) of the Cr. P.C. which requires that witnesses in attendance shall be examined on the same day and continued from day-to-day if the examination was not completed. We cited an earlier judgment in which every High Court was requested to issue a circular to all the trial courts that the above quoted sub section should be strictly complied with and if any particular trial judge violates it, administrative action shall be taken against him. The following observations were made by us in our judgment.

"It is no justification to glide on any alibi by blaming the infrastructure for skirting the legislative mandates embalmed in S. 309 of the Code. A judicious judicial officer who is committed to his work could manage with existing infrastructure for complying with such legislative mandates. The precept in the old homily that a lazy workman always blames his tools, is the only answer to those indolent judicial officers who find fault with the defects in the system and the imperfections of the existing infrastructure for his tardiness in copying up with such directions.

In some States a system is evolved for framing a schedule of consecutive working days for examination of witnesses in each sessions trial to be followed. Such schedule is fixed by the Court well in advance after ascertaining the convenience of the counsel on both sides. Summons or process would then be handed over to the Public Prosecutor in charge of the case to cause them to be served on the witnesses. Once the schedule is so fixed and witnesses are summoned the trial invariably proceeds from day to day. This is one method of complying with the mandates of the law. Of course, the High Court can monitor, supervise and give directions, on the administration side, regarding measures to conform to the legislative insistence contained in the above Section".

I do not know whether the High Courts have followed the aforesaid requests made by the Supreme Court that parliamentary mandates should be complied with for avoiding persecution of witnesses.

44

Can the destiny be so cruel to a damsel ?

I authored the judgment of the bench when a young lady reached the Supreme Court dissatisfied with the judgment rendered by the High Court of Kerala by which compensation awarded to her by the Railway Tribunal was considerably slashed down. It was the case of one Rethi Menon who while travelling in the express train on the night of 3.9.1996 suffered havoc due to a jerk. Her background was, as a child she lost her father and her widowed mother toiled hard to give her education. She passed degree course in commerce and secured a job in Bangalore. As she was in her early twenties, she was in search of better career prospects. Eventually she was called to appear for an interview at Trichur. She boarded the Island Express at Palakkad railway station. That journey finally turned out to be the most cursed one in her life.

When the train took momentum, Rathi Menon moved to the wash basin to have a face wash. During that time the jinxed train jerked violently at a turning and suddenly she was thrown out of the train. In that fall her back hit against a hard portion of the train and consequently her spinal cord was ruptured. In a trice that girl turned into a paraplegic.

She fell down from the train, its wheels ran over her right arm severing it fully from the shoulder point. The train, not knowing what it did to one of its genuine passengers, continued its normal running, leaving the maimed girl on the track itself during that dreadful night. She was unable to move her right leg which remained on the rail track. She would have expected "a good Samaritan" to reach her help but none came and hence the poor girl remained where she fell, bleeding and unattended. Every minute was horrendous to her as she was sinking in full consciousness. Most probably she would have lost all her hopes in life.

Alas !, within half an hour another train came along the same track which, without knowing that a horribly maimed human being was lying ahead, ran over her right leg, amputating that leg also. Thus within a span of less than an hour she became one-handed one-legged paraplegic.

While she remained on the track in such a condition for some more time, she was spotted by the driver of a locomotive who was shunting a railway engine. He stopped the engine and removed Rethi to the nearest hospital and was later shifted to a Medical College Hospital where she remained for a very long period. However, she remained immobile for ever. This was the long and short of the episode which made her to claim compensation.

When she claimed compensation from the railway department, its Tribunal awarded Rs. 6 lacs with the regret that it could not give more on account of a ceiling imposed by the statutory rules. But the mindless railway department dragged the hapless girl to the High Court of Kerala by filing an appeal challenging that award. I do not know whether the claimant would have filed any cross appeal for enhancement of the compensation awarded by the tribunal. When the appeal was boarded before a division bench headed by a senior lady judge, expectations were high from all concerned that merciful largesse would come out of the bench of the High Court. But what happened was just the other way around. It was unfortunate that division bench had chosen to slash down the compensation awarded in a substantial manner on the ground that the amount awarded by the Tribunal was based on the rules which prevailed on the date of the award and not on the date when the accident happened. It was against the said judgment that Rethi Menon moved the Supreme Court.

K. Sukumaran, senior advocate (he was a former judge of the High Court) appeared for Rethi Menon. His presentation evinced curiosity from others sitting in the court room, for, he was assailing the judgment authored by none other than his own better-half (Justice K.K. Usha - an eminent judge later became Chief Justice of Kerala High Court. After her retirement she was appointed Chairman of CEGAT (an acronym for Customs Excise Gold control Appellate Tribunal). After hearing the arguments of both sides, I wrote the judgment for the court. The first paragraph of it reads like this:-

"Misfortunes do not come single" is an old adage but even the author of that adage would not have imagined that multiplicity of misfortunes would visit the same person in a series on the same night, that too within the same hour. One may ask aghast, can the destiny be so cruel to a damsel?"

The claim of compensation was made under the provisions of Railways Act and its rules. As per the relevant rules "the amount of compensation payable in respect of death or injury shall be as specified in the schedule". The rules and the schedule were amended with effect from 1.11.1997. After such amendment the amount of compensation payable in a case of the present nature "shall be rupees four lacs". The division bench of the Kerala High Court said that as the accident happened prior to 1.11.1997, the victim cannot claim at the rate shown in the schedule as it stood on 1.11.1997. But we did not agree with that reasoning. What I said in our judgment is the following:-

"The asinine consequence of accepting the interpretation placed by the Division Bench of the High Court can be demonstrated through an illustration: If a person sustained injury in an accident in a train on 31.10.1997, and another person sustains the same kind of injury in another accident in a train the next day i.e. 1.11.1997, when both persons made separate applications before the same Claims Tribunal for compensation, the Tribunal can award Rs. 2 lakhs only in the first case and Rs. 4 lakhs in the second case. What a woeful discrimination, if not a glaringly unfair differentiation. See the interval between the two accidents of identical features. It was only a few hours, but the difference in the compensation amount is enormously high. Any court should avert an interpretation which would lead to such manifestly absurd fallout, unless the court is compelled otherwise by any mandatory provision.

Why the Central Government decided to make such a vast variation in the amount of compensation? It cannot be conceived that the Government wanted to make discrimination between those victims who suffered an injury in an accident prior to 1.11.1997 and those who suffered an identical injury in a similar accident on or after that date. The raison d'etre for making such variation is easily discernible. The Central Government wanted to update the compensation amount. Rupee value is not an unchanging unit in the monetary system. Students of economic history know that currency value remained static before the Second World War. But the post-Second World War witnessed the new phenomenon of vast fluctuations in money value of currency notes in circulation in each nation. When the US Dollar registered a steep upward rise, currencies in many other countries made downward slip. What was the value of one hundred rupees twenty years ago is vastly different from what it is today. This substantial change has caused its impact on the cost of living also.

The unjust consequences resulting from the interpretation which the High Court placed can be demonstrated in another plane also. If a person who sustained injury in a railway accident or in an 'untoward incident' was disabled from making an application immediately and he made the application a few years hence, is he to get the compensation in terms of the money value which prevailed on the date of the accident ? Suppose a Tribunal wrongly dismissed a claim after a few years of filing the application and the claimant approaches the High Court in appeal. As it happens quite often now, some High Courts could take up such an appeal only after the lapse of many years and if the appeal is decided in favour of the claimant after so many years, what a pity if the amount awarded is only in terms of the figure indicated on the date of the accident. From all these, we are of the definite opinion that the Claims Tribunal must consider what the Rules prescribed at the time of making the order for payment of the compensation".

On the above reasoning we enhanced the compensation very substantially in tune with the schedule prescribed with effect from 1.11.1997 onwards. The amount came to more than Rs. 6 lacs. We ordered that amount to carry interest at the bank rate until payment is made.

The above judgment evoked a lot of publicity. The photo of Rethi Menon was also published in many newspapers as she was moving on a wheel chair. One of the newspapers described the smiling Rethi Menon as she appeared in the photo that she is the real back bone of the office (where she works during the time of the judgment) in spite of the impairment of her back bone. After my retirement I came across articles published in some law magazines eulogizing the judgment in Supreme Court in Rethi Menon case. The articles supported the inclination of the Supreme Court for awarding substantial justice in a bountiful dimension to such deserving victims by adopting meaningful and humane interpretation of the letter of the law.

45

A charlatan in black robe

There are imposters in every profession. They are more in medical profession and less among engineers. But the legal profession too, unfortunately, does have a number of such charlatans. This is more so with the over crowding of legal profession at different levels - mofussils or district centres and the ever increasing tribunals and also the High Courts. I do not mention Supreme Court in this context because of the strict filtering conducted to add to the cadre known as Advocates on Record. Barring the Supreme Court level, imposters have crept into the legal profession at many centres. It is practically difficult to identify those mountebanks. Leaders of the profession have asserted time and again that once such characters are caught there should be no compromise with them. Nevertheless, weeding out such imposters among the professionals has not been taken up in a concerted manner. I had to deal with the case of a charlatan in black robe while sitting with Justice M.K. Mukherjee. In that case, I authored the judgment of the Supreme Court for the bench. It is interesting to narrate the facts of the case.

A young man named Mahalingam approached Nilgiri's Bar Association (Tamil Nadu) for admitting him as a member, representing that he was a qualified legal practitioner, having enrolled himself with the state Bar Council. Without suspecting the bona-fides of the application he was admitted to the membership of the Bar Association. He started his practice at the new station and built up a good clientele and involved himself in all the activities of the Association. Once he contested for the post of Secretary and won it. He continued as a busy legal practitioner in the courts at Nilgiris till 1985. But by then some members of the Bar who developed suspicion about his credentials made secret inquiries and discovered that he was imposturing as an advocate as his credentials were bogus. They brought it to the notice of the other members of the Bar Association who, in an emergent meeting, decided to launch prosecution against him. Mahalingam, sensing the developments against him, ducked out of the scene. A complaint was filed against him with the local police for offences of false personation and cheating etc. The police, after investigation, charge-sheeted him for those offences.

Mahalingam adopted a strategy to skip the punishment by pleading guilty to the charge and he prayed for mercy of the court. That strategy worked. The magistrate accepted the plea made by him and pardoned him with a warning to keep good behaviour in future and allowed him to go free.

Nilgiri Bar Association was not prepared to accept the decision of the magistrate. So they filed a revision petition before the High Court of Madras. That revision remained in limbo for about 10 years on the file of the High Court. Once it was boarded before a single judge, he heard it and pronounced the judgment. The single judge also felt that some leniency could be shown to the accused. He directed Mahalingam to pay Rs. 15,000/- to the Bar Association as donation for buying books to their library. However, the judge appreciated the alacrity and perseverance shown by the Bar and he advised them to forget the past and show magnanimity to the accused. The Judge pointed out two intervening developments which persuaded him to show such leniency. One was, Mahalingam joined a course of law later and passed law degree in 1988 and enrolled himself as an advocate with the Karnataka Bar Council. Second was, he expressed repentance over his conduct and he conducted himself well thereafter. But the Bar Association disputed the authenticity of the law degree claimed by Mahalingam and also his claim that he was conducting himself properly.

When the judgment was pronounced by the High Court, Mahalingam promptly dispatched a bank draft to the Bar Association for the amount but they with a matching promptness spurned down the ill-gotten money donated by the accused. The Bar Association rushed to the Supreme Court for special leave to appeal. We heard arguments of both sides. But we were not prepared to show any leniency to Mahalingam and hence we imposed a punishment of imprisonment for six months and a fine of Rs. 5,000/-. In our judgment I pointed out the following:-

"While adverting to the nature of the offence we bear in mind the necessity to weed out imposters in the professions which require special learning and training, particularly at a time when such imposters are proliferating in the society. Any leniency shown to such wiles would certainly tend to sprout up weeds at menacing scales. The case of the respondent is not one of single lapse or even multiple delinquencies confined to a few days. The long period of eight years during which the mountebank had successfully indulged in interloping as a qualified and learned counsel would have considerably eroded public confidence in the probity of the legal profession particularly in that area and besmirched the reputation of that Bar as the public might be looking upon every other member of the profession with suspecting eyes. The trial magistrate and the learned single Judge of the High Court, who found a repenting mind in the respondent, have failed to notice that repentance had dawned on him, even if that also was not a pretension, only when he reached a cul-de-sac. When he was masquerading himself everyday in sartorial costumes prescribed only for accredited members of the legal profession it did not occur to him even once during the long period of eight years to think of repentance. On the contrary, he was flourishing at large and had even become the secretary of the Bar Association. If the vigilant Bar had not discovered the trickery, perhaps he would still have persisted in his art of cheating. For all these reasons we are of the definite opinion that the crime committed by him should have been dealt with deterrently".

I learned that Mahalingam surrendered to jail and completed the period of imprisonment. A couple of years thereafter, my wife and I spent a few days in the guest house of Ootty. When members of the Nilgiri Bar Association knew about our stay in the summer resort, they approached me with a request to address the members of the Bar. They organised a well attended meeting of the Bar, in spite of being vacation period. The meeting was presided over by Justice P. Shanmugam of the Madras High Court who had the administrative charge of Nilgiri district. He was earlier a Judge of the Kerala High Court and I had the fortune to sit with him hearing many important cases. So his presence at the meeting gave me an added pleasure. In my speech I made a reference to the alacrity shown by the members of the Nilgiri Bar in maintaining the probity of the legal profession.

46

An Advocate was convicted for contempt of court

During the last year of my service as a Judge of the Supreme Court I had to deal with a number of corruption cases including some of the leading politicians in India. As some of these cases are still pending in the courts I do not wish to narrate either the facts or the court proceedings or even to mention the names of the personnels involved in such cases.

But those were the days when the bench of which I was a senior partner had to hear and decide a number of sensational cases. One of them related to a contempt of court proceeding initiated against an advocate of the Madras High Court by name "Sundaram". It arose from the following facts. Ram Jethmalani was a Minister in the Union Cabinet when Atal Bihari Vajpayee was the Prime Minister. He was Law Minister and later he held another important portfolio also. (Jethmalani had argued before me in certain important cases. I would rank him as one of the best lawyers of India on the criminal law side. By his becoming a Minister of the Union Cabinet I felt that the Supreme Court became poorer in the absence of such an outstanding legal luminary). While Jethmalani was the Minister, Dr. Justice A.S. Anand, Chief Justice of India made certain observation during a particular court proceeding and this observation created some ripples. When Jethmalani heard about it he tendered his resignation from the

Union Cabinet. Before he resumed his practice as an advocate he published a book. It contained a passage relating to the age of Dr. Justice A.S. Anand. A few days after the publication of the said book, a practising advocate of the Madras High Court by name Sundaram filed a criminal complaint in the court of a Judicial Magistrate in which the Chief Justice of India was made an accused alleging certain offences including misappropriation of money, fabrication of documents etc. on the premise that Dr. Justice A.S. Anand had already crossed the age of superannuation as narrated in the book authored by Jethmalani. The Judicial Magistrate before whom the complaint was filed dismissed it without taking cognizance of the offences alleged. But the complaint evoked a lot of publicity regarding the allegations contained in the complaint. The registry of the Supreme Court then requested the Chief Justice of India to consider whether the above conduct of Mr. Sundaram amounted to criminal contempt of court. But the CJI (Dr. Justice A.S. Anand) recused himself from considering the said request; instead, he placed the matter for consideration by the bench which, during that time, was dealing with criminal contempt cases. Thus it reached my court as cases like that were ordinarily posted before our bench during the relevant period.

We felt, prima-facie, that the conduct of Sundaram amounted to contempt of court and so we issued notice to him to appear before the Supreme Court to show cause why he should not be held guilty of contempt. Sundaram appeared and contested the charge and at the end of the proceedings we held him guilty of contempt of court. Accordingly we convicted him. We sentenced him to imprisonment for six months. However, a rider was added that if Sundaram filed an affidavit in the High Court stating that he would not commit contempt of court thereafter, the sentence of imprisonment would stand postponed indefinitely, and he would be required to undergo the sentence only in the event of violation of his assurance. Sundaram filed the affidavit before the High Court and thus escaped from jail.

The said judgment of ours was received with mixed reaction. While some applauded it, some others including very renowned persons criticised it mainly on the ground of the severe sentence of imprisonment imposed on him for contempt of court. I do not know why those critics did not appreciate the judicial grace shown in that judgment by putting a rider which helped the condemner to escape from the sentence without undergoing imprisonment even for a day as he availed himself of the option offered to him. Some newspapers published the substance of the judgment without mentioning the rider through which the condemner escaped imprisonment. Publication of such a news in a truncated manner did create the impression that the Supreme Court dealt with the condemner in a very harsh manner. But the truth was the other way around.

As a matter of fact, the question of age of Dr. Justice A.S. Anand had already been determined by the President of India on a previous occasion. The controversy was revived with the publication of the book authored by Ram Jethmalani. During the proceedings for contempt of court initiated against Sundaram, I got the opportunity to scrutinise the papers relating to the question of age of the former CJI. I have to record here that I was fully convinced that his age was what Dr. Justice A.S. Anand had himself mentioned at the time of his appointment as Judge of the Supreme Court of India. It is a sad thing that Dr. Justice A.S. Anand had to face this allegation again and again even after a constitutional authority had found in unambiguous terms that Dr. A.S. Anand did not do anything to camouflage his age.

47

Travelogue

I had the fortune to receive a large number of eminent citizens of this country in my official bungalow at New Delhi. By eminent citizens, I do not mean eminence by virtue of the office they held. No doubt many persons holding gubernatorial and diplomatic as well as sinecure positions visited us, but when I used the term eminence in this context it is on account of their acceptance in the society by the services they rendered. I mentioned the name Kiren Bedi earlier, now I wish to mention the name of V. Kurian. He was the life and soul of the Amul institution at Anand district in Gujarat state. When that institution was a very small co-operative society fostered by Sardar Vallabhai Patel in the early days of his public life, V. Kurian was picked up by him with a special mission to improve the impoverished village called Khera in Gujarat which consisted entirely of cattle graziers. Sardar Vallabhai patel wanted to pool the milk collected by the farmers of the area into one hotchpot for selling it at a reasonable margin to urban population so as to help the poor farmers to get their deserved profit. The society formed by Sardar Vallabhai Patel started growing from year to year and the profit margin earned by the villagers also started swelling up. The society could supply seeds for growing grass in plenty so that cattle could be provided with enough fodder. This enabled to beget better breed and the farmers to grow more yielding cows. Eventually the quantity of milk which each farmer could produce became much larger in quantity and the profit earned by the society started swelling up to high levels. The price for the milk was fixed at a much higher rate than the market price. This system brought about considerable improvement in the prosperity of the area. Larger areas of land were included in the activities of the society and the name of the locality was rechristened as 'Anand'. By the time Sardar Vallabhai Patel shifted his political activities to Delhi. At his instance V. Kurian was chosen as the successor in the milk society. The progress of the society continued to gallop up under his able stewardship. He was sent to England for specialising in milk and other diary products. The surplus garnered by him from the society was utilised to make a factory called "Amul" for producing various products from milk such as milk powder, ghee, butter, chocolates etc. The profit which the society earned from the new endeavour reached phenomenally high level. Again larger areas were included within the domain of the society so that benefits of Amul business were brought to a much larger number of people.

My wife and I visited Amul factory and we were taken around to various sections of one of the most sophisticated manufacturing enterprises in the world using diary products. We could also see the prosperity which the consumers of the factory could enjoy who were cattle herding people. V. Kurian visited me with his wife and gave me two cassettes one showing the various activities connected with Amul establishments and the other was the life of Sardar Vallabhai Patel whom he regarded as his mentor.

Having reached Gujarat I took care to visit particularly three important places associated with the life of the Father of the Nation. One of my long cherished desires was to visit the place of birth of Mahatma Gandhi – whom I regard as the greatest Indian after Sree Budha. I made it on 24th April 1999. It was a long journey from Ahmedabad to Porbandar and the road was not quite motorable. Porbandar was a small princely state in 1869. Today it is a flourishing sea port city abutting the Arabian sea. Gandhiji's father was the Prime Minister of Porbandar and hence his residential house was a palatial bungalow having 22 rooms. The room wherein Gandhi was born on the 2nd of October 1869 is now specially set apart for visitors. We were the only two visitors when my wife and I reached that house. I was sad that the house which should have been a place of pilgrimage for many Indians is not being used as such. We entered the small room wherein we saw a marked spot denoting it as the place where Mahatma Gandhi was born one hundred and thirty years before our visit. No doubt that spot was a blessed one having received the first touch of the one who became the Father of the Nation and attained the position of one of the greatest sages of India.

The second place of importance for me in Gujarat was Sabarmathy Ashram near Ahmadabad. The site of the Ashram was on the banks of the Sabarmathy river flowing about four miles north of Ahmedabad city. Gandhiji bought the land with the help of a merchant. He built a small house which later became the most famous Sabarmathy Ashram. The spinning wheel which eventually became the symbol of the great freedom struggle was actually fabricated at this place. Even today the Ashram and its premises have a solemn atmosphere. This became the real headquarters of Mahatma Gandhi's activities during the tumultuous years of his life.

The third important place I visited was the court room in Ahmedabad wherein the most famous but the shortest judicial trial ever took place, at the end of which Gandhi was sentenced to imprisonment for a period of six years for the offence of treason. The trial took place on 18th March 1922. The statement made by the accused Mohandas Gandhi has now become immortalised as they are now permanently inscribed in that court room. The sessions judge (one Mr. Robert Broomfield ICS) accepted the plea of guilty made by the accused Gandhi and the sentence was passed at the end of the shortest trial which lasted only for less than 100 minutes. The words of the Sessions Judge are quoted below:-

"The determination of a just sentence is perhaps as difficult a proposition as a judge in this country could have to face. The law is no respecter of persons. Nevertheless, it will be impossible to ignore the fact that you are in a different category from any person I have ever tried or am likely to have to try. It would be impossible to ignore the fact that in the eyes of millions of your countrymen, you are a great patriot and a great leader".

On hearing the above words from the judge, Gandhiji made the following submission:

"So far as the sentence itself is concerned I certainly consider it as light as any judge would inflict on me and so far as the whole proceedings are concerned I must say that I could not have expected greater courtesy".

Before the judge stepped down he bowed to the prisoner - a very unusual scene in any court - and the prisoner bowed in return. When I entered the room I read the words spoken by the judge to the prisoner which are now inscribed on a permanent record kept in that room. A shrill passed through my body as though I was present at the famous trial.

There are certain other places of attraction for a visitor in Gujarat such as Somanath Temple, the Gir forest (the largest natural habitat for the lions in India) and Akshar Dham Temple in Gandhi Nagar. When I read the news that three Pakistani militants stormed into the Akshar Dham Temple and killed a number of worshippers therein, I felt very sad. Akshar Dham Temple is probably the most beautiful and the largest of all the places of worship I would have visited in the world. I never knew before I stepped into this wonderful shrine that it was so. Only if one could go and see it the magnitude of the wonder created by human hands could be gauged. (Another Akshar Dham Temple was built in New Delhi by the Swaminarayan Trust. Three years after my retirement from the Supreme Court, we visited this new temple. I must concede that the new temple has, by all means, exceeded in the size and magnificence of the other temple in Gandhi Nagar).

Krishna Temple of Mathura in U.P. is being revered as the birth place of Lord Krishna. When I visited the temple with my wife, we both felt that the temple should have been converted into a stupendous shrine, but I felt sad that now it is being poorly maintained apart from being too small a size for commemorating the birth place of such a great Lord. The legendary stories surrounding the birth of Sree Krishna, his childhood and infantile pranks could be unfurled in and around Mathura, but it is a pity that no care has been taken to commemorate the important events which have come down to us through folklore and epics. But the battle field of Kurukshetra in Haryana is different. It is well maintained. This place is believed to be a terrain whereat the most revered divine exhortations in the celebrated book Geetha were made by Lord Krishna as the charioteer of Arjuna, the valiant brigadier of the battle of kurukshetra. A sprawling park has been created as the background with large number of shady trees. A huge chariot depicting the story of Geetha recitals is kept in the middle portion of the park. Important verses of Geetha are seen inscribed at different spots in the vast garden.

My wife and I could visit two important Buddhist shrines, one at Sikkim near the border of Tibet and the other in the state of Arunachal Pradesh. Both shrines have huge Buddhist monasteries attached to them where monks young and old, with tonsured heads were seen sitting in meditation. They all wore orange coloured cassocks. A statue of Lord Budha is the cynosure at both shrines as the size of them is immeasurably enormous. Adolescent children were seen recruited as trainee monks wearing religious costumes and they were playing around in ecstasy.

"Hazrat Bal" is one of the most important Moslem shrines in the world. It is situated near Sreenagar in Kashmir. It is here that "the holy relic" of the prophet (one strand of hair) is being preserved and hence this shrine acquired very great focus of attraction. The trustee permitted my wife also to get inside the shrine and all that she had to do was to cover her head with the shawl. I wore a fur cap and we both removed our foot wears at the entrance. The shrine was originally not as magnificent as it is now. It was rebuilt in the present form by Sheik Abdullah (the first Prime Minister of Kashmir after India attained independence) who was a great devotee of this shrine. The people say that Sheik Abdullah had even begged for money in order to rebuild the mosque. "Hazrat Ball" has earned world wide publicity in 1958 when the holy relic was stolen from a tight security zone. But fortunately it was recovered very soon. The then Union Home Minister Lal Bahadur Shastry had dashed down to Sreenagar for ensuring that the recovered strand was the same as the original. Had it not been recovered so soon the commotion started with the disappearance of the relic would have snowballed into a wild fire in the valley blowing for weeks if not months. The second episode connected with the Hazrat Bal shrine took place when half a dozen terrorists sneaked into the structure with highly explosive substance and threatened to smash that place of worship unless some of their demands were conceded to by the government. But the government adopted a very stiff stand, the specially recruited commandos surrounded the mosque and gave ultimatum to the terrorists to surrender if they wished to escape. Before the time limit expired the commandos succeeded in killing all the terrorists who were inside the mosque. After a long period of interval a similar incident was repeated by some other terrorists who too were killed before they could destroy Hazrat Bal. When we visited the shrine we had to pass through many filters of security barriers, though we were spared from being checked at close proximity on account of the office I held at that time.

"Golden Temple" at Amritsar is perhaps the most important Sikh shrine in the world. No doubt it is the most beautiful place of worship with its shining golden exterior. We visited golden temple on 5.3.1999. It consists of the main shrine wherein the Grandh Sahib (the sacred book) is kept and the structure is covered by a dome made of gold as the outer layer. It glitters always, particularly during evenings when the sun rays focus on it. This is called Harmandir Sahib. It is surrounded by a rectangular pond the water of which is even potable. Outside the pond is a sprawling array of galleries, on one side of it is the "Akal Takth" which unfortunately got smashed to smithereens during the infamous "Operation Blue Star" performed by the Indian Army for finishing off a large number of militants under the leadership of Bhindran Wala who turned "Akal Takth" into the headquarters of Akal Khalsa for carrying out terrorist activities to establish a new nation called "Khalistan". Akal Takth, after the operation blue star, was re-built by the army people on the orders of Indira Gandhi. But what was so rebuilt had been demolished subsequently by the Sikh devotees and the present Akal Takth has been built in accordance with the principles embodied in their religion. The importance of Akal Takth was understood by me only after it was seen. Akal means 'timeless' which is an attribute to God. Takth means, the 'seat'. Thus Akal Takth was considered to be the seat of God wherefrom edicts of the supreme council of Sikh religion are being pronounced.

My wife and I were honoured by the Jathaders of the Golden Temple by tying a turban on the head and religious precepts were recited. They presented a large framed photo of Golden Temple and also a Kirpan (small sword) as token of the honour conferred on me.

We could visit the rarest sarcophagus (ancient coffin) situated at Rozabal located in the middle of the old town of Sreenagar (Anzimar). The word "Rauza" denotes the tomb of the celebrated saintly personality. This is the tomb wherein the saint by name 'Yuz Asaf' was buried about 2000 years ago. The visit to "Rozabal" was the real motive which gave moving inspiration for undertaking a trip to Jammu and Kashmir at a time when it was risky to do so. The importance of Rozabal is the following:- I happened to read a book written by a German scholar-cum-researcher by name 'Holger Kerston' under the title "Jesus lived in India". The author does not believe that after crucifixion of Jesus he had ascended to heaven as Christians believe, instead Jesus travelled through the "silk route" (an ancient trade route for carrying silk products, started from Antioch and stretched up to China, passing through Damascus, Iraq, Iran, Afghanistan, Tibet and Himalaya) Jesus finally reached Kashmir which, in ancient centuries, gave asylum to the people belonging to one of "the twelve lost tribes of Israel". According to Holger Kerston, Jesus wanted to preach "the Kingdom of God" to all the lost tribes of Israel. One of his disciples (St. Thomas) was deputed by him to the south east Asia (the reference is evidently to Kerala) with the same mission. The author further says that he himself went to Kashmir in search of some relic in order to confirm the theory that Jesus lived in Kashmir during his final stage of life. When the author reached Rozabal he wanted to undertake some excavation work and he obtained permission from Farukh Abdullah, the then Chief Minister of Jammu and Kashmir. He finally came across a cluster of tombs of some ancient spiritual sages who were buried there hundreds of years ago. He says that he came across marks of foot-prints on all the tombs, perhaps as the identification marks given to such tombs by the devotees. One of the tombs in the cluster was proved to be the burial place of a Jew (He gives some reasons to probabilise that theory). When modern scientific standards were applied, it was revealed to be as old as 2000 years. Initially there was no foot print carving available on that tomb as was found on many other nearby tombs. But when further excavation was made vax and mud mixed together had to be removed for a depth of about six feet. When the excavation reached the bottom they noticed two foot prints. The mould of them was taken on plaster of paris and got them photographed. A close look at the photos instilled in the mind of an on looker a shrill as both foot prints contained permanent scar marks. According to Holger Kerston those scars represent nails stricken wounds on the feet. The author propounded the theory that the said tomb could be the place where Jesus Christ was finally buried in Kashmir.

After reading the above book authored by Holger Kerston, I was not only eager to visit the Rozabal but my heart throbbed to see it. I conveyed my desire to Dr Justice B.P. Seraf (who was the Chief Justice of Jemmu and Kashmir High Court) and told him that I have a very great urge to see the tomb, whether the theory is right or wrong. But Justice Seraf cautioned me against the proposed visit on account of tight security reasons. But I insisted on seeing it. The I.G. of Police called on me at the circuit house (where we were accommodated) and finally he agreed to chart out a programme. Justice Seraf also accompanied us. We wore the dress of Kashmiris and went to Rozabal in a taxi car without creating any doubt about us. We reached the enclosure inside of which the cluster of sarcophagus are preserved. We could only remain there for ten minutes as we were warned to return to the car at the earliest.

I must here say a few words about Dr. Justice Seraf. He was first introduced to me as a Judge of the Bombay High Court. He earned a reputation as one of the quick disposing judges of the country. His doctorate is in Income Tax Law, but he authored some of the most useful text books in the law of arbitration. He was surely a fine metal to be elevated to the Supreme Court, but he missed it for reasons not known to me. Eventually, we became good friends and even now we maintain it.

I do not vouchsafe that the tomb mentioned above is a place where Jesus Christ was buried. It is a theory of Holger Kerston which he very emphatically put through in the book mentioned above. After my retirement as Judge of the Supreme Court, I could fulfill a long cherished desire to see the important places concerning Jesus Christ. So my wife and I joined a group and visited Bethlehem, Nazareth, Galilee, Jericho and Jerusalem. We also visited the ancient land of Egypt and saw the landmarks of the gift of Nile including the huge pyramids and the Sphinx. Visiting USA and Canada came into the agenda because we were invited to inaugurate FOKANA Biennial held at Rochester.

Keralites living in America used to form associations in their local cities. All those associations have formed into a consortium called "Federation of Kerala Associations of North America". Its acronym is "FOKANA". Members of the consortium assembled with members of their families once in two years at a selected place. In 1998 the festival of FOKANA was held at Rochester (A city situated about 300 miles north of Chicago). The Vice President of the consortium then was Mr. Mammen C. Jacob @ (Bobby). He came to New Delhi and invited me and my wife to be present at the inaugural function of the festival. I agreed as it was an occasion for my wife to visit USA (She could not accompany me when I went to USA earlier in 1976). But there was an official snag for me because the registry of the Supreme Court told me that Judges of the Supreme Court required sanction of the President of India for going abroad. So I sent a letter requesting the President to grant sanction. I got a reply advising me to avail myself of the fund from the Central government to go abroad. I felt that for attending a private function I shall not draw public money. I approached Justice A.S. Anand (who was then a senior judge and would become Chief Justice of India eventually) He advised me that no sanction of the President was necessary when the judge was invited by friends and relatives of a foreign country. Sanction is required, according to him only when a judge was invited by a foreign government or agency to attend any official function. So I wrote to the President seeking permission to withdraw my request for sanction as the proposed visit was only for attending a function held by an association of Kerala people.

Biennial of Fokana conclave held at Rochester was a very colourful function. Rochester was a beautiful city but its population was very thin. On account of the city's proximity to Niagra Falls, the city has attained tourist attraction. The inaugural function was preceded by a procession of the participants in which they displayed pageant of the Kerala traditional values. In the absence of a live elephant they made a dummy and fabricated it simulating it as a caparisoned tusker. Decorated umbrellas besides some ancient costumes including 'Kathakali; of Kerala were displayed accompanied by 'Panchavadyam'. The procession became a special attraction to the small population of Rochester. The inaugural function was conducted at the banquet hall of a five star hotel. The organisers had requisitioned four such hotels situated close to each other as a large number of participants had to be accommodated for three days. The ceremony of inauguration was by lighting the lamb which task was performed by my wife. Dr. Roy P. Thomas a leading figure of the Malayalee community delivered the welcome speech. He was a renowned speaker both in English and Malayalam. His welcome speech was studded with satire and facts. I delivered the inaugural address. The venue hall was jam-packed with participants. I delivered my speech in English as I sensed that the audience consisted mostly of new generation Keralites in USA who were not familiar with speaking their mother tongue Malayalam. The function was also addressed by Oommen Chandy, (Former Chief Minister of Kerala), T.K. Ramakrishnan, (who was then Home Minister of Kerala), Mammen Mathai M.L.A. and K.M. Roy (a renowned journalist) and Jesudasan (a cartoonist of fame). A music concert was performed under the leadership of Kerala's celebrity singer Jesudas which rendered the function a rare gaiety and splendor. On no other occasion could one see such a huge confluence of Keralites in a foreign country. For them Fokana biennial was not only a festival, it provided occasion for youngsters to meet their counterparts and hence it became a fertile ground for sprouting matrimonial alliances.

A few homely get together were arranged for us at cities such as New York, Houston, Chicago, Boston and Fort Lordale (in Florida). Among them one was arranged by my relatives living in New York and New Jersey. It was organized by T.S. Chacko, His wife (Leelamma) belongs to my family. T.S. Chacko was then the Vice President of FOKANA. He was a very energetic person. My wife and me were thrilled seeing a large number of relatives gathered together in such a far away land to share the joy of having one of their kith and kin in their midst.

When we visited the World Trade Centre in New York and reached the top floor of the tallest structure little could we comprehend that this monstrous twin sky scrapers would become incinerated into ashes with five thousand human beings burnt alive. But it did happen on the 11th September 2001 which transformed the American society into a frightened people. Prior to that episode the security checks for air passengers at all Airports in USA were restricted only to some formalities. I remember when I visited USA in 1976, I could get into the aircraft within five minutes of reaching the domestic airport. Of course in 1998 security checks became much more tightened as the identity of the passenger had to be ensured by the officials.

But after 11.9.2001 a passenger has to undergo not merely stringent and rigorous and very elaborate check procedure, but agonizing hours to have the security checks completed. Journey by air in USA became a harrowing ordeal. How long this would continue cannot be gauged even by the officials.

My wife and I reached the airport of New York to fly to Houston on 27.6.1998. We could make it only a few minutes after the time limit for reporting at the airport i.e. an hour ahead of the time of departure. So the officials of the flight refused to admit us into the aircraft as we were expected to reach there at least one hour ahead. (Now it is expanded to three hours ahead of the departure time even for domestic flights). Late Mammen Mathai MLA was also with us to fly to Houston. We both were to attend a function on the next morning at Houston and so we pleaded with the officials to relax the condition of the time to report at the airport on the ground that we were delayed due to very heavy traffic on the road and that we were quite unfamiliar with the city. But the officials politely answered that heaviness of vehicular traffic in New York city during the evening hours was not an unusual feature, but the fact that luggage carrier of the air craft was already closed and the seats booked for us were already allotted to somebody else prevented the officials from admitting us into the air craft. We moved to another counter and enquired with the official whether he could help us to reach Houston on the same night. He collected our tickets, we found him tapping on the computer buttons several times. He then told us that he had discovered a way out to help us.

There was a flight bound to depart from New York after about two hours destined to Atlanta City and there would be another flight from that city to Houston after an interval of half an hour of arrival there at. However, he cautioned us of the risk involved that if for any reason the first flight was delayed in reaching Atlanta City the other flight would not wait for our arrival. As we had no other alternative we had to take the risk, we requested the officials to clear our passage in the flight bound for Atlanta City. Again there were other two problems. One was, our hosts in Houston might be waiting at that airport expecting us in the flight already booked by us. It would be an uphill task to contact them as we did not have their cell number. The second was, if the flight to Atlanta City was delayed, we had absolutely no idea where to stay during night. The first problem was solved by our friends in New York who succeeded in getting the lines to reach our hosts who were waiting at the airport of Houston. As we reached Atlanta City we noticed, to our surprise, that all arrangements were made for our onward journey to Huston.

But an unforeseen snag cropped up in the meantime, since Mammen Mathai MLA had kept his travel documents including his passport in his luggage which was already consigned to the aircraft. The airport officials wanted him to show his identity when he reached at the door of the aircraft ready to be airborne at Atlanta city. He had carried his identity card issued by the Kerala State Legislature Secretariat, but when he produced it the officials looked at it and asked "what is meant by Kerala ?" He returned the identity card to the MLA and insisted on some other identity document. Evidently that official had not heard about the state called Kerala. It was a tense situation as the security check up had been strictly tightened during those days. When Mammen Mathai was asked to wait out of the queue and other passengers were asked to move in, an idea flashed in my mind that I could help using my diplomatic passport. I offered to identify Mammen Mathai as a state legislator in India. We were relieved when the official agreed to act on what I said because my diplomatic passport did show that I was a judge of the Supreme Court of India.

"Disney World" in Florida was on our itinerary. Mammen C. Jacob made all arrangements for our trips to various places in Florida. Oommen Chandy, his wife and son, besides Mammen Mathai were also with us when we visited different places in Florida. Sight seeing at Disney World was arranged for two days and we were to stay in the nearby city of Orlando during the intervening night. (As I had already seen Disney World in 1976, there was nothing new for me, but this was the first visit of my wife). I do not wish to narrate the various items of magic and marvels we witnessed at Disney World, but I wish to mention a small episode which gave me an inkling of the popularity of Oommen Chandy in the assembly constituency from which he won all the elections for more than three decades. This happened on the evening of the first day. We had a very tiring and hectic day seeing around various spectacular shows in the magic world. We could reach our hotel at Orlando only at 11 p.m., all we then needed was falling into the bed as we were so tired. We had to set out again to proceed to Disney World by early morning and so we decided not to waste any more time to take rest. But alas, two gentlemen (belonging to the constituency of Chandy) were seen waiting to take him to their house situated at a distance of 100 miles away from Orlando. Due to fatigue, another journey covering a total distance of 200 miles up and down was almost out of question for us. But the two gentlemen were found insisting on their MLA to accompany them on the premise that they would be dropped back very soon. I over heard them saying that the road condition in USA was so good that it was an easy drive during night. I then intervened and told as could be heard by all concerned. "However much perfect is the road condition in USA, the distance is 100 miles to your place and that cannot be covered in less than 2 1/2 hours which means a minimum of 5 hours for journey alone and a couple of hours more for the visits at the two houses". Those gentlemen realised the uphill task and therefore they practically gave up the idea of persuading their MLA to go with them. After I had a little sleep for about a couple of hours I woke up and walked through the corridor to see the Orlando city in night. I found Oommen Chandy's son sleeping alone in his room. Mammen Mathai disclosed to me that the boy's parents were waiting till I slept and then they left with the two gentlemen of Puthuppally. Early next morning the couples returned to the hotel after a long car journey up and down the houses of those two men. During the entire night Oommen Chandy and wife would have been in the car. No wonder Oommen Chandy never failed in any election at Puthuppally. Later he became the Chief Minister of Kerala.

My wife and I had to travel by air from Houston (which was almost far in the south of U.S.A.) to Chicago. We boarded our flight after informing Dr. Roy Thomas our friend who was a very prominent Malayali living in Chicago. But our flight could reach only up to a midway city called Cincinnati as the pilot got a message that the airport of Chicago was closed down due to a tornado. As we reached Cincinnati late in the night we were told that no flight to Chicago would take off until the airport was cleared. However, I contacted Dr. Roy over the phone and he moved the airport authorities to see that we were accommodated in the first flight to be flown from Cincinnati destined to Chicago. But there was no sign of any improvement of the weather at Chicago for hours together. We were really stranded at the airport of Cincinnati. By about 3 a.m. a lady from the counter called out my name saying that Dr. Roy Thomas was on the line. Roy informed me that airport at Chicago would be reopened very soon and that we would be accommodated in a flight scheduled to leave Cincinnati around 4 a.m. These things were arranged by Dr. Roy remaining at the airport of Chicago. We heaved a sigh of relief after getting into the aircraft. Dr. Roy Thomas was seen waiting for us with a smile at the airport of Chicago to receive us without even pretending that he had to sacrifice his sleep during the entire night. Our stay in Chicago for a few days was made very pleasant by the hospitality arranged by Dr. Roy and his wife Elsie. In fact, we owed to the couple for a very memorable visit to that part of USA from where we proceeded to Rochester to attend Fokana functions. Three years later I visited USA again. I was invited to deliver key note address at the biennial of "Kerala Medical Graduates in North America". They are a big group. They with their families assembled in the auditorium of Hiat Regency hotel, Chicago. The conference was preceded by a wonderful cruise in a ship through the Michigan Lake. This time I first went to Houston as guest of Mathew Daniel. He and his wife arranged very nice sight seeing around. We went to San Antonio by car and on the way visited the famous "Natural Bridge Cavern". It is a net work of natural caves containing the rarest natural formulations of transparent rocky substances. Once you get into the cavern you have to walk even miles far into a depth seeing around amazing formulations in different shapes. One of them is named "the Peacock throne" as per its shape. The aquatic scenes at San Antonio were amazing. They are all man made wonders attracting lot of tourists to that area. I visited one of the trial courts in the state of Illinois to acquaint myself of how the American Judicial system provides help to the litigants at the grass root level. Of course, with the advent of the information technology the evidence collecting process has registered significant progress. I could witness the Video Conferencing by which oral evidence of witnesses was collected without they being physically brought to the court room. I am glad that Video Conferencing has now been adopted in India, though it remains only in a nascent state.

We could visit Russia officially on the invitation of the President of the apex Court of Russia. Chief Justice of India Dr. A.S. Anand, Justice S.P. Barucha and myself with our spouses were received at Moscow airport by the Indian Ambassador and staff. My nephew Pradeep who is settled down in Russia also reached the airport. He felt thrilled when he found his name specially printed at the banquet hosted by the Indian embassy at Moscow. The city of Moscow impressed me as one of the most beautiful cities in the world, particularly the Moscow river flowing through the middle of it was enchanting as our visit was during the summer season. We were told that during winter all those places would look like a white cloth covered around. Nobody in Russia could speak English, hence we required translators at all official functions. We attended the receptions hosted by the Judges of the Supreme Court of Russia, the Speaker of the Parliament and the law Ministry of Russia. As I was very eager to see "Kremlin" which created history during Stalin's reign we spent a lot of time seeing it and the Red Squire situated near thereto. Except the mausoleum of Lenin there is nothing to remember about the long rule of the Communist Party of Soviet Union as everything else had been erased. The Cathedrals, built during "Emperor Iwan the Terrible", was described by the guide as a place where many were persecuted during the Czarist rule. We visited the most beautiful cathedral in Moscow. During Stalin's regime this Cathedral had been converted into a "Bale Theatre". After Stalin's death the administration reconverted it as cathedral. It is called "Jesus the Savior cathedral". St. Peters Burg was the capital of Russia during the pre communist era. It is truly one of the most beautiful cities in the world. The huge palaces and cathedrals, particularly St. Issac Cathedral, provided a special charm unlike other western cities. In my view, St. Issac cathedral excelled in many respects the cathedrals situated elsewhere. During Stalin's rule the city was rechristened as "Leningrad", but now the original name St. Petersburg has been restored. The geographical location of the city rendered it a peculiarity. The city would be in dark practically without sun rays on many days during winter. Conversely, the city would be always in day light during nights in summer. In fact, the sun never sets on a particular day in the month of July and they call it "White day". We were fortunate in seeing the city on one of those days when it was almost a white day, as there was no nightfall at all. The huge palace where the Czars of Russia lived with their family has now been converted as a museum and hence a great tourist attraction. The monetary unit of Russia "rubble" was earlier competing with the US dollar when Soviet Union was in the zenith of its power, but when we visited Russia the rubble was even cheaper than the Indian rupee.

48

Attack on the Parliament House fizzled out

It happened on December 13, 2001. It could have been a terrible national calamity, but the republic of India escaped only on account of providential care. During the forenoon I was hearing arguments in a three Judge bench of the Supreme Court. Senior advocates Ram Jathmalani, Kapil Sibal and Additional Solicitor General Mukul Rotagi were engaged in the arguments on the question whether bail could be granted to Lalu Prasad Yadav and Dr. Jagannathan Misra, both of whom were former Chief Ministers of Bihar state. The Central Bureau of Investigation registered a number of cases against them for offences under the Prevention of Corruption Act in the infamous "animal fodder scam". Our bench had ordered the accused to be released on bail on a previous occasion in some of the cases involved in the fodder scam. As soon as those accused were released on bail they were again arrested in connection with some of the remaining cases in the same batch. While arguments reached full swing, the Attorney General for India (Soli Sorabjee) rushed into the court hall and requested us to retire to the chambers immediately as he had information that Parliament House was being besieged by a gang of armed terrorists. It was reported that both chambers of Parliament (Lok Sabha and Rajya Sabha) were almost fully occupied by Members of Parliament and that the terrorists were armed with highly explosive and lethal substances. The Supreme Court building is situated within calling proximity from the parliament complex. On being alerted, we the judges suddenly retired to our chambers. The advocates rushed out of the court halls. I learnt that in the same way all judges of the Supreme Court in different courts retired to their chambers on being alerted. The few minutes which followed thereafter were full of suspense as we had no news of what exactly was happening out side. But hardly half an hour passed, officers of the Registry of the Supreme Court informed us that the attack was thwarted successfully by the security police and all those involved in the attack of parliament were killed. Thus we heaved a sigh of relief, though we did not get details of all what happened.

When learnt the details later we realized that it was a well orchestrated scheme prepared by highly trained terrorists to capture parliament and keep the members thereof as captives to bargain for certain non-negotiable issues concerning the nation. The terrorists reached the parliament complex in an Ambassador car which was painted with the colour resembling the vehicles of the security personnels. A huge quantity of RDX (highly explosive substance which can smash even a huge building into smithereens) was concealed inside its dickey. A very thin wire was used to connect the RDX stock with the switch of a battery fitted on the person of one of the terrorists. He was trained to press the switch immediately on getting a particular signal and had he done so, the RDX would have exploded and in a minute the entire parliament complex would have turned into a heap of rubbles. I cannot say whether such an explosion would involve the Supreme Court complex also. Some people said that it would have. There were about six terrorists who formed into a suicide squad. When their vehicle entered the parliament complex, the official car of the Vice President of India (who was ex-officio Vice Chairman of the Rajya Sabha) was in the process of being negotiated by its chauffer to keep it ready for the dignitary to enter. But this was not anticipated by the terrorists and hence their car accidentally collided with the vehicle of the Vice President. Perhaps, in that collision the wire which connected the RDX with the suicide would have got snapped. In a daring counter attack made by the security personnels, all but the last among the terrorists were killed. Then the last man pressed the battery switch, but the RDX in the dickey of the car did not explode because the wire was already snapped a few minutes ago. Had it not been so, what would have been the extent of the calamity. It could not be estimated by any one, particularly because about 300 Members of Parliament were then inside the building. Even today it is an enigma to me why the crucial wire was broken at the most crucial minute and saved the Indian Parliament from total ruination.

Though all the Parliament Members were saved and all the attackers were killed, the cost which the nation had to pay for the salvage operation was the lives of six daring patriotic policemen. The striking feature is that they knew that they all would be killed in the course of the blitz launched against the terrorists. Still they acted and sacrificed themselves on the altar of the nation and the Republic was saved by them. They deserve to be remembered by the nation. The Parliament complex should contain monuments to immortalise them. At least the busts of their statues should be erected at a suitable spot of the sprawling Parliament complex for the future generation to know the personnel who saved our Parliament by sacrificing their lives and to pay homage to them.

Apart from those who were caught and killed by the security policemen in the daring action there were men who worked behind the curtain to chalk out a plan to capture the Parliament with the members inside, Central Bureau of Investigation finally caught almost all of them and charge sheeted them. They were tried for various offences. The trial court convicted some of them. The conviction of one among them gave rise to a controversy regarding his involvement in the conspiracy. There was school of thought which propagated his non-involvement in the conspiracy, while a contrary school held out that he was one of the kingpins. Anyway, such controversies came to a rest when the apex court finally absolved him from the charges. Still one main accused Afsal Guru continues to create headlines as the Supreme Court finally confirmed the death sentence passed on him. While one set of people demand the execution of the death sentence without further delay, another set of people clamour for Presidential clemency in favour of commuting death sentence to life imprisonment. Political as well as communal colour is seen reflected in the controversy regarding the capital punishment imposed on Afsal Guru.

Thus the fizzled out attack on the Indian Parliament still continues to have the embers burning in one form or the other. But the nation is miraculously saved by the unseen hand of the Almighty when the thin wire which connected with RDX stock with the switch on the battery of the suicide got snapped in the encounter.

49

The last sitting as a judge

My last sitting as a judge, whatever hierarchical level I functioned, was on 29.1.2002. This was because, by mid-night of 29th January, I attained the age of 65. According to Article 124(2) of the Constitution of India, a judge shall hold office in the Supreme Court of India only until he attains the age of 65. Nevertheless my last sitting, for hearing regular appeals in the Supreme Court, happened to be on Thursday the 24th January 2002. Normally, there would be nothing special to be remembered about the last day of sitting in the court as that would be a winding-up day. But in my case that day turned out to be one of most exciting days in my judicial life on account of a particular case. I heard arguments in that case along with Mr. Justice Pukhan.

When the case was taken up, the time was about 3.30 p.m. and then neither me nor Justice Pukhan was prepared to take up any new appeal as we had only thirty minutes more to reach the end of the sitting hours. A lady advocate stood up and reminded us that on a previous occasion we agreed that this case would be taken up out of turn as the accused in that case was remaining in jail for nearly eight years. So we thought we could at least hear the facts of the case and thus reach the time limit of 4 p.m. But when the facts of the case were narrated in brief, a flash of thought passed through my mind that it was not a case to be left half baked. The facts in that case, briefly stated, were the following:-

Two accused were convicted of murder and both were sentenced to imprisonment for life by a Sessions Judge. In appeal filed by them, the High Court confirmed the conviction and sentence as against both. The second accused alone filed Special Leave petition in the Supreme Court, but that petition was dismissed at the admission stage itself as the Supreme Court found no merit in it. Subsequently the other accused in the case filed Special Leave Petition as against the judgment of the High Court, in so far as, it related to his conviction and sentence. During arguments the advocates said that the plea would be confined to a limited point regarding the nature of the offence for which he could have been convicted. Hence notice was issued on that Special Leave Petition to the state concerned. The state of Maharashtra entered appearance through their state counsel.

When the lady advocate began to narrate the facts of the case, a spark of thought kindled in my mind that unless the appeal was allowed in the case, there would be mis-carriage of justice. The admitted prosecution version in that case was like this:-

The victim (the deceased) walked down a staircase while the two accused were standing at the bottom. The deceased asked the accused, "why did you implicate me in a false case ?" On hearing this utterance, both assailants took out their knives and stabbed the deceased on the chest. He died later in the hospital. Before he died he gave a dying declaration, in which he narrated the incident which was the same version as the prosecution case. When the postmortem examination was conducted the doctor smelt alcohol from the body.

After hearing the narration of those facts I asked the counsel for the state of Maharashtra; "if the synopsis of the prosecution case was as narrated, was it not a case for reducing the conviction to the second degree murder. (in which it is not a case of murder under law, but only culpable homicide not amounting to murder). I asked the counsel whether it was possible for the accused to fear that the deceased was then in a quarrelling mood.

If the accused had ventured to answer the query of the deceased by saying either yes or no, the situation would have been aggravated. If the answer was 'yes' the deceased could have felt greatly angered and if the answer was 'no' that would also have made the deceased angry. In such a situation the accused would have developed apprehension that the deceased might assault them, at least by pushing them down, if not a grievous assault. If the accused apprehended that grievous hurt would be caused to the accused, then the right of the accused under law, being the right of self-defense, could even stretch up to causing the death of the deceased. But, on the contrary, if the conduct of the deceased was not enough to instill the apprehension that grievous hurt would be caused, the right of self-defence would not entitle him to inflict fatal injury to the deceased. Nevertheless, in such an event, the right of self-defence would be restricted to a much lesser degree. Had the accused inflicted only bodily hurt to the deceased the law would protect the accused. So if the accused in such a situation, had inflicted fatal injuries to the deceased, he was liable to be convicted for a lesser offence. (it is known as "exceeding the right of self-defense"). The offence then would go down to a lower degree which is called 'culpable homicide not amounting to murder'. In the present case the situation was such that the accused could have feared that the deceased was in an aggressive mood and hence accused would be justified in giving him a push to thwart the aggression. But the accused inflicted fatal injuries and thus exceeded his right.

When the above legal position was discussed in open court, the counsel for the state of Maharashtra very fairly expressed that he did not intend to take up a different stand. As my colleague Justice Pukhan also concurred with my thinking, we decided to alter the conviction from first degree murder to the lesser degree of culpable homicide and reduced the sentence of life imprisonment to the period which he had already undergone. I dictated judgment of the court and ended it by directing the jail authorities "to set the first accused free forthwith".

Normally the case would have ended with the said judgment. But I had another flash of thinking. If the legal position was what we held regarding the first accused, how the legal position was different as for the second accused on the same set of facts. But the hurdle for the second accused was that the Special Leave Petition filed by him earlier happened to be dismissed without going into the merits of the case. This created an unsavoury situation. On the same set of facts, one of the two accused could be convicted only for the second degree homicide, then how could the other accused be convicted for a higher degree of homicide and direct him to suffer a sentence of a much longer term of imprisonment. This became a baffling question before us.

We then reminded ourselves of the fundamental right enshrined in Article 21 of the Constitution "No person shall be deprived of his life and liberty save in accordance with the procedure established by law". If according to the procedure established by law, he could only have been convicted of a lesser offence, could he be deprived of his liberty for a period beyond what he would be legally liable. Would the fact that the conviction and sentence passed on him were confirmed by the court earlier render the Supreme Court helpless in granting his fundamental right under Article 21.

After discussion at the Bar we decided to extend the same benefit to the second accused as well. For that purpose I dictated the following portion also in open court. "The spirit of Article 21 beckons us, notwithstanding the finality attached to the earlier order of the Supreme Court by which the Special Leave Petition filed by the first accused was dismissed. He could not be detained in prison even one day more than what he would have been liable under law. Hence we apply the same benefit to the second accused which we had granted to the first accused. We therefore, direct the jail authorities to release the second accused also forthwith, unless he was required to be detained in any other case".

After the above dictation was given I looked at the clock of the court, the needle showed that it was 4 p.m., the end of the day.

I cannot, but record here a comment which the Maharashtra state counsel passed in open court.

"Your Lordship cannot have a more befitting finale for the glorious judicial carrier than what it took place now".

50

Prelude to departure

The Central Bureau of Investigation (CBI) is truly the premier investigating agency in India. It attracted great confidence of the people of India over the years regarding a high calibre investigation conducted by them into serious criminal offences involving important personages. This might be on account of a unique position which the CBI enjoyed in India as no other agency was fixed above them. The only drawback which I have noticed in the functioning of the CBI is its disability to carry out investigation totally free from all political strings. CBI sometimes could not act contrary to the dictates of the Prime Minister of India or the Home Minister of India. This is not because of any illegal compulsion exerted on them but due to practical applications. When CBI was headed by Dr. C.R. Raghavan, who was one of the best police cops in India, the prestige of the CBI reached its zenith. Supreme Court on many occasions engaged the CBI in a profitable manner by directing them to conduct investigations into a number of sensational episodes. Dr. Raghavan as Director of the CBI conducted a conference at Vigyan Bhavan to commemorate the name of CBI's founder Dr. Kohli. I was invited to deliver "Dr. Kohli memorial lecture" on a volatile subject "Anatomy of Corruption". The Vigilance Commissioner of India Sri. Vittal presided over the function. It was attended by almost all the top officers of the CBI working in different parts of the country. The speech which I delivered was well received and its text was published on the editorial page of "The Hindu".

When I reached near the termini of my career as judge of the Supreme Court of India the CBI produced a special work by printing a book compiling all my judgments on criminal law which I pronounced in the Supreme Court. Mr. Loknadh Behra, a senior officer of the CBI was assigned the task to make the compilation and also to give a final shape of the book. It was presented to me by Dr. P.C. Sharma, the Director of the CBI. That book is meant "for in-house use only" by the CBI. The introduction in the book contains, among other things, the following:-

"These judgments mark a significant shift in Criminal jurisprudence of our country; and such judgments have important and far reaching effect on the police investigation and trial of cases".

After the book was presented to me and when I opened it, I could find out that it was well edited and well chronicled and well indexed work as anybody could enter into the different subjects detailed therein, without much effort. I became much elated when I noticed that I rendered such a large number of judgments on the subject of criminal law during my tenure in the Supreme Court.

I must mention here with a sense of gratitude that a large number of persons invited me to offer felicitation to me on completion of my tenure as judge of the Supreme Court of India. They included judges, past and present, senior advocates and associations of advocates besides some from outside also. But I regard the felicitation accorded to me by the Bar of Punjab and Haryana High Court as a unique one which was unprecedented.

Mr. Gagan Pradeep Singh Bal, as President of the Punjab and Haryana Bar Association called on me along with some of his colleagues and requested me to attend a function organized by the Bar at Chandigarh to facilitate me. They said that the purpose was to honour me as most of the members of that Bar were citing the judgments authored by me before various courts but none of them had occasion to see me personally. I was really moved by the sentiments expressed by them, but I told them of my difficulty to spare a day for undertaking journey to Chandigarh. A couple of days later they suggested to me that they proposed to arrange a function at New Delhi and requested me to spare a convenient day. A meeting was arranged at Punjab Bhavan, New Delhi to which they invited not only the members of their Bar but all the sitting judges of the Supreme Court also. The turnout in the meeting was quite impressive, considering the trouble which the advocates of that Bar undertook to reach New Delhi. K.T.S. Tulsi, the senior advocate of the Supreme Court who was former Solicitor General of India (who hailed from Punjab Bar Association) spoke on behalf of the advocates. He said as follows:-

"Justice Thomas in his long and distinguished tenure had his share of resolving political conflicts through judicial process in the High Court of Kerala as also from the forum of last resort. While his judgments proved that the high and mighty were not more equal than others, yet his approach to the problems was neither populist nor unconventional. He did not load the dice against the litigants, merely because they were the high and the mighty. In his court they were neither more nor less equal than others. Justice Thomas decided numerous cases full of controversy between the Centre and the States and between one Government and other. Yet not one of his judgments created controversy. They were universally accepted and respected. There was not one incident in his court which might have created any inconsistency between the popular Government and judicial supremacy. The power and the prestige of the Supreme Court rested safely in the hands of Justice Thomas. His contributions in the process of interpretations of criminal cases will continue to serve the nation for decades and centuries. After the legendary Justice Krishna Iyer, the southern most State of the Country gave to us another illustrious judge whose contribution, particularly in the field of criminal law will be regarded as even more legendary".

The members of the Bar of Punjab and Haryana High Court presented me with a beautiful memento. I price it as one of the most valuable trinkets. In my reply I said that such gesture shown to me by the members of the Bar Association with which I had no past acquaintance, really touched the cockles of my heart.

51

Farewell to Law

Three farewell functions are usually customary for every judge nearing retirement in the Supreme Court which became the accepted practice. I too had the privilege of being accorded with those three. One was the function organised by "the Supreme Court Advocates on Record Association". It was a farewell dinner held at Hotel Claridges, attended by almost all the advocates on record practising in the Supreme Court, besides a large number of senior advocates, all the sitting and former judges stationed in New Delhi. The President of the Association made a moving farewell speech in which he said that the large gathering in the dinner farewell was the reflection of the popularity of the retiring judge. I replied in a humorous tone, saying that the year 2002 would be recorded as the year of the largest evacuation from the Supreme Court because eight judges were to retire during that year and I claimed leadership of the evacuees of 2002, because I was the first to retire in that year. I also said, as a banter, that the year 1937 would be remembered because eight mothers gave birth to eight would-be-judges of the Supreme Court of India among whom my mother would posthumously be conferred with primordiality. The gathering expected my reply speech in a tone of emotion but I made into an occasion for laughter.

The second function was truly the main farewell as it was organised by the Supreme Court Bar Association. It was held on the sprawling lawns in front of the magnificent building of the Supreme Court of India. As usual a special shamiana and dais were erected at the venue. As it had to be held on 29th January 2002, being my last working day in the Supreme Court, I had a foreboding that the function would be thinly attended because another grand function as the finale of the Republican Day celebrations called "Beating the Retreat" was to be held at Vijay Chouk (in front of Rashtrapathi Bhavan) It is usually a colourful pageant when the all personnels of the band set of the Army, Navy and Air Force who attended the Republic Day parade would play military band to bid farewell to the Commander-in-Chief who, under the Constitution of India, is the President of India. During all the years we were in Delhi, we never missed even one occasion to attend "Beating the Retreat" programme held on the evening of 29th January, except on this last occasion as my own farewell function happened to fall at the same time. Naturally, I expected only a thin attendance at the farewell meeting, but the gathering swelled up to be one of the largest ever for such a function. The organisers told me later that they did not expect more than 1,500 persons and hence they arranged sandwiches only for that number but every piece had to be cut into two for catering double the number which turned up at the function.

The Chief Justice of India (Justice S. P. Berucha) delivered a customary speech on behalf of all Judges bidding me farewell. He was followed by Soli Sorabji, the Attorney General for India. He spoke in very moving terms. He was followed by the address of the Vice President of the Supreme Court Bar Association Mr. Raju Ramachandran (Mr. Kapil Sibal was the President of the Association, he was out of India during then and hence he called on me before his departure and bade good bye) A poem composed by Kapil Sibal was read out at the function and then it was presented to me in a framed casket. I crave permission of my readers to bear with me for reproducing the poem below:-

Dear Justice Thomas you have been known
To be a judge with a straight backbone
Some say you lacked the gentle touch
That hardened criminals like so much.

You set in motion, evolved a craft
To deal with those involved in graft
Occasionally some of us did feel
An over-abundance of judicial zeal

The loopholes of the law you plugged
Had many a politician bugged
Interpreted with judicial tack
The Prevention of Corruption Act.

Many an accused you'd oft berate
Make them appear before the Magistrate
Surrender before you ask for bail
For sometime cool your heels in jail.

The High and Mighty clearly saw
That they were not above the law
Counsel in the midst of discourse
Were told the law must take its course

Prosecutions commenced without much ado
Allegations make be taken as true
The charge be framed as appeal shall lie
None has the right to question why ?

For the lure of graft is unique indeed
Driven by avarice and greed
Be dealt with harshly in the strongest terms
In response to societal concerns.

Your conscience was your only guide
Your response, to the voice inside
Your pens command guided by God
Without fear or favour, ill-will or reward.

You adorned the Bench, full of grace
Can someone fill up this Judicial Space ?

You leave us in a blaze of glory
Others are bound to tell your story.

The presence of Shanti Bhooshan, one of the tallest doyens of the Indian Bar, at the farewell function was noted with dismay by many judges and advocates because he was not seen in such functions on earlier occasions. He remained until all the speeches were over. Before he left the venue he conveyed to my wife (who was sitting in the front row of the audience) the reasons for his presence at this function. He told my wife thus:- "I have been practising here for more than three decades. Among many judges who were here, I regard your husband as one of the best. I noted four special features in him. First, his extremely polite manners, second - this high office did not get into his head, the third - his grip on criminal law was amazing and the last is that his integrity was not even doubted by any". My wife conveyed this to me even before Shanti Bhooshan left the venue. So I rushed to him and expressed my gratitude for the kind words spoken about me.

In my reply speech I referred to the legendary story of "the honeybees of Solomon" (narrated in the first paragraph of this book) and said that my good God mercifully sent such honeybees to me on many occasions, sometimes in the form of a document, some times as an answer to a query or as the submission made at the Bar etc. I ended my reply speech bidding adieu to my colleague judges, members of the Registry, my personal staff and to all the learned members of the Bar. Lastly I bade farewell to "the legal profession itself which sustained me for forty-two years of my life".

The third customary farewell function was a dinner hosted by my colleague judges and their spouses on the night of 29th January 2002. A silver plaque inscribing the names and signatures of the Judges was presented to me and a similar one containing the names and signatures of all the spouses of the judges was presented to my wife. Those farewell mementoes now adorn on the show case of our drawing room.

When I reached our bungalow from all the customary farewell functions I noticed one envelope lying on my table waiting to be opened by me. It was a letter addressed by Fali S. Nariman, the President of Bar Association of India who is truly one of the most respected lawyers in India. The words in that letter are the following:-

"My dear Justice Thomas,

I will hate to see you go, and you know why, the court will be much the poorer for the loss of a fine upright judge with robust commonsense.

Bapsi joins me in sending you and dear Mrs. Thomas our fond regards - but not farewell !

Yours sincerely,
Fali S. Nariman.

Epilogue

I wrote many things in this book. I am sorry, in most of them I projected myself. The discerning reader may pardon me for any excesses, some even bordering on megalomania, in my writings. But here is my excuse – after all, those were about my own experiences, on what I heard, saw and did. It is inevitable in such recollections for the author to self-propel. But sometimes, it goes out of proportion and may appear dissonant. If such self-flinging emanated from noble men who deserve to be emulated, it could serve for the improvement of the society. But when it concerns men of mediocrity that could become counter-influencing on impressionable minds. Without being formally humble, I would include myself in the latter category.

I left New Delhi within a few days after laying down office as Judge of the Supreme Court of India and am now living in my hometown Kottayam (Kerala). This is a fantastic small town which lit the light of learning in the country, claiming primordiality among all the educational institutions. (I belong to the alumni of the oldest college in India – C.M.S. College, Kottayam) The flora and fauna are resplendent here. The daily stroll of more than an hour before sun rise with my contemporaries of student days has been, thus far, rejuvenating. I declined to accept all the assignments offered to me which involved shifting my residence to New Delhi. However, I accepted certain other challenging work which kept me busy and engaged so far.

Tharuni, whom her parents and my parents brought to me as my life partner on 29th October 1962 remains my sole companion at home now. Our children, settled elsewhere, visit us with their children as often as they can. Our Heavenly Father has been merciful to us.

Index

Y